Risk Communication

People today must make decisions about many health, safety, and environmental risks. Nuclear power, HIV/AIDS, radon, vaccines, climate change, and emerging infectious diseases are just some of the issues that may face them in the news media, ballot box, or doctor's office. In order to make sound choices they need to get good information. Because their time is limited, that information has to be carefully selected and clearly presented. This book provides a systematic approach for risk communicators and technical experts hoping to serve the public by providing information about risks. The procedure uses approaches from risk and decision analysis to identify the most relevant information; it also uses approaches from psychology and communication theory to ensure that its message is understood. This book is written in nontechnical terms, designed to make the approach feasible for anyone willing to try it. It is illustrated with successful communications, on a variety of topics.

M. Granger Morgan is Lord Chair Professor of Engineering and Head of the Department of Engineering and Public Policy at Carnegie Mellon University, where he also holds academic appointments in Electrical and Computer Engineering and in the H. John Heinz III School of Public Policy and Management.

Baruch Fischhoff is University Professor in the Department of Social and Decision Sciences and the Department of Engineering and Public Policy at Carnegie Mellon University. He serves on the editorial boards of several journals and is a member of the Institute of Medicine of the National Academy of Sciences.

Ann Bostrom is Associate Professor in the School of Public Policy at the Georgia Institute of Technology.

Cynthia J. Atman is Director of the Center for Engineering Learning and Teaching in the College of Engineering at the University of Washington, where she also holds an academic appointment as Associate Professor of Industrial Engineering.

RISK
COMMUNICATION
A Mental Models Approach

M. Granger Morgan
Carnegie Mellon University

Baruch Fischhoff
Carnegie Mellon University

Ann Bostrom
Georgia Institute of Technology

Cynthia J. Atman
University of Washington

CAMBRIDGE
UNIVERSITY PRESS

PUBLISHED BY THE PRESS SYNDICATE OF THE UNIVERSITY OF CAMBRIDGE
The Pitt Building, Trumpington Street, Cambridge, United Kingdom

CAMBRIDGE UNIVERSITY PRESS
The Edinburgh Building, Cambridge, CB2 2RU, UK
40 West 20th Street, New York, NY 10011–4211, USA
10 Stamford Road, Oakleigh, Melbourne 3166, Australia
Ruiz de Alarcón 13, 28014 Madrid, Spain
Dock House, The Waterfront, Cape Town 8001, South Africa

http://www.cambridge.org

First published 2002

Printed in the United States of America

Typeface Garamond 3 10.5/14 pt.   *System* QuarkXPress[R]   [GH]

A catalogue record for this book is available from the British Library.

Library of Congress Cataloguing-in-Publication Data

Risk communication : a mental models approach / M. Granger Morgan ... [et al.].
      p. cm.
   Includes bibliographical references and index.
   ISBN 0-521-80223-7 – ISBN 0-521-00256-7 (pbk.)
      1. Risk communication. I. Morgan, M. Granger (Millett Granger), 1941–

   T10.68 R58 2001
   658.4'08 – dc21   00-067448

ISBN   0 521 80223 7   hardback
ISBN   0 521 00256 7   paperback

CONTENTS

PREFACE

Do-it-yourself books typically help readers to perform physical tasks, such as installing energy-efficient windows or growing aphid-free roses. This do-it-yourself book offers help on an intellectual task: developing risk communications using a mental models approach. Such communications are designed to contain, in readily usable form, the information that people need to make informed decisions about risks to health, safety, and the environment. Some of these decisions involve risks that individuals face in their everyday lives. Others involve risks that they must address as citizens in a modern society.

The public health and safety communities have long attempted to tell people about risks such as home fires, infectious disease, and auto accidents. The design of most of their communications relies primarily on intuition and conventional wisdom. Some of these communications have worked well, especially those with inherently simple messages, such as "don't smoke in bed." Although people may not have followed this advice, that is not because they did not understand *what* they were supposed to do, although not understanding *why* may have reduced compliance. Other communications have been less successful, even with ostensibly clear-cut messages (e.g., "Just Say No"). These messages have much simpler content than attempts to explain such complex, novel risks as those posed by modern technical systems or environmental pollution.

Our method was created to meet this challenge, with an approach that reflects both the natural science of how risks are created and controlled and the social science of how people comprehend and respond to such risks. In the original project, Greg Fischer, Baruch Fischhoff, and Emilie Roth represented the theories and methods of psychology. Lester Lave brought the perspective and analytical methods of economics. Granger Morgan and Indira Nair offered the skills and substantive knowledge of natural science and engineering. All contributed their experiences with policy analysis and contacts with the communities in which these results might be used. Several doctoral students and postdoctoral fellows provided backgrounds in engineering, management, law, policy analysis, and applied social science; they include Cynthia Atman, Ann Bostrom, Keith Florig, Gordon Hester, Urbano Lopez, Michael Maharik, Jon Merz, and Marilyn Jacobs Quadrel.

Together, we developed the approach presented here. At its heart are commitments to the scientific facts of risk, the empirical understanding of human behavior, and the need for openness in communication about risk. We sought an approach that would treat diverse problems with a common set of methods and theories, as well as one that would be readily usable by the professionals entrusted with communicating about risks. The method presented here has been applied to such diverse topics as the potential risks from radon in homes, nuclear energy sources in space, electromagnetic fields, climate change, and sexually transmitted diseases. Some of the resulting communications have been professionally published and widely distributed to the public. We have also benefited from the experiences of Sarah Thorne and Gordon Butte, of Decision Partners, with whom we have tested and adapted these methods in a variety of applications.

This book is designed to share what we have learned. In our work, we have found that each communication task creates new challenges, reflecting either the nature of the risk or people's intuitive beliefs about it. As a result, while this is a do-it-yourself book, use it as a field guide rather than a cookbook! Don't hesitate to innovate when our standard methods do not fully address the particular situation you face — and, please, share your experiences with us.

In addition to the people just listed, a number of others have helped to make our work possible. Patti Steranchak provided extensive administrative support and assisted in the development of many of the materials, the production of most of the communication brochures, and the preparation of this manuscript. Connie Cortés conducted many of the mental models interviews in the early years of the project. Claire Palmgren picked up where she left off. Other significant contributions have come from Jack Adams, Tony Bradshaw, Wändi Bruine de Bruin, Irene Brychcin, Stephanie Byram, Caron Chess, Wendy Davis, Julie Downs, George Duncan, Dan Geisler, Dan Kovacs, David Lincoln, Donald MacGregor, Kevin Marsh, Denise Murrin-Macey, Karen Pavlosky, Richard Puerzer, Daniel Reed, Donna Riley, Karen Schriver, Paul Slovic, Tom Smuts, Ola Svenson, and Rosa Stipanovic, as well as from dozens of experts who reviewed our draft communications, and hundreds of individuals who participated in a wide variety of experimental studies.

Finally, we thank our spouses, Betty Morgan, Andi Fischhoff, Doug Bostrom, and Mike Meyer, for the patience and support that have made this work possible.

Creating such a broad-based and interdisciplinary method would not have been feasible without core support from the National Science Foundation (under grants SBR-9521914, SES-8715564, SES-9309428, SES-9022738, SES-9209940, SES-9209553 and SES-9975200) and supplementary support from the Electric Power Research Institute (under contracts RP 2955–3, RP 2955–10, and RP 2955–11), the Carnegie Corporation of New York, the Environmental Protection Agency (under grant CR 824706-01-2 and R8279200-1-0), the National Institute for Alcohol Abuse and Alcoholism (under grant IU19AI 38513), the National Institute of Allergies and Infectious Disease (under grant IU19 AI 38513), and the Scaife Family Foundation.

Risk Communication

I

INTRODUCTION

1.1   The Context of Risk Communication

There are many different kinds of risk. In one study, we asked a group of citizens to "make a list, in whatever order they come to mind, of the risks that most concern you now" (Fischer et al., 1991). The most frequent nominations were everyday threats to life and limb, such as accidents, disease, and crime. Also listed were economic risks, such as the possibility of losing a job or making a bad investment. Some people listed personal concerns, such as their love life going sour or their child flunking out of school. The risk of eternal damnation was also mentioned. Only 10% of the risks cited were from environmental hazards, natural hazards (e.g., floods and earthquakes), or technology. Clearly "risk" is a very broad topic. In a subsequent study, when we asked people to focus specifically on "health, safety, and environmental risks," they readily provided many such hazards. However, as shown in Table 1.1, even then, everyday risks, such as drugs, auto accidents, and conventional pollutants, dramatically outranked more exotic ones.

Whereas professional risk experts devote many hours to considering rare and unusual hazards, most people do not share this preoccupation. With jobs, family, friends, and the other demands of daily living, their lives are filled with more immediate concerns. Of course, given that modern life is awash in risks, people must deal with them in one way or another. When they do, their attention is most often directed toward com-

1

mon day-to-day hazards. For eminently sensible reasons, the time that most people can devote to rare or unusual risks is usually very limited.

In some cases, people can exert direct personal control over the risks they face (e.g., through diet or driving habits). In other cases, they can only act indirectly, by influencing social processes (e.g., the allocation of law enforcement funds, the enactment of environmental legislation, the siting of hazard facilities). In all cases, they need a diverse set of cognitive, social, and emotional skills in order to understand the information that they receive, interpret its relevance for their lives and communities, and articulate their views to others. They can acquire those skills through formal education, self-study, and personal experience. However, as diligent as they might be, individuals are helpless without trustworthy, comprehensible information about specific risks.

Fortunately, many people are engaged in providing such information. Doctors' offices are full of brochures and posters about ways to control risks. In 1988, the Surgeon General mailed a pamphlet about AIDS to every home in the United States. The 1986 reauthorization of the Super-fund Act requires notifying local communities about both routine chemical emissions and potential catastrophic actions. The Centers for Disease Control have conducted a massive campaign to inform Americans about the risks (and nonrisks) of HIV/AIDS. The Food and Drug Administration has created nutritional labels for all food products and is in the process of creating standardized risk labels for over-the-counter drugs. Workers handling chemicals are entitled to see Material Safety Data Sheets, informing them about the nature and handling of risks.

All these communications aim to supply people with the information that they need in order to make informed decisions about risk. For risks under personal control, successful communication can help people to identify those risks that are large enough to warrant some of their very limited time and attention. It can help them to identify the "best buys" in risk, where there are large compensating benefits for taking risks and no missed opportunities for cheaply reducing risk – or gaining great benefits by accepting a little more risk. For risks under societal control, successful communication can help ensure the "diffusion of knowledge among the people," which Thomas Jefferson argued is the only sure strategy "for the preservation of freedom and happiness."

Table 1.1 Types of risk mentioned when subjects were asked to "make a list, in whatever order they come to mind, of the health, safety, and environmental risks that most concern you."

Type of Risk	Percentage of Mentions
Health (22.9%)	
Cancer, heart disease	4.8
Sexually transmitted diseases	5.9
Drugs, alcohol, and smoking	7.4
Other	4.8
Safety (22.4%)	
Motor vehicles	6.7
Other transportation	2.8
Natural hazards	2.4
Fire and explosion	3.3
Other, including home and workplace	7.2
Environment (44.1%)	
Conventional air pollution	7.6
Conventional water pollution	7.0
Conventional solid waste and other	6.5
Toxic/hazardous chemicals	5.2
Pesticides, fertilizers	2.0
Ionizing radiation	4.8
Large ecological	8.0
Human ecology	2.0
Other	1.0
Society (10.6%)	
War	3.0
Other	7.5

Adapted from Fischer et al. (1991).

1.2 The Goals of Risk Communication

As practiced today, risk communication is often very earnest but also surprisingly ad hoc. Typically, one cannot find a clear analysis of what needs to be communicated nor solid evidence that messages have achieved their impact. Nor can one find tested procedures for ensuring the credibility of communication.

The stakes riding on public understanding are high for those who create risks, as well as for the public that bears them. With many risks, it takes little imagination to identify the individuals and institutions who would like others to exaggerate or underestimate risks. As a result, there are significant disagreements about the content of risk communications. To many of the manufacturers or managers of technologies that create risks, "risk communication" means persuading the public that the risk from a technology is small and should be ignored. In such contexts, according to Sheila Jasanoff (1989), "risk communication is often a code [word] for brainwashing by experts or industry."

As used here, "risk communication" means communication intended to supply laypeople with the information they need to make informed, independent judgments about risks to health, safety, and the environment (Fischhoff, 1990; Gibson, 1985; Gow and Otway, 1990). Given people's time constraints, effective communication should focus on the issues that recipients most need to understand. If a communication omits critical information, then it fails the most obvious responsibility of communicators. It may leave recipients worse off if it creates an illusion of competence, so that recipients erroneously believe themselves to be adequately informed. If it presents irrelevant information, then it wastes recipients' time and diverts their attention from more important tasks.

Once they have determined the appropriate content, the developers of a risk communication need to ensure that this message is understood as intended. Failing that test wastes recipients' time (not to mention the resources invested in the communication). It denies them empowerment for dealing with the risk. Recipients may resent the communicator if they feel that they are being denied an opportunity to understand. They may doubt themselves if the experience leaves them feeling incapable of understanding. Failed communications can also contribute inadvertently to controversy and conflict. In all these ways, poor risk communications can create threats larger than those posed by the risks that they describe. We should no more release an unproven communication on people than an unproven drug.

Effective risk communications require authoritative and trustworthy sources. If communicators are perceived as having a vested interest, then recipients may not know what to believe. They may accept the message at face value or reinterpret it in ways that attempt to undo perceived biases. As a result, the impact of communications will be blurred, and the communication process further complicated. Not knowing whom or what to believe can make risk decisions seem intractable (Fischhoff, 1992). Such confusion and suspicion can erode relations between experts and the public, as well as open the door to less credible sources.

Such failures of communication can be deliberate, as when communicators attempt to manipulate the public or simply fail to take their duty to inform seriously. However, they can also be inadvertent, as when communicators fail to realize the complexity of their task or the opportunities for failure.

1.3 The Goals of Communication Recipients

What a risk communication should contain depends on what audience members intend to do with it. Sometimes recipients just want a trustworthy expert to tell them what to do. Sometimes they want to make their own choices but need quantitative details (such as probabilities or prices) in order to do so (Fischhoff, Bostrom, and Quadrel, 1997). Sometimes, they want help in organizing their thinking. We consider each situation briefly in turn.

Advice and answers   People who are poised, waiting to be told what to do, just need explicit instruction, summarizing the conclusions that they would reach if they had sufficient time and knowledge. It is not hard to imagine sometimes wanting a trusted doctor, lawyer, insurance agent, or investment counselor to spare us the details and tell us what we should do.

When the same advice is given to many people, all should have similar goals, which the experts attempt to help them achieve. That is, the advice should reflect the best available technical knowledge, applied in a normatively defensible way. Experts should not have a vested interest in how members of their audience behave, beyond wanting to help them to act in their own best interests. For example, a financial expert appearing on a television investment program should not recommend a stock with plans to sell it in a few days, hoping to get many viewers to buy it and drive the price up.

Responsible advice helps recipients understand how their options are shaped by social forces – and how the creation of additional options may require collective as well as individual options. It should help people to create new options for themselves and contribute meaningfully to public debate (Fischhoff, 1992).

Numbers   People often want to make choices themselves. Rather than instruction on how to choose, they want quantitative summaries of expert knowledge. For example, they may need to know the costs, probability of success, and probability of adverse side effects associated with alternative medical treatments. Having received such information, they can plug the values into their personal decision-making model and make the choice that makes the most sense for their personal situations. To serve that process, communicators must analyze the decisions that their audience members face and then determine the information that is most relevant.[1] Assuming that the resulting estimates can be made credible and comprehensible, this might reduce the expert knowledge that people need to a few well-chosen numbers (or ranges) – rather than the "core dump" of, say, the typical patient package insert.

Processes and framing   In some cases, people need to know more than just a few numbers. They need to learn how a risk is created and how it can be controlled. That information allows them to monitor their own surroundings, identify risky situations, and devise appropriate responses. Such knowledge allows people to follow (and join) the public debate and be competent citizens. A risk communication that provides such information assumes that its audience is motivated to obtain such understanding and invest the effort required to gain it (when they believe that their efforts will be rewarded).

Communications intended to provide such broad understanding face an enormous selection problem, insofar as any fact with some arguable connection to the risk might be transmitted. Our approach addresses this need for

[1]Merz, Fischhoff, and Mazur (1993) have used this approach to identify the most relevant information for patients facing the prospect of carotid endarterectomy, a procedure for scraping out an artery leading to the brain in order to reduce the risk of strokes. Only a few of the many possible side effects were found to matter to any more than a tiny fraction of potential patients.

selecting and presenting information. We recognize that there are situations calling for the more modest but still challenging goals of communicating numbers and advice. We have treated them in other writing (e.g., Fischhoff, 1992, 1999; Fischhoff, Bostrom, and Quadrel, 1997; Fischhoff et al., 1998). Speculatively, even those goals might be advanced by a more comprehensive approach, so that people have an understanding of why they are being told to follow a particular course of action or what basis there is for a quantitative claim. More specifically, our goal is to create an adequate mental model of the risky process, allowing people to know which facts are relevant and how they fit together. That knowledge should help them to make sense out of any new facts that come their way and their own direct observations. Within this general framework, their attention should be focused on those facts that make the greatest difference in determining risk levels.

1.4 Criticisms of Risk Communication

We have met risk specialists who, at least in private, argue that the Jeffersonian ideal of a well-informed public is naïve, making risk communication for the general public mostly a waste of time. Some of these skeptics assert that people are technically illiterate and ruled by emotion rather than by substance – hence education is hopeless. Others argue that all important decisions about risk are made by special interests and power elites – hence education is pointless, even if possible. Our reading of the evidence is that neither assertion is true.

Because people's time is short, they can't learn about, much less influence, all risks. As a result, people often want specialists to make sure that life doesn't get too hazardous. Yet the history of democratic countries shows that when they see experts failing, laypeople can effectively assert their desire to affect both personal and political decisions. These battles for control may not be quick or tidy processes. Technical specialists often resist communication with the public, in ways that erode their credibility. Table 1.2 summarizes the historical stages through which communication often evolves when organizations discover that they have a risk problem. Once specialists lose the trust needed to serve as credible sources, the public's learning process becomes much more complicated. Laypeople no longer know where to go for information. Their interactions with risk specialists may be colored by emotional reactions by all parties.

Risk specialists may not like to acknowledge their own emotional involvement nor to deal with that of the public. However, emotion is often a natural part of high-stakes choices. The specialists have a job to do and find it frustrating to have to deal with the public – a task that few envisioned when they chose technical careers and for which few are properly trained. For their part, citizens should not like risks imposed upon them, especially without consultation. Nor should they like to assume risks so that other people can become rich and powerful. Nor do people like the feeling of being lied to. Anyone would (and perhaps should) become emotionally involved when they see themselves in such situations.

Such emotions need not mean that risk communication is hopeless, nor that people are incapable of making reasoned decisions about risks. Indeed, emotion can provide motivation for acquiring competence – even if it makes people more critical consumers of risk communications. Although citizens may begin their learning process with relatively little technical understanding, we believe that most can understand the basic issues needed to make informed decisions about many technically based risks – given time, effort, and careful explanation. Unfortunately, when a message is not understood, the recipients, rather than the message, often get blamed for the communication failure. If technical experts view the public as obtuse, ignorant, or hysterical, the public will pick up on that disrespect, further complicating the communication process.

As mentioned, some critics argue that risk communication is typically manipulative, designed to sell unsuspecting recipients on the communicator's political agenda. Of course, some consultants make a good living approaching risk communication in this way, and sometimes they succeed. In an open society, however, there are often multiple sources of information. The fact that some risk communication is cynically manipulative doesn't mean that all risk communication must be. Our goal is to help those hoping to develop balanced materials, providing lay audiences with the information that they need to make informed, independent decisions. In Chapter 2, we will argue that such design must start with an examination of the choices people face, the beliefs they hold, and experts' relevant knowledge. It must be assumed that the principal obstacles to understanding are lay time and attention, not intelligence.

Table 1.2   Historical stages in risk communication.

One way to think about risk communication is as an evolutionary process in which communicators gradually reach higher levels of understanding about the nature and complexity of their task. Communicators at each stage lack some of the understanding of public concerns that become apparent at later stages.

---

1. *All we have to do is get the numbers right.* The simplest communications rely on words rather than deeds. If risks are well managed, or obviously worthwhile, or have no clear substitutes, then no one may ever be interested in hearing about them. Indeed, many risk managers aspire to this status, hoping to do their job well and be left alone. If this strategy works, then time and trouble have been saved by all parties. However, if it fails, then people may ask awkward questions about the long silence. Was something being hidden? Or did the experts just not care?

2. *All we have to do is tell them the numbers.* The quickest response to the demand for information is to share one's work. As a result, when risk managers discover that they have a public risk perception problem, they may be tempted to present the research that convinced them that the risk was acceptable – in something close to the form in which it was produced. Although there can be something touching and forthright in such a straightforward delivery, it is unlikely to be very effective. Moreover, not understanding the public's perspective may be interpreted as not caring about it.

3. *All we have to do is explain what we mean by the numbers.* When risk estimates do not speak for themselves, an obvious next step is to explain them. That can be a difficult task with an audience that shares no common vocabulary or conceptual background with the risk experts. For example, a candid disclosure of risk information will include the degree of scientific uncertainty surrounding it. However, accomplishing that task for a specific risk requires a prior understanding of the general nature of scientific inquiry and disputation. Without it, the candid communicator may seem to be evasive, equivocating, or contentious. Furthermore, the numbers alone do not tell the entire story about risks. Often, people need to understand how a risky process works, in order to devise strategies for dealing with it or to feel competent to follow public debate.

4. *All we have to do is show them that they've accepted similar risks in the past.* Having done their best to get the numbers across, communicators may be frustrated to find that little is resolved. One common expression of their frustration is to argue something like, "the risks of technology *x* [which we promote] are no greater than those of activity *y* [which you already accept], so why not accept *x*?" Although such comparisons can be worth considering, they are no more than suggestive. Acceptability depends on benefits as well as risks. Those who advocate consistency in risk levels too vociferously endanger their own credibility.

5. *All we have to do is show them that it's a good deal for them.* Considering both risks and benefits in communication means, in effect, adopting recipients' full perspective, because they will have to live with both kinds of consequences. Doing so may lead to changing the activity in question so that it actually provides a better balance of risks and benefits. Explaining benefits encounters difficulties that are analogous to those involved in explaining risks, along with some added twists. For example, logically equivalent ways of presenting the same options can produce systematically different choices (known as "framing effects").

6. *All we have to do is treat them nicely.* People judge communications by their form and their substance. The form suggests, among other things, how much faith to place in the content and how respectfully the communicator regards them. If people do not feel respected, then they have more reason to suspect that they are not being fully informed. They also have more reason to fear that risks are not being managed on their behalf and that the risk-management process is part of a larger trend to disenfranchise them. Although sympathetic delivery is no guarantee of respect, it does show that one is recognized as a person with feelings (even if those are being manipulated).

7. *All we have to do is make them partners.* Stages 1 through 6 involve increasing stages of viewing the recipients of the message as individuals with complex concerns. However, the understanding is cultivated in order to get across a message whose content has been determined by the communicator. That means seeing recipients as individuals but not engaging them as such. This stage takes on the public as partners in risk management. It means providing them a seat at the table and allowing them to communicate their own concerns. In effect, it means opening a communication channel in the opposite direction.

Source: Fischhoff (1995).

When evaluating the success of communications and the competence of citizens, it is important to be realistic about the path from understanding to action. For example, it took many of us several years to install smoke detectors after learning about them. Although carbon monoxide detectors are now quite cheap, many of our homes still lack them. These delays don't reflect lack of understanding of the risk of fire or lack of caring about the safety of our families. Nor do they result from an emotional approach that ignores or rejects the facts. They occur because people have other pressing things to do. Changes just take a while.

1.5   How People Think about Risk and Uncertainty

Experts sometimes describe "risk" in terms of the expected numbers of deaths. Viewed this way, the accident risk of a technology can be obtained by multiplying the probability of an accident by the number of people who will be killed if it occurs (summed over all possible accidents). When members of the public rank activities and technologies in terms of "risk," the lists often deviate considerably from those generated by best-guess statistical estimates of expected fatalities. Some experts have cited this disparity as evidence of public stupidity or ignorance. When anecdotal observation is replaced with systematic study, a rather different picture of lay risk perceptions emerges. It shows that people use more complex, "multiattribute" definitions of risk, which include additional considerations beyond the expected numbers of deaths (Slovic, Fischhoff, and Lichtenstein, 1980). When laypeople order well-known hazards in terms of deaths in an average each year, they tend to agree with the statistics. When they order hazards in terms of how *risky* they are, laypeople produce a somewhat different order. The difference reflects the inclusion of additional factors such as how well the risk is understood, how equitably the risk is distributed across the population, how well individuals can control the risk they face, and whether the risk is assumed voluntarily or is imposed on people without their approval (Fischhoff et al., 1978; Slovic, 1987). Using the statistical technique of factor analysis, these attributes can be organized in terms of a small number of factors, as shown in Figure 1.1. The location of a hazard within this "factor space" says quite a lot about how the public is likely to

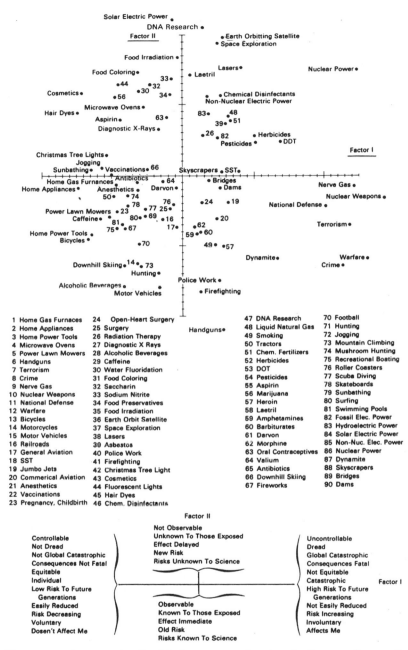

Figure 1.1. An example of a risk-factor space, showing the first two factors of a three-factor structure derived from the interrelationships among the ratings of 90 hazards on each of 18 risk characteristics in the extended study. Factor 3 (not shown) reflects the number of people exposed to the hazard. *Source:* Slovic, Fischhoff, and Lichtenstein (1980).

respond to it (Slovic, 1987). For example, the further that a hazard falls to the right, the greater the chance that the public will want to see active regulatory intervention.

Lay judgments of annual fatalities can be directly compared to the best available statistics. Such comparisons typically reveal a strong ordinal correlation but some systematic errors in the absolute estimates. It is as if people generally have a good idea about which risks are bigger and which smaller, but not so good an idea of by how much. A common pattern is for the frequency of very common causes of death, such as stroke, to be underestimated while the frequency of very rare causes of death, such as botulism poisoning, is overestimated (Lichtenstein et al., 1978). Typical results are illustrated in Figure 1.2. The exact estimates that people produce depend on the details of the elicitation procedure (Fischhoff and MacGregor, 1983; Poulton, 1989).

Experimental studies have found that people often make judgments, such as estimating the frequency of an event, in terms of how easily they can recall past examples or how easily they can imagine such occurrences. Psychologists call this "the availability heuristic" (Tversky and Kahneman, 1973). It appears to explain some of the systematic errors observed in people's quantitative estimates of risks. Thus, while stroke is a very common cause of death, most people only learn about it when a close friend or relative or a famous person dies. On the other hand, every time anyone in the developed world dies of botulism, we may read and hear about it in the news.

Experimental psychologists have identified several other cognitive heuristics (Kahneman, Slovic, and Tversky, 1982). One, termed "anchoring and adjustment," involves beginning the estimation process by choosing a salient value, then adjusting from there in the light of whatever other considerations come to mind. It can be illustrated with the results shown in Figure 1.2. These respondents were told that motor vehicle accidents produce about 50,000 deaths per year in the United States.[2] A second group of respondents was told that there are about 1,000 deaths per year in the United States from accidental electrocution. Their responses

[2]While the mileage driven by U.S. drivers has continued to increase, since this study was completed in the late 1970s motor vehicle deaths have fallen, hitting a low of 40,300 in 1992 and rising only slightly since them.

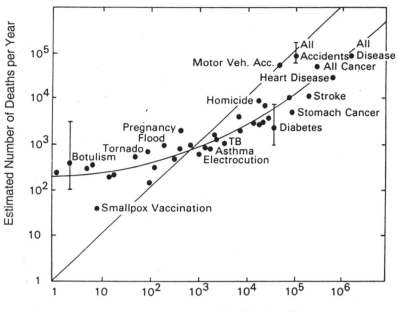

Figure 1.2. Plot showing the geometric mean of lay estimates of the numbers of deaths from a variety of causes (vertical axis) versus comparable statistical estimates (labeled as "actual" on the horizontal axis). In general, the rate of frequent causes of deaths is underestimated and that of less frequent causes is overestimated. Deviations from the best-fit curve can be interpreted in terms of reliance on the availability heuristic. Much of the "scatter" of the points is systematic across studies using different methods. The figure is redrawn from Lichtenstein et al. (1978).

shifted down, by a factor of 2 to 5, as shown in Figure 1.3. Thus, the absolute value of estimates was influenced by whether respondents had heard the high or the low number. They "anchored" on the number that they had been given, then did not "adjust" their answers sufficiently when estimating other values.

There are a number of excellent reviews of the literature on human judgment under uncertainty. One that is particularly well suited for readers with limited background in experimental social science is Plous (1993). Another very good but more technical treatment can be found in Hastie and Dawes (in press). Although the subject of much less systematic study, decision making by experts may also reflect such processes (e.g., Fischhoff, 1989; Henrion and Fischhoff, 1986; Kammen and Hassenzahl, 1999).

1.6   What Kinds of Communications Are We Considering?

The mental models approach described in this book attempts to solve the communication problems faced by risk specialists working at the middle stages of the developmental sequence displayed in Table 1.2. It offers a way to ensure that, if they choose to, laypeople can understand how the risks they face are created and controlled, how well science understands those risks, and how great they seem to be. Accomplishing this task is a necessary condition for establishing a partnership with the public and laying the foundations for mutual trust sought at the latter stages in the developmental sequence. Reaching this goal requires both a consideration of how the public intuitively thinks about the risks and a determination of which aspects of the scientific literature actually matter to the public. Then those topics must be presented in a balanced, credible, and comprehensible manner. Communicating effectively about risk does not, however, in itself fulfill risk managers' obligation to the public. It falls short of hearing the public out on the issues that interest them, nor does it create socially acceptable decision-making processes (Canadian Standards Association, 1997; National Research Council, 1989, 1996). Thus, we are proposing a public-centered approach to developing risk messages. It is a necessary, but not sufficient, condition for public-centered risk management.

We judge the success of the approach by its ability to improve the understanding of those who attend to the communications that it produces. Doing so cannot ensure that recipients like the risks any more: some risks look better the more that one knows about them, others look worse. Better understanding cannot guarantee changes in behavior; those depend on how people perceive benefits as well as risks, and on their resources and constraints. Having better risk communications cannot even ensure a broader audience for those communications. People have a lot on their mind and many other communications clambering for their attention. All that we can realistically seek is to be ready for laypeople if they

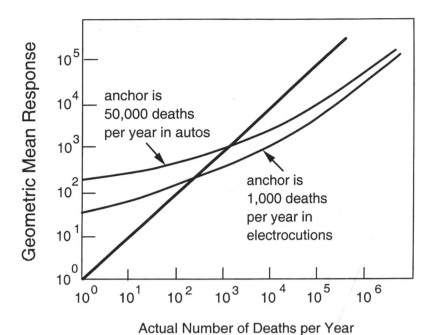

Figure 1.3. Comparison of best-fit quadratic curves for two versions of the experiment in Figure 1.2. In one, subjects were told that roughly 50,000 people died annually in traffic accidents in the United States. In the second, subjects were told that roughly 1,000 people died annually in the United States from accidental electrocutions. The downward shift in the mean response reflects the anchoring-and-adjustment heuristic. The figure is based on data from Lichtenstein et al. (1978). "True" frequency reflects best available statistical estimates.

become interested in a topic that we have treated systematically. Over time, if communications improve, people might be more eager to listen to them.

It is common for some participants in risk debates to blame a lack of public support on poor understanding. Such "dumb-public" arguments have been a frequent element in debates about the risks of nuclear power, genetically modified organisms, and the electric and magnetic fields associated with electric power systems. However much some participants might wish all disagreements to be the result of ignorance or factual misunderstanding, the reality is that they often spring from fundamental disagreements about political power, institutional trust, or the ethical appropriateness of contested activities. A clearer understanding of the facts may allow a more focused debate, but it will typically not resolve such underlying disagreements.

Chapter 2 offers a conceptual overview of our approach. Chapter 3 discusses the creation of the expert model that analyzes the risk situations and decision options facing recipients. Chapter 4 describes the open-ended interview procedure used to capture lay beliefs in something like their natural formulation. These together provide the foundation for message development. Chapter 5 shows how the results of these interviews can be translated into structured questionnaires, which can be more efficiently administered when assessing the need for risk communication or its impact. Chapter 6 outlines our process for converting these empirical observations of information needs into communications, and their evaluation. Chapter 7 summarizes several worked examples applying the method to diverse environmental risks. Chapter 8 describes applications to health risks. Chapter 9 returns to the broader issues to discuss briefly risk communication in the political and ethical context of risk analysis and management.

In this book, we focus on written communications. Many of the same steps are necessary to develop and refine the substantive content of radio or TV messages, an interactive Internet message, or a museum display.

References

Canadian Standards Association. (1997). *Risk Management Guidelines* (CSA-850). Canadian Standards Association, Ottawa.

Fischer, G. W., Morgan, M. G., Fischhoff, B., Nair, I., and Lave, L. B. (1991). "What Risks Are People Concerned About?" *Risk Analysis,* 11:303–314.

Fischhoff, B. (1989). "Eliciting Knowledge for Analytical Representation," *IEEE Transactions on Systems, Man and Cybernetics,* 13:448–461.

(1990). "Psychology and Public Policy: Tool or Tool Maker?" *American Psychologist,* 45:57–63.

(1992). "Giving Advice: Decision Theory Perspectives on Sexual Assault," *American Psychologist,* 47:577–588.

(1995). "Risk Perception and Communication Unplugged: Twenty Years of Process," *Risk Analysis,* 15:137–145.

(1999). "Why (Cancer) Risk Communication Can Be Hard," *Journal of the National Cancer Institute Monographs,* 25:7–13.

Fischhoff, B., Bostrom, A., and Quadrel, M. J. (1997). "Risk Perception and Communication," in R. Detels, J. McEwen, and G. Omenn, eds., *Oxford Textbook of Public Health.* Oxford University Press, London, pp. 987–1002.

Fischhoff, B., and MacGregor, D. (1983). "Judged Lethality: How Much People Seem to Know Depends upon How They Are Asked," *Risk Analysis,* 3:229–236.

Fischhoff, B., Riley, D., Kovacs, D., and Small, M. (1998). "What Information Belongs in a Warning? A Mental Models Approach," *Psychology and Marketing,* 15:663–686.

Fischhoff, B., Slovic, P., Lichtenstein, S., and Combs, B. (1978). "How Safe Is Safe Enough? A Psychometric Study of Attitudes Towards Technological Risks and Benefits," *Policy Sciences,* 8:127–152.

Gibson, M., ed. (1985). *To Breathe Freely: Risk, Consent, and Air.* Rowman and Allanheld, Totowa, N.J.

Gow, H. B. F., and Otway, H., eds. (1990). *Communicating with the Public about Major Accidents Hazard.* Elsevier, London.

Hastie, R., and Dawes, D. M. *Rational Choice in an Uncertain World.* 2nd ed., Sage, in press.

Henrion, M., and Fischhoff, B. (1986). "Assessing Uncertainty in Physical Constants," *American Journal of Physics,* 54:791–798.

Jasanoff, S. (1989). "Differences in National Approaches to Risk Assessment and Management," presented at the Symposium on Managing the Problem of Industrial Hazards: The International Policy Issues, National Academy of Sciences, Washington, D.C., February 27.

Kahneman, D., Slovic, P., and Tversky, A., eds. (1982). *Judgment under Uncertainty: Heuristics and Biases.* Cambridge University Press, New York.

Kammen, D., and Hassenzahl, D. (1999). *Shall We Risk It?* Princeton University Press, Princeton, N.J.

Lichtenstein, S., Slovic, P., Fischhoff, B., Layman, M., and Combs, B. (1978). "Judged Frequency of Lethal Events," *Journal of Experimental Psychology: Human Learning and Memory,* 4:551–578.

Merz, J. F., Fischhoff, B., and Mazur, D. J. (1993). "Informed Consent Does Not Mean Rational Consent: Cognitive Limitations on Decision Making," *Journal of Legal Medicine,* 11:321–350.

National Research Council. (1989). *Improving Risk Communication.* National Academy Press, Washington, D.C.

(1996). *Understanding Risk.* National Academy Press, Washington, D.C.

Plous, S. (1993). *The Psychology of Judgment and Decision Making.* McGraw Hill, New York.

Poulton, C. (1989). *Bias in Quantitative Judgment.* Lawrence Erlbaum and Associates, Hillsdale, N.J.

Slovic, P. (1987). "Perceptions of Risk," *Science,* 236:280–285.

Slovic, P., Fischhoff, B., and Lichtenstein, S. (1980). "Facts and Fears: Understanding Perceived Risk," in Schwing, R. C. and Albers, W. A., Jr., eds., *Societal Risk Assessment: How Safe Is Safe Enough?* Plenum, New York, pp. 181–214.

Tversky, A., and Kahneman, D. (1973). "Availability: A Heuristic for Judging Frequency and Probability," *Cognitive Psychology,* 4:207–232.

2

OUR MENTAL MODELS APPROACH

2.1 The Need for a Systematic Approach

An effective communication must focus on the things that people need to know but do not already. This seemingly simple norm is violated remarkably often in risk communications. Rather than conduct a systematic analysis of what the public believes and what information they need to make the decisions they face, communicators typically ask technical experts what they think people should be told. Rather than subject draft communications to rigorous empirical evaluation by individuals like those who will use them, communicators pass them around to staff or expert committees for approval. Those passing judgment may know very little about either the knowledge or the needs of the intended audience.

Under such conditions, it is not surprising that audiences often miss the point and become confused, annoyed, or disinterested. If the communicators feel that they have done everything that is expected of them, they may conclude that their audience was responsible for the communications failure. If the public is blamed for being stupid, irrational, or hysterical, it is deprived of both information and respect in the future.

In some cases, the failure to inform reflects willful neglect or disinterest. Communicators would just as soon not have the public know the facts, or they may lack the resources needed to take this part of their job seriously. More often, though, we suspect that the failure reflects the lack of systematic procedures for finding out what people know and need to know, and for confirming empirically that a communication has been effective. As a result, communicators depend upon "conventional wisdom" regarding what to say and how to say it.

To overcome these problems, we have developed a five-step method for creating and testing risk messages in a way that is faithful to the sciences of risk and communication:

Step 1. Create an expert model Review current scientific knowledge about the processes that determine the nature and magnitude of the risk. Summarize it explicitly, from the perspective of what can be done about the risk, allowing external review and the analysis of information relevance. The formal representation that we have chosen is the influence diagram, a directed network drawn from decision theory, which allows representing and interpreting the knowledge of experts from diverse disciplines. Once created, the expert model is reviewed by technical experts with differing perspectives in order to ensure balance and authoritativeness. Note that the term "expert" refers to the individuals creating it, without implying that their beliefs are perfect or even superior to lay beliefs in all respects.

Step 2. Conduct mental models interviews Conduct open-ended interviews, eliciting people's beliefs about the hazard, expressed in their own terms. The interview protocol is shaped by the influence diagram, so that it covers potentially relevant topics. It allows the expression of both correct and incorrect beliefs and ensures that the respondents' intent is clear to the interviewer. Responses are analyzed in terms of how well these mental models correspond to the expert model captured in the influence diagram.

Step 3. Conduct structured initial interviews Create a confirmatory questionnaire whose items capture the beliefs expressed in the open-ended interviews and the expert model. Administer it to larger groups, sampled appropriately from the intended audience, in order to estimate the population prevalence of these beliefs.

Step 4. Draft risk communication Use the results from the interviews and questionnaires, along with an analysis of the decisions that people face, to determine which incorrect beliefs most need correcting and which knowledge gaps most need filling. Then draft a communication and subject it to expert review to ensure its accuracy.

Step 5. Evaluate communication Test and refine the communication with individuals selected from the target population, using one-on-one read-aloud interviews, focus groups, closed-form questionnaires, or problem-solving tasks. Repeat this process until the communication is understood as intended.

The remainder of this chapter provides a brief elaboration of these steps. Chapter 3, "Creating an Expert Model of the Risk," considers the steps involved in constructing a consensus description of expert knowledge about the risk, expressed in terms of an influence diagram. Chapter 4, "The Mental Models Interviews," and Chapter 5, "Confirmatory Questionnaires," address Steps 2 and 3, respectively. Chapter 6 considers Steps 4 and 5, developing and evaluating communications. Chapters 7 and 8 apply the general method to specific communications.

2.2   The Mental Models Metaphor

Before we turn to a practical step-by-step description of the process, a little philosophy may be helpful. By definition, the audience for a communication lacks a complete understanding of its subject matter. Yet for most risks, people have at least some relevant beliefs, which they will use in interpreting the communication. They may have heard some things about the risk in question. It may remind them of related phenomena. Its very name may evoke some associations. If they must make inferences about the risk, such as how big it is, how it can be controlled, or who manages it, they will assemble their fragmentary beliefs into a "mental model," which they will then use to reach their conclusions.

This is not a model in a formal sense. It does not involve a strict mapping between things in the real world and elements in the model; nor does it have fixed operations for combining those elements. However, it shares some features with formal models. People need to figure out what things in a complicated situation are worthy of attention. They need some general principles for judging how these things interact with one another. They must recognize how well their abstraction captures the complexities of the actual process.

We will describe lay beliefs about a risk in terms of mental models,[1] which can then be compared with the formal, or "expert," model capturing the pooled beliefs of technical specialists about the same phenomenon. The comparison shows both the gaps between the models and the current knowledge that can be built upon.

This metaphor is not novel to our method. It has been used extensively in cognitive psychology and cognitive science, for phenomena as diverse as how people solve brainteasers to how they troubleshoot steam boilers. For each domain, investigators must find a way to represent beliefs. That can be very different for areas with clearly identified elements and operations (e.g., how people play chess) and poorly defined areas like most risk problems. Representations may differ, too, for deterministic and probabilistic relationships.

2.3   Constructing the Influence Diagram

What experts believe about a risk provides one basis for determining what laypeople need to know. We have chosen to summarize these beliefs in influence diagrams, a formulation that allows (a) integrating diverse forms of expertise and (b) assessing the importance of different facts. Section 3.2 explains influence diagrams in greater detail.

The objective is to construct a single description, summarizing the pooled knowledge of the community of experts, not the views of any one

[1]For discussion of mental models and their application in a variety of different contexts, see Carroll and Olson (1987), Collins and Gentner (1987), Craik (1943), di Sessa (1983, 1984), Doyle and Ford (1998), Driver and Easley (1978), Galotti (1989), Gentner and Stevens (1983), Jungermann, Schütz, and Thüring (1988, 1989), Kempton (1986, 1988), Kempton, Feuermann, and McGarity (1992), Norman (1983), Nussbaum and Novick (1982), Rouse and Morris (1986).

expert. Where there are disagreements and uncertainties, the summary must capture them as well.

The expert model is an attempt to pool in a systematic manner everything known, or believed, by the community of experts that is relevant for the risk decisions the audience faces. It leads to talking with experts repeatedly, showing them interim summaries of what we have heard them say, asking them to review our work. As a result, despite the name, the model need not exist in any one expert mind. Even were a single expert to have such comprehensive knowledge, this expert modeling procedure is a reactive one; it forces the experts to think more systematically about their beliefs than they might have otherwise. As a result, they may have different beliefs at the end of the interview process than they had at its beginning. If they believe that the process has furthered their understanding, then such changes should be reflected in the influence diagram. In contrast, the mental models interviews, described in the next section, try to avoid reactivity and obtain a "snapshot" of what laypeople currently believe, in the absence of external influences. The expert model also provides the general structure for those interviews.

2.4   Eliciting Mental Models

A common way to elicit current beliefs is to administer a questionnaire. However, doing so presumes that one knows in advance the full set of potentially relevant lay beliefs and misconceptions, as well as the terms in which they are intuitively phrased. Structured tests also run the risk of inadvertently communicating experts' knowledge, providing cues in cases where respondents are unsure of the answer. If interviewees are changed by the process, then their views no longer represent those of the population from which they are chosen. Researchers who study the survey process have increasingly demonstrated what an active intellectual process it is (National Research Council, 1981; Schwarz, 1999; Turner and Martin, 1984). Unless they have very sharply defined beliefs about the precise question being asked, and no reason to lie, respondents may engage in complex inferences. They may try to discern just what a question means, what they think about it, what the interviewer expects them to say, what other people are saying, and how to translate their (perhaps complex) beliefs into the available response options (Fischhoff, 1991; Poulton, 1989; Schwarz, 1996).

To minimize such problems, we use an open-ended interview procedure designed to control reactivity. It begins with a very general question, like "Tell me about radon." No hints are given regarding what topics should be addressed. No constraints are imposed on the language used. We are looking for a "core dump" of whatever comes to respondents' minds on the topic. Each topic they raise, they are later asked to elaborate. For example, "You mentioned that radon can come into a house through the cellar, tell me more about that." This allows us to extend the interview without adding content of our own. It also helps us to be certain that we know what respondents mean. It is not uncommon, in this expansion, to discover that respondents are using a scientific term, such as "radioactive," "gas," "death rate," "clean needles," or "safe sex," without having any precise meaning in mind, or with an interpretation quite different from that used by experts.

Administering this kind of interview requires practice and a procedure for keeping track of what respondents have said and what issues require follow-up. Because the interviewer typically knows a great deal about the risk and is trying to conduct the interview in something close to a conversational style, there is often a temptation to introduce new words or ideas. When we review the tape recordings of trial interviews, such inadvertent help is a focal concern. See Chapter 4.

A well-trained interviewer can sustain a surprisingly long conversation, even with respondents who initially claim to know very little about the topic. Eventually, though, the follow-ups and follow-ups to follow-ups produce nothing new. If we stopped at this point, we would have little risk of reactivity but some risk of missing important parts of respondents' mental models, simply because the interview happened to go in other directions.

As a result, the next stage of the interview is somewhat more intrusive. It increases the risk of putting something into respondents' minds while reducing the risk of missing something that was already there. In it, we ask respondents to tell us about each major area in the influence diagram. For example: "How can people control their exposure to this risk?" "Is there any way of reducing the damage if you have been exposed?" If respondents have not already mentioned such basic issues, then there is a good chance that they just slipped their minds – insofar as control and treatment are such fundamental concepts in thinking about any hazard. As before, respondents are asked to elaborate on everything that they say. In order to ensure that the interview neither misses important topics nor needlessly repeats them, interviewers use various aids to help keep track of which topics they have visited (Chapter 4).

The final stage of the interview is more intrusive still, making sure that we have not missed anything important. To this end, we have used several different strategies. One asks respondents to sort photographs, indicating whether each is "relevant" or "irrelevant" to the topic, describing the pictures and explaining their sorting choices as they proceed. A second asks respondents to solve problems, using their beliefs (and not just reporting them). A third asks for explicit definitions of commonly used terms, such as "radioactive" or "safe sex."

Because the later parts of the interview are progressively more reactive, responses to each section are analyzed separately.

2.5 The Value of Open-Ended Interviews

Each time that we have conducted mental models interviews, we have discovered surprising beliefs and formulations, begging treatment in risk communications. For example, we found that some people believe that houses containing radon are permanently contaminated. While incorrect, this inference is reasonable for someone who has heard that radon is radioactive and has followed the national controversy over radioactive waste disposal. However, while radon is a radioactive gas, it decays into other materials that lose their radioactivity in a matter of days. Thus, once a house's source of radon is closed off, the remaining radioactivity will soon be gone.

People who expect permanent contamination might also believe that remediation is impossible or at least prohibitively expensive. They might choose not to test, so as to retain the psychological power of denial or to avoid the legal requirement of disclosure, should they want to sell the house. Without a test, they can at least imagine that their house is radon-free. Given its prevalence, the erroneous belief that radon contamination is permanent should be a primary objective of risk communication. It was, however, absent from the EPA's initial *Citizen's Guide to Radon* (1986). The EPA deserves much credit for taking the unusual step of empirically evaluating the impact of this communication (Smith et al., 1988, 1990). However, the design of the *Guide* lacked an open-ended "mental models" stage. As a result, its central message, *you should test your house for radon,* may have been undermined by the belief that testing was futile.[2]

2.6   The Cost of Open-Ended Interviews

Although necessary, open-ended interviews are more expensive than structured surveys administered to similar samples. In addition to the interview itself, there is the cost of creating verbatim transcripts of the tapes and systematically analyzing their content. As a result, it can be tempting to skimp on the process. However, we have found that the discipline of looking at the details of what people say provides much of the utility of the approach, distinguishing it from the impressionistic analyses of, say, most focus-group work. The price of looking hard at people's beliefs is that with a given budget, one can look at fewer people in this way, both before the design of a risk communication and after its administration. Fortunately, much of the value of the open-ended interviews can be obtained with a relatively small sample. An appropriate sample of 20–30 individuals should reveal most of the beliefs held with any substantial frequency in the population from which they were selected. However, it can give only the most general notion of the relative frequency of those judgments. Periodically, a respondent will relate a fascinating misconception (or insight) that we will never hear again. For example, when asked about health risks from high-voltage power lines, one person said that radiation leaks out of nuclear power plants, travels along the lines, and thereby reaches people. If common, such a mental model would be important to address in communications. However, in follow-up studies, that did not

---

[2]As a result of the EPA's review of results from our work, a later edition of the *Citizen's Guide* addressed contamination.

prove to be the case, either in further open-ended interviews or in structured ones like those described in the next section.

2.7 Confirmatory Questionnaires

Knowing how frequently different beliefs are held allows us to focus communications on the most widely held misconceptions, as well as to evaluate their impact. As a result, the next stage in our process develops a questionnaire that explores issues that have been identified as potentially important through the mental models interviews. Such a questionnaire can be efficiently administered to larger samples of people in order to achieve statistically reliable prevalence estimates.

Such a comprehensive assessment of lay knowledge will include items addressing (a) important beliefs, as defined by the significant elements in the expert model, (b) significant misconceptions, identified in the open-ended interviews, and (c) critical terms, used in describing a risk. Like everything else in our approach, these questionnaires go through iterative testing to reach a form that will be understood by respondents as intended. In principle, this might require creating different forms for different populations, in order to ensure that the questions are functionally equivalent – even if they use somewhat different wording.

In addition to allowing us to estimate the population prevalence of various beliefs, these questionnaires also provide a form of *convergent validation* for our procedures. We acknowledge the imprecision of the prevalence estimates obtained from the open-ended interviews. Nonetheless, there should be some rough similarity between the prevalence observed in the two settings. Indeed, we have usually found such agreement. In one of our first mental models efforts, for example, 88% of interview respondents and 74% of questionnaire respondents believed that radon is a gas; 58% of interview respondents and 57% of questionnaire respondents erroneously believed that radon affects houseplants; just over 20% of both groups erroneously believed that some radon exposure comes from "rotting garbage." However, given the small number of open-ended interviews, the agreement should not always be that good, even if the two procedures tapped exactly the same beliefs. For example, while just over 80%

of those interviewed said radon comes from underground, only about 60% endorsed that belief on the structured questionnaire (Bostrom, Fischhoff, and Morgan, 1992). We cannot know whether that disparity reflects method difference or random variation. If both estimates lead to similar communication design choices, the gap need not be resolved.

2.8   Creating Communications

At this point in the process, the content of the communication should be pretty well determined. In effect, the message should help people to pass the test provided by the structured questionnaire. To that end, it must reinforce pertinent correct beliefs and discourage important incorrect ones.

In presenting that information, we are guided both by studies on the specific topic and by general research on document design and cognitive processes. For example, that research shows that effective communication requires an obvious logical structure. The expert influence diagram provides one such natural structure: how risks are created, how one gets exposed to them, what they do to one's body, how one can prevent them from happening or mitigate their effects. Chapters 6, 7, and 8 show other structures.

In order to ensure a coherent structure for the communication, it is usually essential to give one individual ultimate editorial authority for the entire product. Committee-written communications often serve no one's needs, especially if they are subject to continual fiddling by many hands. One institutional arrangement to manage the many-hands problem is to create an editorial committee, whose members divide responsibility for specific tasks. For example, one person might review the content for scientific accuracy, another for any liabilities that it creates for the issuing organization, another for how it addresses social and cultural sensitivities. However, their authority should be restricted to these domains of competence. Once committee members have passed judgment on their respective topics, a communication specialist should have final authority for creating the message with the best chance of getting across the jointly approved content. Thus, most of those involved in the process will have to smother their stylistic instincts at some point.

A single final author also has the best chance for creating a communication that speaks with a single voice. We try to have that voice be respectful and neutral. The communication should not talk down to its audience. It should assume that the audience is interested in and capable of mastering the material. It should concentrate on providing the information that people will need to form their own independent opinions and reach their own conclusions. It should authoritatively reflect the state of the science and explain uncertainties and controversies in a balanced, scientifically accurate manner.

These preferences reflect the intellectual roots of our approach in decision theory, which emphasizes helping people to make the choices that they view as in their own best interests. Communications derived from a public health perspective often adopt a rather different stance, seeing their goal as getting people to do what some experts, perhaps aided by some lay advisers, have determined to be good for them. In such contexts, a persuasive tone is entirely proper. With proper institutional oversight and control, there may even be an ethical case for manipulating or compelling recipients to adopt specific actions for their own good or that of society (e.g., smoking, storm evacuation). However, we believe that a neutral stance is appropriate for communicating about socially controlled risks and for most other risks under people's individual control. We believe that giving people the information they need, and the help needed to process that information, is often the most effective way of achieving "appropriate behavior," even where persuasion is legitimate. Good communication should help people to see what is right for them. This may take time. However, as the persistent decline in the rate of smoking and the persistent rise in the rate of seat belt use indicate, faced with clear and compelling risk information, collectively and individually many people eventually decide they should overcome old habits and do the safe thing. Even when this is not the case, the long-term health of relations between experts and the public argue for candor (Fischhoff, 1998; National Research Council, 1989).

2.9 More Testing

As they are developed, communications require systematic empirical testing. Initially, this will require open-ended procedures, allowing diverse responses to emerge. To the extent possible, these tests should simulate the conditions under which the communications will eventually be used. For example, if people will study the messages by themselves, test subjects should be asked to take the drafts home and mark them up with questions, then report back on their impressions, confusions, and so on. Or, individuals might be asked to think aloud as they slowly read through the draft. If people will eventually discuss the risk in groups, then appropriately composed focus groups might be used.

Often, these lay evaluations are sobering experiences. Drafts that looked sound to us end up being trashed by readers who were confused, misled, or offended by passages or pictures that we thought were entirely straightforward or innocuous. The larger the ensuing changes are, the greater need there is to involve substantive experts in ensuring that nothing has gone awry in the revisions – and to go back for further testing.

Once the developmental work seems complete, the communication should be evaluated, using the confirmatory questionnaire. This test not only assesses overall knowledge levels but also provides diagnostics regarding particular areas needing additional attention. It might reveal population differences in comprehension, with one version of the communication working better with some people and another version with others. If multiple, targeted messages are not possible, then a policy choice may be needed, deciding whom to reach on which issues. If audience comprehension is still incomplete, even after processing the message, then a decision will have to be made regarding the acceptable level of misunderstanding: Is the best possible communication adequate for the task assigned it? If not, then ancillary methods (e.g., personal counseling, banning products) might be necessary.

2.10   Is It Worth It?

A crude version of this process can be accomplished in a calendar month, with a couple of person-months of personnel time – especially within an organization having permanent professional and communication staffs. A full effort, done to scientific quality standards, requires between three months and a year, depending on how focused the effort is and how complicated the problem is found to be. That effort might cost on the order of $100,000. The attractiveness of this investment depends on the consequences of misunderstanding. These will vary with the risk, audience, and institutions involved. Many risk decisions involve millions or even billions of dollars. A small fraction of this, spent on helping the public to become better informed decision makers, may save much larger amounts down the road – by reducing regulatory conflict, product liability suits, irate consumers, needless casualties, perceptions of callousness, unnecessary alarm, lost credibility, and the other costs associated with avoidable conflicts.

The revealed preference of many organizations is that risk communication is worth much more than a mental models project costs. Many organizations have much larger budgets for advertising, public relations, annual reports, label design, and other efforts with risk communication objectives. We believe that the return on this investment can be substantially increased (and the chance of it backfiring substantially reduced) by spending some of it on the sort of systematic research that we advocate here. We believe, too, that its use will improve not only the production of individual communications but also the communicators' ability to learn from their own experiences. Its tools offer ways to collect evidence documenting that experience. Its structure offers a systematic way to pool what is learned and to organize staff work in ways that should be relatively efficient and satisfying. It provides ways to resolve otherwise frustrating differences of opinion about communication. And finally, it creates modular solutions that might be used in addressing new problems.

We still learn something from each application (and, because we work at universities, are drawn to applications that have something new and general to teach us). Nonetheless, we think that anyone should be able to master the procedure and join us on the learning curve.

References

Bostrom, A., Fischhoff, B., and Morgan, M. G. (1992). "Characterizing Mental Models of Hazardous Processes: A Methodology and an Application to Radon," *Journal of Social Issues,* 48(4):85–100.

Carroll, J., and Olson, J. R., eds. (1987). *Mental Models in Human-Computer Interaction: Research Issues about What the User of Software Knows.* National Academy Press, Washington, D.C.

Craik, K. (1943). *The Nature of Explanation,* Cambridge University Press, Cambridge.

Collins, A., and Gentner, D. (1987). "How People Construct Mental Models," in D. Holland and N. Quinn, eds., *Cultural Models in Language and Thought,* Cambridge University Press, Cambridge.

di Sessa, A. (1983). "Unlearning Aristotelian Physics," in D. Gentner and A. L. Stevens, eds., *Mental Models,* Lawrence Erlbaum Associates, Hillsdale, N.J.
(1984). "Learning About Knowing," in E. Klein, ed., *Children and Computers,* Jossey-Bass, San Francisco.

Doyle, J. K., and Ford, D. N. (1998). "Mental Models Concepts for Systems Dynamics Research," *System Dynamics Review,* 14(1):3–29.

Driver, R., and Easley, J. (1978). "Pupils and Paradigms: A Review of Literature Related to Concept Development in Adolescent Science Students," *Studies in Science Education,* 5:61–84.

Fischhoff, B. (1991). "Value Elicitation: Is There Anything in There?" *American Psychologist,* 46:835–847.
(1998). "Communication unto Others . . . ," *Reliability Engineering and System Safety,* 59:63–72.

Galotti, K. M. (1989). "Approaches to Studying Formal and Everyday Reasoning," *Psychological Bulletin,* 105(3):3:331–351.

Gentner, D., and Stevens, A. L. (1983). *Mental Models.* Lawrence Erlbaum Associates, Hillsdale, N.J.

Jungermann, H., Schütz, H., and Thüring, M. (1988). "Mental Models in Risk Assessment: Informing People about Drugs," *Risk Analysis,* 8(1):147–155.
(1989). "How People Might Process Medical Information: A 'Mental Model' Perspective on the Use of Package Inserts," in R. E. Kasperson and P. J. M. Stallen, eds., *Communicating Health and Safety Risks to the Public, International Perspectives.* Reidel, Dordrecht.

Kempton, W. (1986). "Two Theories of Home Heat Control," *Cognitive Science,* 10:75–90. Reprinted and expanded in *Cultural Models in Language and Thought,* D. Holland and N. Quinn, eds., Cambridge University Press, New York, 1987.
(1988). "Folk Models of Air Conditioning and Heating Systems: Summary of Findings." Paper presented at AAAS Symposium on Cognitive Ethnography of Industrial Society, Boston, February 14.

Kempton, W., Feuermann, D., and McGarity, A. (1992). "I Always Turn It on Super: User Decisions about When and How to Operate Room Air Conditioners," *Energy and Buildings*, 18:177–192.

National Research Council. (1981). *Surveys of Subjective Phenomena*. National Research Council, Washington, D.C.

(1989). *Improving Risk Communication*, National Research Council, Washington, D.C.

Norman, D. (1983). "Some Observations on Mental Models," in D. Gentner and A. L. Stevens, eds., *Mental Models*. Lawrence Erlbaum Associates, Hillsdale, N.J.

Nussbaum, J., and Novick, S. (1982). "Alternative Frameworks, Conceptual Conflict and Accommodation: Toward a Principled Teaching Strategy," *Instructional Science*, 11:183–200.

Poulton, C. (1989). *Bias in Quantitative Judgment*. Lawrence Erlbaum Associates, Hillsdale, N.J.

Rouse, W. B., and Morris, N. M. (1986). "On Looking into the Black Box: Prospects and Limits in the Search for Mental Models," *Psychological Bulletin*, 100:349–363.

Schwarz, N. (1996). *Cognition and Communication: Judgmental Biases, Research Methods, and the Logic of Conversation*. Lawrence Erlbaum Associates, Hillsdale, N.J.

(1999). "Self-Reports: How the Questions Shape the Answers," *American Psychologist*, 54:93–105.

Smith, V. K., Desvousges, W. H., Fisher, A., and Johnson, F. R. (1988). "Learning about Radon's Risk," *Journal of Risk and Uncertainty*, 1:233–258.

Smith, V. K., Desvousges, W. H., Johnson, F. R., and Fisher, A. (1990). "Can Public Information Programs Affect Risk Perceptions?" *Journal of Policy Analysis and Management*, 9:41–59.

Smith, V. K., and Johnson, F. R. (1988). "How Do Risk Perceptions Respond to Information? The Case of Radon," *The Review of Economics and Statistics*, 70:1–8.

Turner, C. F., and Martin, E., eds. (1984). *Surveying Subjective Phenomena*. Russell Sage, New York.

U.S. Environmental Protection Agency and Centers for Disease Control. (1986). *A Citizen's Guide to Radon: What It Is and What to Do about It* (OPA-86-004). U.S. Government Printing Office, Washington, D.C.

3

CREATING AN
EXPERT MODEL OF
THE RISK

If communications are to be authoritative, they must reflect expert understanding. To that end, the first step in developing risk communications is creating influence diagrams that summarize the relevant expert knowledge. As mentioned, although it is called an "expert model," the information that it contains need not reside in the mind of any one expert, especially not in such explicit form. Indeed, the creation of an expert model can be a complex, creative act, forcing participating experts to reflect systematically on the structure of their domain.

Even when chosen for expertise about a specific risk, such as indoor radon, an expert is likely to know a lot more than most of us need to know about that risk. Some expert knowledge is likely to be arcane or simply irrelevant to the decisions that risk communication recipients face. Much expert knowledge is too detailed or peripheral to guide risk communication development. The decision or set of decisions that your communication will inform may be defined in part by the experts you consult, who have specialized knowledge about risk mitigation. But once that decision set is defined, it should guide your expert model development as well. In Section 3.2, we discuss converting scientific information about risk into a decision model, such as an influence diagram.

3.1 Influence Diagrams

Influence diagrams were developed by decision analysts as a convenient way to summarize information about uncertain decision situations, allowing effective communication between experts and decision makers and the conduct of information-related analyses (Howard and Matheson, 1981; Shachter, 1988). We have chosen to use them in our work on risk communication because they can be applied to virtually any risk, are compatible with experts' conventional ways of thinking, are easily understood and readily subjected to peer review, and fit with a decision-making perspective. In creating an influence diagram, it is essential to follow the formalisms that we are about to describe. In communicating one, it may be adequate, at least initially, to look at its parts more heuristically – showing which factors matter and how they are interrelated.

An influence diagram is a directed graph, with arrows or "influences" connecting related "nodes." Simple influence diagrams contain nodes of two kinds: ovals, which represent uncertain circumstances or "states of the world," and rectangles, which represent choices made by a decision maker. An arrow between two nodes means that the node at the arrow's tail exerts some "influence" on the node at the arrow's head; more formally, knowing the value of the variable at the tail node helps one to predict the value of the variable at the head node. For example, an influence diagram of the weather might include an arrow from an oval representing sunshine to an oval representing air temperature, because sunshine is a factor that influences air temperature (and knowing how sunny it is helps in predicting the temperature).

The easiest way to explain influence diagrams is with an illustration. Suppose that we want to construct a model of the risk that a resident of a two-story home will trip and fall on the stairs.[1] That process involves two stages. Before they can fall, stair climbers must lose their balance by tripping. After losing their balance, they either recover their balance or fall. Thus, the diagram starts with two ovals labeled "trip on stairs" and "fall on stairs," as shown in Figure 3.1a.

---

[1]There are a number of other reasons, in addition to tripping, that someone may fall on the stairs. For ease of illustration, we will leave these other causes out of this example.

This two-node model is too simple to be very helpful for either estimating or communicating the risks. It does not show any of the factors influencing the likelihood that someone will trip or the likelihood that, having tripped, that person will then fall. It does show how irreversible tripping is, in the sense of how doomed one is to fall, once tripping has begun. If that conditional probability is high, then one should avoid tripping at all costs. One way to make the model more useful is by elaborating the factors influencing the likelihood of such tripping. These might include the stair climber's agility, the stairs' height and width, the floor covering, the kids' tendency to leave toys on the stairs, and the cat's preference for sleeping on the stairs. Lighting may, in turn, affect the chances of seeing the cat or toys. Figure 3.1b adds these factors. "Children's behavior" is a predictor of "toys on the stairs." Others are certainly possible.

Figure 3.1c adds two factors influencing the likelihood of not recovering one's balance after tripping. One is the person's agility, already implicated in influencing the probability of tripping; this is shown by the second arrow from "agility" to "fall on stairs." The second is whether there is a railing to grab.

Finally, there are decisions that people can make that will influence the outcome. For example, a person might decide to stop using the stairs and live just on the ground floor. Figure 3.1d shows this decision with the rectangle labeled "use the stairs," which influences the chance of tripping. The homeowner might also decide to remodel, affecting factors that influence the chance of tripping (e.g., floor covering and lighting), or the chance of falling (e.g., having a railing). Finally, while changing the cat's sleeping habits is unlikely, the family probably has some chance of persuading the children not to leave their toys on the stairs. Because the influence here is not directly on the toys but on the children, it appears as a two-step process; the decision to discipline the children influences the children's behavior, which, in turn, influences where the toys are left.

Clemen (1991) has pointed out that people often confuse influence diagrams with flowcharts, in which each node represents an event or activity in a process, such as making bread. An influence diagram can be thought of as a snapshot of all the factors that influence the state of the world, including the decisions that can trigger or shape the processes cap-

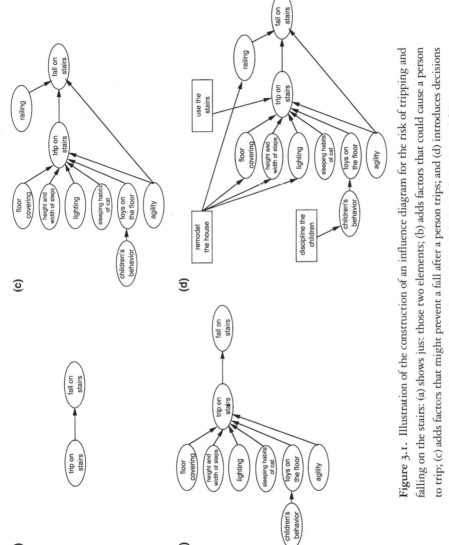

Figure 3.1. Illustration of the construction of an influence diagram for the risk of tripping and falling on the stairs: (a) shows just those two elements; (b) adds factors that could cause a person to trip; (c) adds factors that might prevent a fall after a person trips; and (d) introduces decisions that residents could make that would influence the probabilities of tripping and falling.

tured in the nodes. In contrast, a flowchart shows a deterministic process that is stepped through one box at a time. In a flowchart, the outcomes of all previous nodes are known at the time that a particular box is reached. In an influence diagram, many nodes can be involved simultaneously and involve uncertain outcomes – so that the outcome is unknown until the process has played itself out.

The formalisms underlying influence diagrams allow including both causal and noncausal (or indirectly causal) influences. For example, high levels of radon are more prevalent in certain parts of the country. If a certain ethnic group disproportionately lives in those parts, then knowing residents' ethnic background would help to predict their radon levels. However, there would be no causal relation between ethnicity and radon exposure. In some such cases, there is a common cause between the two indirectly related factors. If so, then it may be possible to model the underlying causal structure, for example, where prejudice leads members of an ethnic group both to be poor and to live in an area with high risk levels. Being able to include both causal and noncausal relationships allows influence diagrams to accommodate whatever information is available. However, because causal relations can be easier to understand, other things being equal, they might be preferred in communications.

Our descriptions of influence diagrams here are typically informal. By imposing a few structural rules, attaching actual mathematical relationships to the influences, and describing the value of the uncertain variables in terms of probability distributions, influence diagrams can be given much more precise meaning. Indeed, when properly constructed, an influence diagram can be converted into a decision tree, a standard tool in the field of decision analysis (Miller et. al, 1976). The boxed section "Influence Diagrams and Computer Models" elaborates further on the relation between influence diagrams and decision trees. Experience with our mental models method naturally leads to mastery of these procedures. For the simplest uses, though, all one needs to ask is whether the value of the variable at Node B depends on the value of the variable at Node A. If so, then draw an arrow from A to B.

The goal in constructing an expert model is achieving sufficient clarity that the influence diagram could be converted into an executable computer model. Even when that next step is not taken, formally creating an

Influence Diagrams and Computer Models

The computer environment Analytica* uses influence diagrams as the interface for building computer models. Variables in these models are represented as nodes in an influence diagram, which the modeler can construct by clicking on icons, dragging them into place, and connecting them with arrows to indicate influences. Below this graphical layer, the modeler can specify the mathematical relationships indicating the nature of the influences. Importantly, Analytica allows the introduction of uncertainty regarding the values of the model variables. Suppose, for example, that we wanted to build an Analytica model to compute the volume of a rectangular building. We start by creating an influence diagram that looks like this:

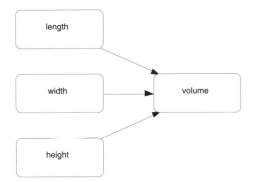

If we double click on the node labeled "length," the computer gives us an opportunity to specify a mathematical definition. For example, we could define length as 10 meters, if we knew it with precision. We can do the same thing for width, or we might specify a "vector" of three values [10, 20, 30], which tells the computer to run the model once for each of the three widths: 10, 20, and 30 meters. Suppose we are uncertain about the height. If our knowledge allowed us, we could specify our uncertainty as a probability distribution, such as a lognormal distributed with a geometric mean value of 10 meters, and a geometric standard deviation value of 1.5. The computer's evaluation of the model would produce a result like this:

---

*Analytica is distributed by Lumina Decision Systems, Inc., 59 N. Santa Cruz Avenue, Suite Q, Los Gatos, CA 95030; info@lumina.com.

(continued)

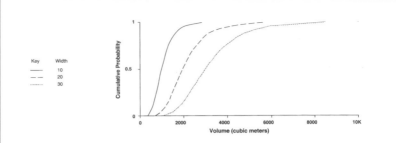

The first curve shows the cumulative probability distribution for volume when length is 10 meters, width is 10 meters, and height has the specified uncertainty distribution. The second and third curves show the distributions for volume when the width is 20 and 30 meters, respectively.

Alternatively, we could ask the computer to show us how uncertainty changes as we vary the width from 10 to 30 meters:

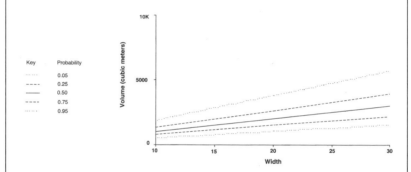

In this case, the five lines show a range of confidence from 5% at the bottom to 95% at the top.

In building a model of a complex system, the influence diagram can quickly become extremely complicated. In order to deal with this complexity, it is convenient to group parts of the diagram together as submodels, then organize them hierarchically. For example, models of climate change need to include physical processes (in the atmosphere and oceans), social processes (population, economic consumption and production), and biological and ecological processes (in managed and unmanaged contexts). It also should include human actions (emissions, taxes, and various forms of adaptation) that can feed back upon the system and influence its future course.

Figure 3.10 on page 59 illustrates a portion of such a hierarchically organized model, the Integrated Climate Assessment Model (ICAM) developed in Analytica by Hadi Dowlatabadi at Carnegie Mellon (http://hdgc.epp.cmu.edu). In this illustration, heavy ovals contain submodels, which are elaborated at a lower level in the hierarchy.

The upper-left corner of the illustration shows the top level of the hierarchical family of influence diagrams and associated computer models. Economic processes produce emissions to the atmosphere, which influence climate through various geophysical processes. These provide feedback to the natural world and the economy. When uses run the model, they can specify various combinations of three broad policy options (abatement, adaptation, and geoengineering). Figure 3.10 illustrates what users would see if they were to explore the submodel labeled "demographic and economic processes." If, instead, users double clicked on the node labeled "energy and emissions" in the top-level representation of ICAM, they would see a screen that displays several different kinds of emissions, such as carbon dioxide, methane, and fine particles. If they double clicked on the node for "methane," they would move one level further down in the model hierarchy and see separate nodes for natural and human (anthropogenic) sources. Double clicking on this last node would produce a screen like this:

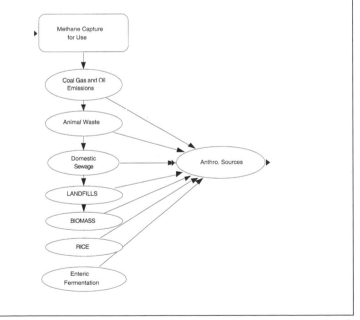

(continued)

41

Here, all the principal human sources of methane release are indicated. Under each of the left-hand nodes in this diagram is a set of mathematical relations and numerical data from measurements made around the world. By choosing the methane emissions node, and asking the computer to evaluate it, the user could ask the computer model to plot a (probabilistic) projection of methane emissions for the next century.

expert model inevitably involves some (at least implicit) quantification. The experts must at least run some numbers in their heads when pruning minor influences in order to keep the diagram to a manageable size.

The scientific use of influence diagrams allows the calculation of risk levels associated with different states of nature, and with different human actions. For example, it might predict the lung cancer rate for houses with a given ground concentration of radon and the effect on that rate of various changes in ventilation. In some cases, there will be firm scientific evidence, providing the estimates needed to obtain these numerical solutions. In other cases, expert judgment will be needed. Such analyses can also help to direct and evaluate interventions. For example, an influence diagram for the risks of AIDS would include the effects of drinking on people's exposure to the virus (Fig. 8.1 on page 163). One arrow might reflect the effects of alcohol on the user's physical ability to take protective measures; a second arrow might show the effects on evaluating the risks and benefits of behaviors. A formal analysis of such an influence diagram could show the effect of, say, eliminating all drinking or creating fail-safe condoms (so that clear thinking is less necessary).

3.2   Strategies for Creating Influence Diagrams

There is no simple recipe for converting the scientific information on a risk into an influence diagram. Even among the most experienced risk analysts, the process is an iterative one, as specialists from the relevant disciplines review one another's work and reflect on their own. The construction of each new diagram poses different, and often interesting, challenges. Section 3.3 provides some examples of influence diagrams, along with discussions of their properties. Before turning to them, we sketch several generic strategies in this section. These can be used in isolation or in combination, as a way of providing converging approaches to a common problem.

A full influence diagram, developed through repeated iterations with multiple experts, can be a daunting place to begin the study of a problem. Indeed, looking at some of the worked examples in this volume might lead some readers to conclude that this is all too complicated for those without a staff having deep analytical experience. However, we encourage readers to stay the course. The complete diagrams here all began as simple ideas. Moreover, even a rough approximation will provide much of the guidance needed for creating effective risk communications. These diagrams do not require the detail and precision required for performing formal quantitative analyses. Nonetheless, pushing the analyses as far as possible helps to refine thinking about a risk (see the boxed section "Influence Diagrams and Computer Models").

Technical experts are often happy to assist risk communicators to develop diagrams that capture the key elements of their knowledge. Directed graphs, such as influence diagrams, are common devices in many technical fields. Once the particular formalism has been explained to them, experts often demonstrate considerable facility in using it. Jointly creating the diagram also provides a structured and mutually respectful way for communicators and technical experts to ensure that they understand one another.[2] It is also a good way to communicate with technical specialists, by listening to them first. It can make communication with laypeople seem more tractable to skeptical experts, by decomposing the task into more manageable pieces.

---

[2]There are also several computer programs that can be used for mounting influence diagrams. Some just make it easier to create the physical representation than with conventional drawing programs (by treating arrows as relationships, and not just lines). Others, like Analytica and DPL (Decision Programming Language), allow the user to build a full computer model underneath the diagrams and provide help, such as consistency checks.

The assembly method   In one sense, an influence diagram is just a set of linked factors. As a result, it can, in principle, be assembled by listing all relevant factors and then figuring out how they are related. The listing step might be done alone or as a group brainstorming effort. Members of the team might even conduct mental models interviews with one another. The factors that emerge could then be sorted into related categories, keeping an eye out for functionally equivalent ones. If an overall structure does not emerge spontaneously, then it might reveal itself by making pair-wise comparisons among factors. One strategy that we have sometimes used is to write the factors on Post-it notes and then put them on a blackboard, so that they can be moved around easily, with chalk arrows being drawn and erased until an appropriate structure has been found.

The materials/energy balance method   Many risks involve physical processes. The laws of physics say that under normal circumstances both energy and materials are conserved – that is, the same amount goes in and comes out. Thus the total mass of all the raw materials flowing into a manufacturing plant must equal the mass of the products and wastes flowing out of it and permanently stored there. The same sort of calculation can be done with energy (although the form of the energy may change, as when mechanical or electric energy ends up as heat). Technical experts often rely on such physical conservation laws when they analyze risks.

For example, many risks are created by exposure to particular materials, such as lead. Tracking that (fixed) quantity allows an expert to set an upper limit on possible exposures. The influence diagram then becomes a summary of the factors affecting the amount of the material available for human contact. Those factors might include natural processes, concentrating or dispersing the material, and deliberate human interventions. Once the exposure has occurred, an effects model is needed to show which health effects are possible and how their progress depends on medical treatment, self-care, and so on (Morgan and McMichael, 1981; Morgan, 1993).

The scenario method   Most risks can be described in terms of a causal chain of events. The risk literature contains several discussions of such chains (Morgan, 1981; Hohenemser, Kates, and Slovic, 1983; Hohenemser,

Kasperson, and Kates, 1985; Earle and Cvetkovich, 1983; Kammen and Hassenzahl, 1999). Something happens (e.g., people get exposed to pollution), then another thing happens (e.g., they ingest the pollution), and, eventually, someone gets hurt. The occurrence of each event affects the probability of the next, thereby meriting a link in the influence diagram. Branches leading into each event can then capture the other factors that increase or decrease its probability of occurrence. The chain might be traced forward and backward, hoping that these complementary perspectives reveal a more complete picture. That is, a situation may look different when worrying about how one thing can lead to another and when worrying about where specific problems might come from. Scenarios can be used to test models created by other methods for completeness, by tracing them through the diagram.

The template method   When risk processes have similar structures, each need not be analyzed separately, based on first principles. Rather, one can create modules capturing recurrent exposure and effects processes. For example, as Figure 3.2 illustrates, exposure processes typically precede effects processes. How each operates may be influenced by similar environmental, physiological, and behavioral factors – and, in turn, by the choices made by risk managers or others.

Figure 3.3 applies this general template to the specific risk of infection by Lyme disease. The portion of the diagram to the left of the vertical dashed line describes the processes influencing a person's chances of being bitten by a disease-infected tick. The portion of the diagram to the right of the vertical line describes the processes that influence whether a bitten person becomes infected and, if so, how serious the resulting disease is.

Lyme disease is carried by deer ticks. Adult ticks live and feed on a variety of animals, including white-tailed deer. After mating in the fall, the ticks drop off to lay eggs. Deer tick eggs hatch and develop into larvae, which feed on small animals, such as white-footed mice. If the mouse happens to be infected by Lyme disease, the tick nymphs also become infected and may go on to infect other mice. From mid- to late summer, tick nymphs lie in grass and on bushes, waiting to attach themselves to a passing animal, such as a deer, pet, or person.

The rectangles show control strategies. Habitat influences the popula-

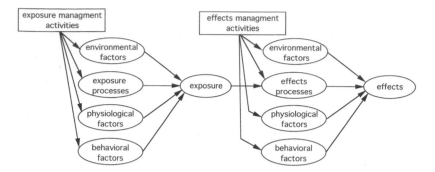

Figure 3.2. Example of a basic template for an influence diagram of risk processes. The left side shows the factors that influence exposure. The right side shows the factors that determine whether and how exposure results in effects.

tion and distribution of deer and mice; controlling either species will reduce risks. Distributing containers of insecticide-impregnated cotton, which mice find attractive as bedding for their nests, can reduce the populations of tick nymphs and ticks among mice. The probability that people will be bitten (exposed) depends on where they go, how they behave, what they wear, and whether they frequently inspect exposed skin for ticks. These behaviors might be affected by educational efforts. When a person is bitten by an infected tick, it takes some time before the infection is passed. Hence, how quickly people discover ticks and how effectively they remove them can affect their risk of infection. Once infection occurs, how quickly it is diagnosed and how effectively it is treated affect the progression of the disease and the severity of its symptoms. If untreated, patients may develop heart problems, headaches, stiff neck, and facial paralysis after a few months. The organization of medical services can affect these processes.

Although the specifics will vary from one risk to the next, many have an underlying structure like that in Figure 3.2.

At first glance, the examples in the next section may seem dauntingly complicated. However, they typically yield to a few minutes of patient study. Start somewhere and go forward or backward, asking the reason for each connection. Then, see what other things are connected to each node.

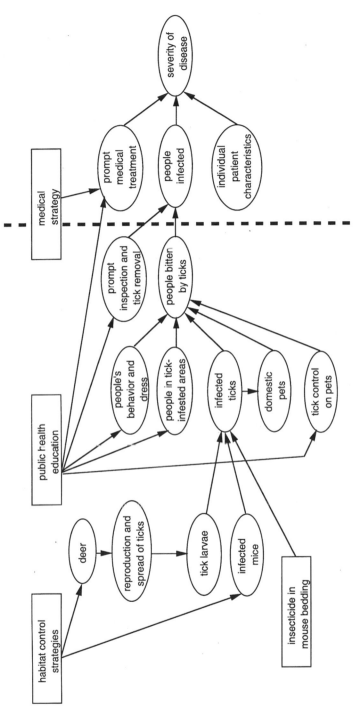

Figure 3.3. Illustration of applying the basic template of Figure 3.2 to the specific risk of infection by Lyme disease. The portion of the diagram to the left of the vertical dashed line deals with exposure processes. The portion to the right of the dashed line deals with effects processes. The diagram has been simplified for illustrative purposes.

47

Gradually, the overall structure will emerge. In some cases, a simple story ties it all together. In other cases, the reality is just complicated, and the diagram reflects that.

3.3   Examples of Influence Diagrams

This section presents several of the influence diagrams that we have used in developing risk communications.

Indoor air pollution   Figure 3.4 describes radon exposure in homes. It was developed primarily by Keith Florig, an engineer with a background in nuclear and environmental topics, in consultation with members of our research group and external reviewers. To make it easier to follow the diagram, large boxes bracket the major processes, showing the hierarchical structure of the model.

The diagram is for a home with a crawl space. Four different sources of radon are included. Usually, the most important is the soil under the building, labeled "radon from soil gas" (in the lower-left corner of Figure 3.4). Second, radon can diffuse out of building materials containing naturally occurring radium. Third, radon dissolved in water can be released when the water is used in the home (e.g., in showering). Because radon is short-lived, it is seldom found in municipal water systems, but it is not uncommon in well water in locations with high radon concentrations. Finally, radon is sometimes found in natural gas. Although it is uncommon in commercially supplied gas, it can be significant in rural homes with small private gas wells.

The diagram shows the variables that influence the intensity of the source. These factors lead to a node that represents the flow rate, or "flux," of radon from each source into the home.

After radon flows into a home, things happen to it. The gas undergoes radioactive decay into very small particles (called radon "daughters" or "progeny"). Some of these decay products can be harmlessly lost by attaching to or "plating out" on surfaces in the home; others are inhaled and attach to people's lungs. These processes, by which radon and its decay products leave the air, are described in the lower-right corner of the

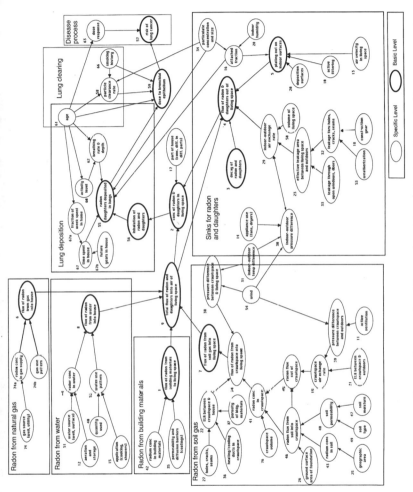

Figure 3.4. Influence diagram for risks produced by radon in a house built over a crawl space. Basic high-level concepts are represented with bolder ovals. *Source*: Bostrom, Fischhoff, and Morgan (1992).

decay products leave the air, are described in the lower-right corner of the diagram, labeled "sinks for radon and daughters."

The concentration of radon and its by-products in the living space depends on both the sources (the four boxes along the left side of the diagram) and the sinks (the box in the lower right).

The three overlapping boxes in the upper-right portion of the diagram contain elements that determine what gets into people's lungs, how much stays there and for how long, and whether the resulting exposure of lung tissue to ionizing radiation ultimately produces lung cancer many years later.

Throughout the diagram, the most important determinants of risk level and, hence, topics for communication are represented by heavy ovals.

Although the causal relations in the diagram are straightforward, it is easy to imagine laypeople not thinking of them spontaneously. Even specialists with technical expertise in one part of the diagram might overlook factors in another.

Our construction of this influence diagram used a combination of the scenario method, the materials-balance approach, and the exposure-to-effects template. In order for health effects to occur, people need to be exposed to radon. For that to happen, radon needs to come from somewhere and then reach them, without being removed by any intervening processes. Thus, we asked ourselves and our experts where the radon comes from and where it goes, what determines the rates of these processes, and, finally, what damage it can do while in contact with people. Given the limited success of medical treatment for lung cancer, we did not elaborate on the disease processes. Because the source of lung cancer has no effect on its progress, a standard disease module could be used here and in related applications. Facts like radon being a gas and radioactive do not appear directly in the influence diagram. Rather, they are background concepts, knowledge of which is essential to interpreting the links that are shown.

In a diagram that we developed for another indoor air pollutant, perchlorethylene, used as dry-cleaning fluid, we had to elaborate the health impacts portion of the diagram in much greater detail. Perchlorethylene differs from radon in having several possible health effects (i.e., it may be a carcinogen, teratogen, and neurotoxin). These effects have, in turn, a different set of covariates (e.g., pregnancy is a risk factor in some contexts, but not others) (Fischhoff et al., 1998).

In developing an influence diagram for other indoor or outdoor air pollutants, one would follow a similar process. The diagram would need to describe where the material comes from; the processes (e.g., loss, chemical reaction) that determine its concentration; the behavioral, physiological, and other factors that determine the amount of exposure; and various health, environmental, or other consequences that such exposure can produce. In some cases, air may not be the only route of exposure. For example, water can be a secondary source of exposure to the perchlorethylene used in dry cleaning. When more than one "medium" (air, water, soil) is involved, it may be necessary to construct parallel diagrams for each.

Problems that involve water pollution can be diagrammed in much the same way. The specific details of the sources, transport, conversion, loss, and exposure processes may all be different, but the basic structure applies.

Catastrophic failure of an engineered system   Figure 3.5 shows an influence diagram for the risks created by nuclear energy sources on spacecraft. Sometimes, these sources are used as a matter of engineering convenience. More typically, they are a necessity, providing the only way to deliver large amounts of power or to support missions far from the sun, where photocells are impractical. This example provides a mixture of technologies that, for many people, evoke feelings that are good (spacecraft) and bad (nuclear power). The risks arise from the breakdown in an engineered system. As a result, the influence diagram follows the scenarios initiated by various possible breakdowns. The probability of each path depends on how the system is engineered (affecting the kind of breakdown and attempted containment), where the breakdown happens (affecting its proximity to people and its dispersal properties), and how various people respond to it (either issuing warnings or taking indicated precautions).

The diagram was primarily developed by Michael Maharik, an engineer with a background in aerospace systems (Maharik, 1992; Maharik et al., 1993). Figure 3.5 reproduces a simplified version. Figure 3.6 shows the

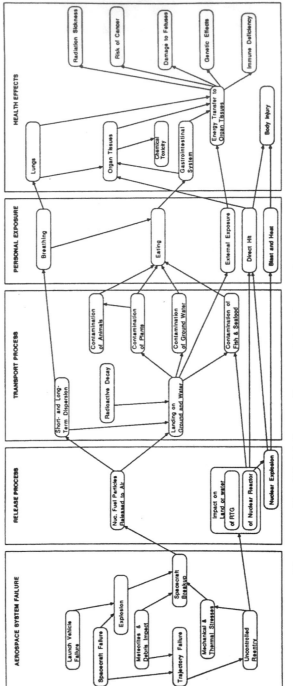

Figure 3.5. Simplified influence diagram of risks from nuclear energy sources on space-craft. *Source:* Maharik and Fischhoff (1992).

full diagram. As with radon, boxes have been added to help the viewer follow the overall structure. Moving from left to right, the first box displays influences that can result in the failure of the system (e.g., the launch vehicle may blow up and destroy the spacecraft or the spacecraft may crash to earth through other failures). The second box shows processes that can result in the release of radioactive materials into the environment. The third box shows how released materials might be transported to other locations and expose people. The final box, on the right-hand end of the diagram, shows how exposures can produce adverse health consequences.

This structure is fairly typical for failures resulting in environmental releases from engineered systems. The first section of the diagram involves processes that are unique to the particular system (oil tanker, chemical plant, waste storage facility). The subsequent exposure and effects processes develop in the same general way as with other forms of pollution.

Failures of engineered systems often can immediately affect people and property (by impact, fire, or explosion), as seen in the bottom of Figure 3.6. With some engineered systems, such as transportation, physical injury is often the principal source of health risk.

Infectious disease Infectious diseases, transmitted through either direct person-to-person contact or various intermediaries (or "vectors"), such as insects or contaminated needles, are an important class of risks. Figure 3.3 showed a simplified influence diagram for Lyme disease, with the movements of deer, mice, ticks, and people combining to create exposures.

Figure 3.7 provides a more elaborated diagram, describing the risks associated with AIDS. There are several parallel transmission processes for this disease, requiring either several separate diagrams or a single one formulated in general terms. This diagram adopts the latter strategy. As a result, it has the "clutter" of factors that are irrelevant for some modes of transmission. For example, alcohol consumption is very important for sexual exposures but irrelevant to transfusion exposures. Because human behavior is involved, some of the factors conceal extraordinarily complicated processes under a single label. For example, "motivation" appears as a single factor. Although it may be analytically efficient to reduce the variety of underlying processes affecting motivation to an aggregate measure, doing so provides little insight into how motivation might be antici-

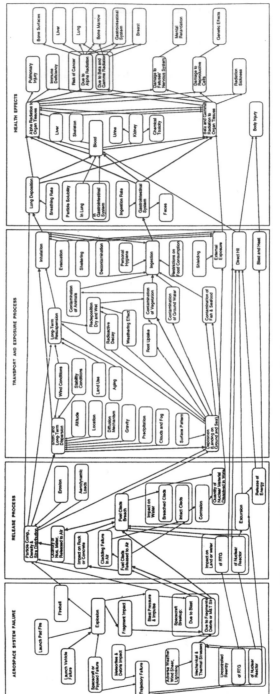

Figure 3.6. Full influence diagram of risks from nuclear energy sources on spacecraft.

Source: Maharik (1992).

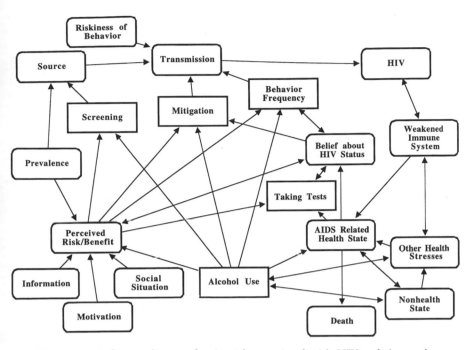

Figure 3.7. Influence diagram for the risks associated with HIV and the resulting disease, AIDS. *Source:* Fischhoff and Downs (1997).

pated or controlled. This node is, in effect, a placeholder for these contributing factors.[3]

The AIDS diagram differs from the others presented so far in having significant feedback. People who have, or fear that they have, HIV may change their behavior in ways that affect others' risk. The extent of their fears should be affected by test results or, more specifically, by their interpretation of those results. Analogous distinctions between perceived and actual risks can be found elsewhere in the diagram. For example, the actual prevalence of HIV affects the probability that an individual will come into contact with a source of the virus (e.g., a sex or drug partner). That individual's perception of that prevalence will affect how potential

[3]In a project on other sexually transmitted diseases, we expand this section of the AIDS influence diagram (Fischhoff, Downs, and Bruine de Bruin, 1998).

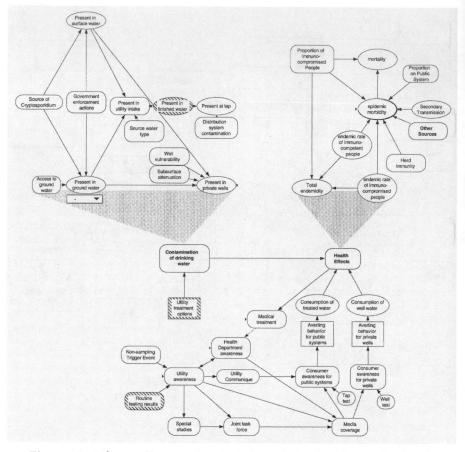

Figure 3.8. Influence diagram using Analytica to depict the risks associated with the contamination of drinking water by cryptosporidium. In this case, a full computable model has been developed. See Figure 3.9 for details of the structure that underlies the node "present in surface water." *Source:* Casman et al. (2000).

sources are screened, if at all; the effectiveness of that screening will determine the ultimate probability of exposure to a source having the virus.

Another quite different infectious disease is cryptosporidiosis. This disease is primarily transmitted to people in runoff from agricultural land that has become contaminated with cryptosporidium oocysts from infected cattle. The oocysts are so small and robust that once they contaminate water, it is quite difficult to filter or kill them with standard methods, such as chlorina-

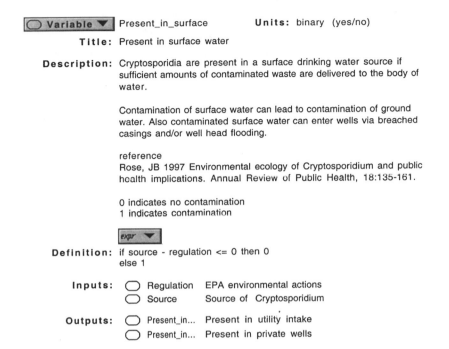

Figure 3.9. If a user were to "double click" on any variable in the Analytica model represented by the influence diagram in Figure 3.8, a "dialogue box" would open up, explaining the variable, the mathematical definition of the variable, and a list of the variables that feed into this variable (inputs) and are fed out from it (outputs). See Chapter 10 of the 1998 printing of Morgan and Henrion (1990) for more details on Analytica, or go to info@lumina.com.

tion. Our work has focused on the water treatment and public warning portions of the problem. Figure 3.8 displays the influence diagram, developed in Analytica with an executable computer model underlying the diagram. Figure 3.9 illustrates the details associated with the node labeled "present in surface water." A user can display this information by "double clicking" on that node in Figure 3.8. Even when actual calculations are not anticipated, creating such work sheets helps to ensure that each node has been clearly and consensually defined – not to mention documenting what was intended.

Global change   We have created expert models of several complex environmental problems, including acid rain (Rubin et al., 1992) and climate change (Morgan and Dowlatabadi, 1996). In these cases, our influence diagrams are so complicated that they would look like a plate of spaghetti if condensed to a single sheet of paper. Like the cryptosporidium example, such diagrams must be organized hierarchically, displaying just a few key pieces at the top level and adding detail as one moves down the hierarchy. Programs like Analytica have features to facilitate keeping everything organized in such a hierarchy. Figure 3.10 provides an illustration of how this particular one works. Although the full influence diagram is material for a course rather than a risk communication, some portions might be more appropriately sized.

When we undertook the development of risk communications on climate change and nuclear energy sources on spacecraft, we based our work on a simplified diagram. However, in contrast to the spacecraft example, the climate change diagram adopted a somewhat different organization than the one in the computer model, so as to emphasize the issues that were most central for general public understanding – which has different foci than some policy making and climate science. Figure 3.11 shows that diagram (Bostrom et al., 1994; Read et al., 1994). Thus, there is no single correct influence diagram for a given risk. The structure should be chosen to represent important expert knowledge in a form that addresses the audience's informational needs.

3.4   Summary

Influence diagrams provide a convenient way to summarize the expert knowledge upon which a risk communication will be built. The influence diagrams use a language that experts often find easy to understand and use. Because a well-designed influence diagram is compatible with more detailed decision or risk analyses, its rigor can build expert support for the communication process. However, a qualitative description is all that is needed for many communications. The discipline involved in constructing an influence diagram can help the risk communicator to ensure that nothing important is overlooked, that only decision-relevant information is included, and that a framework is created for obtaining systematic assistance from experts, as well as documenting the assumptions underlying the communication.

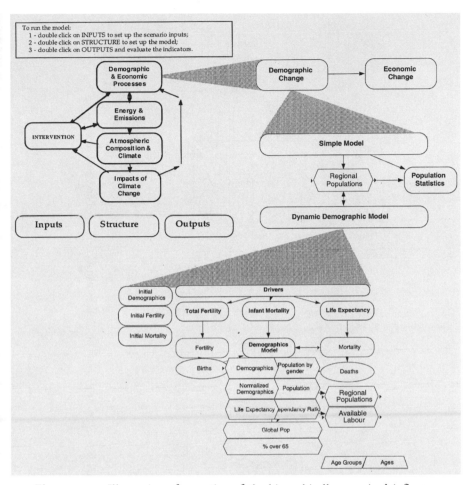

Figure 3.10. Illustration of a portion of the hierarchically organized influence diagram for the Carnegie Mellon Integrated Climate Assessment Model implemented in Analytica. Heavy boxes indicate submodels. Here we illustrate what users would see if they first double clicked on the submodel labeled "demographic and economic processes," then on the submodel labeled "demographic change," and finally on the submodel labeled "dynamic demographic model." Overall, the influence diagram that describes the ICAM computer model contains >1,800 objects, making a hierarchical organization absolutely essential. Note that in the first screen (upper-left portion of figure) there are three disconnected boxes across the bottom. They are *dialogue boxes* in which the user chooses inputs, outputs, and alternative model structures (such as a simple or dynamic demographic model).

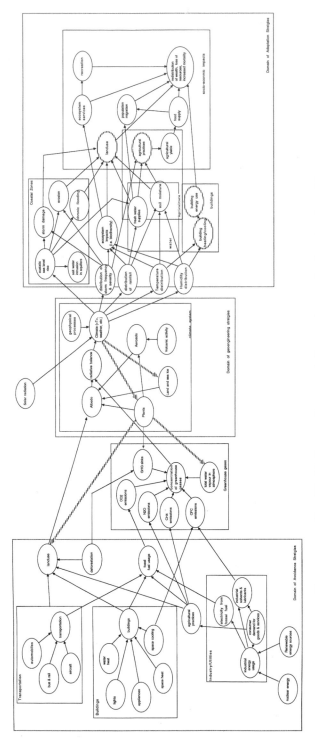

Figure 3.11. Simplified influence diagram of climate change, developed and used in mental models studies.

References

Bostrom, A., Atman, C. J., Fischoff, B., and Morgan, M. G. (1994). "Evaluating Risk Communications: Completing and Correcting Mental Models of Hazardous Processes, Part 2, *Risk Analysis,* 14:789–798.

Bostrom, A., Fischhoff, B., and Morgan, M. G. (1992). "Characterizing Mental Models of Hazardous Processes: A Methodology and an Application to Radon," *Journal of Social Issues,* 48(4):85–100.

Casman, E. A., Fischhoff, B., Palmgren, C., Small, M. J., and Wu, F. (2000). "An Integrated Risk Model of a Drinking-Water-Borne Cryptosporidiosis Outbreak." *Risk Analysis,* 20:495–511.

Clemen, R. T. (1991). *Making Hard Decisions: An Introduction to Decision Analysis,* 2nd ed. PWS-Kent Publishing, Boston, Mass.

Earle, T. C., and Cvetkovich, G. (1983). *Risk Judgment and the Communication of Hazard Information: Toward a New Look in the Study of Risk Perception.* Battelle Human Affairs Research Center, Seattle, Wash.

Fischhoff, B., and Downs, J. (1997). "Accentuate the Relevant," *Psychological Science,* 8(3):1–5.

Fischhoff, B., Downs, J., and Bruine de Bruin, W. (1998). "Adolescent Vulnerability: A Framework for Behavioral Interventions," *Applied and Preventive Psychology,* 7:77–94.

Fischhoff, B., Riley, D., Kovacs, D., and Small, M. (1998). "What Information Belongs in a Warning? A Mental Models Approach," *Psychology and Marketing,* 15(7):663–686.

Hohenemser, C., Kasperson, R. E., and Kates, R. W. (1985). "Causal Structure," in R. W. Kates, C. Hohenemser, and J. X. Kasperson, eds., *Perilous Progress.* Westview Press, Boulder, Colo., pp. 25–42.

Hohenemser, C., Kates, R. W., and Slovic, P. (1983). "The Nature of Technological Hazard," *Science,* 220:378–384.

Howard, R. A., and Matheson, J. (1981). "Influence Diagrams," in *The Principles and Applications of Decision Analysis,* Vol. II. Strategic Decisions Group, Menlo Park, Calif.

Kammen, D., and Hassenzahl, D. (1999). *Shall We Risk It?* Princeton University Press, Princeton, N.J.

Maharik, M. (1992). "Public Perception of the Risks of an Unfamiliar Technology: The Case of Using Nuclear Energy Sources for Space Missions." Ph.D. dissertation, Department of Engineering and Public Policy, Carnegie Mellon University.

Maharik, M., and Fischhoff, B. (1992). "The Risks of Nuclear Energy Sources in Space: Some Activists' Perceptions," *Risk Analysis,* 12:383–392.

Maharik, M., Fischhoff, B., and Morgan, M. G. (1993). "Risk Knowledge and Risk Attitudes Regarding Nuclear Energy Sources in Space," *Risk Analysis,* 13:345–353.

Miller, A. C., Merkhofer, M. W., Howard, R. A., Matheson, J. E., and Rice, T. R. (1976). *Development of Automated Aids for Decision Analysis.* Stanford Research Institute, Menlo Park, Calif.

Morgan, M. G. (1981). "Probing the Question of Technological Risk" and "Choosing and Managing Technology-Induced Risk," *IEEE Spectrum,* 18(11):58–64 and 18(12):53–60.

———. (1993). "Risk Analysis and Management," *Scientific American,* (July):32–41.

Morgan, M. G., and Dowlatabadi, H. (1996). "Learning from Integrated Assessment of Climate Change," *Climatic Change,* 34:337–368.

Morgan, M. G., and Henrion, M., with a chapter by Small, M. (1990). *Uncertainty: A Guide to Dealing with Uncertainty in Quantitative Risk and Policy Analysis.* Cambridge University Press, New York.

Morgan, M. G., and McMichael, F. M. (1981). "A Characterization and Critical Discussion of Models and Their Use in Environmental Policy," *Policy Sciences,* 14:345–370.

Read, D., Bostrom, A., Morgan, M. G., Fischhoff, B., and Smuts, T. (1994). "What Do People Know about Global Climate Change? Part 2. Survey Studies of Educated Laypeople," *Risk Analysis,* 14:971–982.

Rubin, E. S., Small, M. J., Bloyd, C. N., and Henrion, M. (1992). "Integrated Assessment of Acid Deposition Effects on Lake Acidification," *Journal of Environmental Engineering,* 118(1):120–134.

Shachter, R. D. (1988). "Probabilistic Inference and Influence Diagrams," *Operations Research,* 36(4):589–604.

4

MENTAL MODELS
INTERVIEWS

Our approach assumes that sound risk communication requires an understanding of both the risk and audience members' current beliefs about it. Chapter 3 explored how to develop the expert description of the risk in the form of an influence diagram. This chapter describes how to design and conduct mental models interviews, the critical first step in learning what people know already. Chapter 5 explains how to develop structured, confirmatory questionnaires that can be easily and quickly administered to larger samples of people, in order to estimate the prevalence of the beliefs revealed in the mental models interviews.

4.1 Designing and Testing the Interview Protocol

4.1.1 Strategy

The expert influence diagram must be substantially completed before designing the interview, because it guides the topics to be covered.

The goal of the mental models interview is to get people to talk as much as possible about how they think about the risk while imposing as little as possible of other people's ideas, perspectives, and terminology. Our strategy for accomplishing this goal – and the name used for our overall approach – draws on the long tradition in cognitive psychology of studying people's mental models. As early as the 1930s, experimental psychologists realized that understanding behavior in complex, uncertain environments required considering the tacit theories that people (and even other animals) developed to cope with them (e.g., Bartlett, 1932; Tolman, 1932). Mental models have been examined in many different domains, ranging from operators' understanding of engineered systems (Rouse and Morris, 1986) to patients' beliefs regarding their own symptomatology and treatment (Leventhal and Cameron, 1987), physics students' intuitions about mechanics (diSessa, 1988), laypeople's theories of psychology and sociology (Furnham, 1990), children's beliefs about dinosaurs (Chi, Hutchinson, and Rotin, 1989), indigenous people's typologies of the natural world (Atran, 1990), and subjects' beliefs about the solutions of constructed problems (Johnson-Laird, 1983). These different domains have required different elicitation methods, as well as different standards of proof. With highly constrained tasks, it has sometimes been possible to create computational models that simulate the behavior following from the beliefs that investigators have proposed as constituting the mental models (Newell and Simon, 1972). In less constrained domains, investigators have tested their theorized mental models by predicting the behavior that would follow from them, or by looking at converging patterns of belief for mental models elicited with multiple methods (Gentner and Stevens, 1983).

Given the complexity, uncertainty, and unclear bounds of the "systems" that are the focus of many risk communications, our approach most closely resembles the last of these approaches. In such cases, one cannot assume that laypeople bound the system in the same way as technical experts (who might not agree among themselves) nor even that they conceptualize its components similarly. As a result, we use a form of think-aloud protocol that provides as much freedom of expression as possible, within the constraints of directing attention to the focal topics (Ericsson and Simon, 1994). Our procedure uses what might be called a "funnel design." It starts very generally, then proceeds to increasingly focused questions. At the beginning, we run the risk of missing important beliefs because respondents' train of thought has drifted off in other directions, or they are unsure about whether an idea would be considered on topic – but we run little risk of putting ideas in their heads. Toward the end, we pick up beliefs that might otherwise have been lost – but we run the risk of suggesting beliefs or inducing their creation. The intermediate stages direct respondents to the major areas of the influence diagram – in the hopes that bringing up such core topics as exposure, effects, and treatment will correct oversights rather than reveal hitherto unknown topics. Where appropriate, responses from different segments of the interview can be analyzed separately.

The next sections show how these general design principles are expressed in the concrete circumstances of a typical study.

4.1.2 Design Details: A Radon Example

The first step in an interview is to create a simple opening question that encompasses the risk of interest but avoids prejudging the answer. Thus, "tell me about climate change" or "tell me about radon in homes . . ." would be good opening requests. However, "tell me about the risks of radon," "tell me how to reduce radon risks," or "tell me where radon comes from and how it hurts people" would not. Whether radon is a problem represents a judgment that should come from the respondent, not the interviewer, as should any beliefs about potential solutions or problems. Focusing respondents' thinking about radon sources or health threats presumes a similarity between lay and expert beliefs – although there is always some chance that raising a topic in an interview situation will suggest that something is awry (why else would we be asking?).

Often, the opening request will prompt only a few sentences from interview subjects. In order to keep the conversation going, the interviewer must have two things ready: (a) a way to keep track of the topics that the respondent has already mentioned, so that they can be systematically explored with follow-up questions; and (b) a set of standard phrases with which to ask these follow-up questions. Without such phrases, the interviewer risks inadvertently providing information about the topic or using terms that put respondents ill at ease. The language of the prompts should be nonjudgmental. Akin to the strategy of client-centered therapy, follow-up questions are intended to clarify what respondents had in mind, without questioning its legitimacy.

Things move quickly once an interview has started. Both to avoid

unforeseen problems and to give the interviewer an opportunity to practice, it is important to prepare materials ahead of time and to test them,
first on friends and colleagues, then with test subjects.

Figure 4.1 reproduces the work sheet that we developed for interviews on radon in homes.

In order to minimize confusion during the interview, we attempt to fit
the entire work sheet on one side of a page. The topics are arranged hierarchically, following the structure of the influence diagram. As the respondent starts to talk, the interviewer checks the topics that have been mentioned, making other brief notations. These notes allow the interviewer to
keep track of what has been covered and help to ensure that follow-up
questions address all topics that the respondent has mentioned. A standard
notation can help. For example, in Figure 4.1, a check on the left side of a
topic means that it has been raised. A check on the right side means that
the follow-up questions have been completed. For telephone interviews, it
may be convenient to make notes directly on the influence diagram. (With
in-person interviews, respondents might extract cues from seeing the size
or structure of the diagram, or from the location of notes made on it.)

At some point, the interviewer will have followed up on all the topics
that the respondent has mentioned. Further prompts are unlikely to produce additional beliefs and may increase the chances of the interviewer
introducing new ideas or encouraging the respondent to invent beliefs, in
order to have something to say. At this point, the interviewer moves on to
the second phase, in which attention is drawn gently to the major
untouched areas of the influence diagram. The full set of such potentially
relevant topics should be summarized in the work sheets, which are constructed by going through the expert model and identifying topics critical
to the decisions that the subject may face. A few of the topics in the example of Figure 4.1 did not pass the test of importance. Marked with an
asterisk, they were listed so that if a respondent mentioned them, the
interviewer could note that fact and follow up. However, if the subject
does not mention them during the first stage of the interview, the interviewer does not pursue them in the second.

When raising new topics, the interviewer should use the standard,
neutral wording on the interview work sheet. Unlike the first part of the
interview, these questions can introduce new information, although that

should be kept to the minimum needed to make the topic clear. At times, topics overlooked in the first phase will now be expressed clearly. Those might be thought of as topics that are not part of people's working knowledge but could readily be understood if brought to their attention – say, in a risk communication.

Some judgment is required in deciding whether to raise, during the second part of the interview, topics that respondents have already discussed during the first part. If they have little to add, then asking them again may undermine the rapport needed to complete the interview. However, trying too hard to avoid suggesting anything increases the risk of missing something.

Although these two stages of the interview can get at many of respondents' beliefs, they may still have knowledge that they didn't think to mention because nothing triggered that part of their memory. Some way is needed to see if such associations can still be triggered without unduly "leading the witness."

One strategy that we have used is asking individuals to sort a stack of photographs, telling us what each photo shows and whether they see any relationship between it and the topic. They are then asked to explain their choice. To prepare for this task, we assemble a set of about 50 photographs showing varied topics, such as retail stores (e.g., hardware, supermarket meat and produce counters), factories (e.g., process industries, oil, gas and coal facilities), farms and ranches, transportation modes, schools, playgrounds, a day-care center, recreational facilities (e.g., a ski slope and a beach), offices, a trash truck, a city dump, and a chemical waste dump; medical facilities and equipment, drugs, and blood products; and people of various ages, doing common things such as preparing food, caring for children, playing cards, watching television. In short, we seek a cross section of human life and activities. One easy way to assemble such a set of pictures is to use a close-up lens on a good camera and spend a couple of hours in a bright sunny window with some encyclopedias and back issues of varied magazines. Black-and-white can be adequate.

We have used the same core set of photographs for studies of different risks, adding about a dozen pictures special to each application (based on the expert model, pretest interviews, or previous research). Thus, in the case of radon, our pictures included someone taking a shower (because that

RADON

What I'd like to ask you to do is just talk to me about radon: that is, tell me what you know about radon and any risks it poses.

Basic Prompts:
- "Anything else?",
- "Can you tell me more?", *or*
- "Anything else -- don't worry about whether it's right, just tell me what comes to mind."
- Can you explain why?

Draw a Blank (try in order):
1. Have you ever heard the word radon? Can you remember anything at all about it?
2. Let me see if I can jog your memory a bit. Radon is a colorless and odorless gas that can seep into the basements of homes. Does that help?
3. O.K., let me try a little more. Once radon gas has seeped into a home it can cause risks to the health of people who breath it. Have you every heard of such a thing?

EXPOSURE PROCESSES

__|__ **Source Of Radon**
- __ Can you tell me (more) about where radon comes from?
- __ Can you tell me (more) about how radon gets into homes?
- __ You told me that ____ (e.g. radon leaks in through the basement), can you tell me more about that? notes: _____
_____

__|__ **Concentration And Movement In Home**
- __ Can you tell me (more) about the things that determine how much radon there is in a home?
- __ Can you tell me (more) about how radon moves around in a home once it gets in?
- __ Is the level of radon usually the same in all parts of a house?

__|__ **Uncertainty About Exposure**
- __ Is radon found in all homes?
- __ Can you tell me (more) about how much variation there is in the amount of radon in different homes?

EFFECTS PROCESSES

__|__ **Nature Of Effects**
- __ Can you tell me (more) about the harm that can result from radon exposure ?
- __ How else can radon affect you?
- __ Does radon affect some people more than others?
- __ You told me that ____ (e.g. radon causes cancer). Can tell me more about that? notes: ____
_____

__|__ **Uncertainty About Effects**
- __ Do you have any sense of how certain or uncertain scientists are about the health risk of radon?

Figure 4.1. Example of a work sheet for guiding mental models interviews. An interviewer's check in the left side of the ___|___ icon means that the topic has been raised. A check on the right side of the icon means that the follow-up questions have been completed. Topics preceded by stars are of secondary importance and are covered only if brought up by the respondent.

68

Figure 4.1. *(continued)*

EFFECTS PROCESSES (Only If brought up.)

*__|__ **Radon Daughters (Use only If brought up.)**

__ Can you tell me more about radon daughters and their role in the risks that radon poses? (Use only if specifically mentioned.)

__ You said that radon _____ (e.g. decays into small radioactive particles), can you tell me more about that? notes: _____

_____

*__|__ **Role Of Dust (Use only If brought up.)**

__ Can you tell me more about how the presence of dust in the air affects risk from radon?

*__|__ **Role Of Smoking (Use only If brought up.)**

__ Can you tell me more about the difference in radon risk for smokers and non-smokers?

RISK ASSESSMENT AND MANAGEMENT

__|__ **Learning About Radon, Sources Of Information**

__ Where have you heard or read about radon risks?

__ Where have you heard about things that can be done about managing radon risks?

__ Have you heard about any government or private programs to deal with radon risks?

__|__ **Testing For Radon**

__ Is there any way someone can learn what the level of radon is in their house?

__ You said there are radon test kits. Can you tell me how somebody would go about getting one of these kits?

__|__ **Reducing Radon Risk**

__ If somebody finds they have a lot of radon in their house, is there anything they can do about it?

__ You told me _____ (e.g. that there are things someone can do to reduce the level of radon in their house), can you tell me more about that? notes: _____

_____

__
How effective are the measures that you have mentioned for controlling the level of radon in a house? Do they always work equally well?

RISK COMPARISONS (Ask at end whether brought up or not.)

__ Is radon really a significant risk in society, or is it one of those risks that's not all that important?

__ Can you give me some idea of how the risk of radon compares with other risks such as the risk of smoking?

PERSONAL RISK (Ask at end whether brought up or not.)

__ What (more) can you tell me about radon in your own home?

__ Do you have any reason to believe that your own risk from radon is low or high? (Can you tell me why?)

__ Have you ever had your house tested for radon? (Can you tell me why (not)?) (Have you ever thought about doing it?)

__ Have any of your friends or neighbors had radon problems, had their house tested, or done things to reduce the radon level in their house?

__ Complete the interview data sheet!

can release radon gas dissolved in the water), a window and an attic fan (because ventilation affects radon concentration), and a large mill tailings pile (because, in a few places, the processed sand from uranium mining and milling operations produces local concentrations of radon). At least half the photos should be unrelated to the topic, making it clear to respondents that they need not find some way to make every photo relevant.

The picture-sorting task typically uncovers some additional beliefs and misunderstandings not found during the earlier parts of the interview. For example, in the radon study, a picture of the supermarket produce counter prompted some people to say how food might be contaminated by growing in soil containing radon. Because plants do not pick up radon, this is, in fact, not a problem. However, our respondents knew that bioaccumulation is a problem for some toxic materials and made what seemed like a reasonable extrapolation.

Because of its risk of reactive measurement (i.e., inducing inferences), the picture-sorting task should be dropped, rather than abbreviating the first two stages of the interview, if time is short. However, it can go quickly and often yields interesting insights.

We have occasionally used other strategies to explore issues that might be important but which the first two phases of the interview might not adequately raise. In the case of climate change, we concluded by posing several specific questions (see Figure 7.1 on pages 127–128) and then ran a follow-up study that posed definitional and process questions shown in Figure 4.2. In our AIDS interviews (Chapter 8), we asked for definitions of terms like "safe sex" where we suspected that people had false fluency, using the language of risk without really understanding its content (e.g., McIntyre and West, 1992).

4.2 Conducting the Interview

4.2.1 Strategy

Mental models interviews are demanding. They must appear to be almost conversational, so as to keep respondents engaged on a topic that may be complex and unfamiliar. Yet the interviewer must still control the process and maintain a nonjudgmental tone. If you can afford professional inter-

Part II: This section asks general true/false questions. Please answer each question below by checking the one box that best describes what you think:

9. Climate means average weather:

    ❑ True ❑ Probably true ❑ Don't know ❑ Probably false ❑ False

10. Weather means average climate:

    ❑ True ❑ Probably true ❑ Don't know ❑ Probably false ❑ False

11. Climate often changes from year to year:

    ❑ True ❑ Probably true ❑ Don't know ❑ Probably false ❑ False

12. Weather often changes from year to year:

    ❑ True ❑ Probably true ❑ Don't know ❑ Probably false ❑ False

13. Climate means pretty much the same thing as weather:

    ❑ True ❑ Probably true ❑ Don't know ❑ Probably false ❑ False

14. The earth's climate has been pretty much the same for millions of years:

    ❑ True ❑ Probably true ❑ Don't know ❑ Probably false ❑ False

Part III: This section asks true/false questions about the causes of global warming. Please answer each question below by checking the one box that best describes what you think:

29. Burning fossil fuels (e.g., coal and oil) is a major cause of global warming:

    ❑ True ❑ Probably true ❑ Don't know ❑ Probably false ❑ False

30. The space program is a major cause of global warming:

    ❑ True ❑ Probably true ❑ Don't know ❑ Probably false ❑ False

31. Ozone in cities (e.g., smog in Los Angeles) is a major cause of global warming:

    ❑ True ❑ Probably true ❑ Don't know ❑ Probably false ❑ False

Figure 4.2. Examples of definitional and process questions asked in a follow-up to the mental models interviews on climate change.

(continued)

Figure 4.2. *(continued)*

32. The hole in the antarctic ozone layer is a major cause of global warming:

☐	☐	☐	☐	☐
True	Probably true	Don't know	Probably false	False

33. Deforestation is a major cause of global warming:

☐	☐	☐	☐	☐
True	Probably true	Don't know	Probably false	False

34. Aerosol spray cans are a major cause of global warming:

☐	☐	☐	☐	☐
True	Probably true	Don't know	Probably false	False

viewers, consider using them. They should have experience in avoiding common interviewing pitfalls, but will still need to be trained to conduct mental models interviews (Fowler and Mangione, 1990).

Success requires practice. You might ask a few friends to act as guinea pigs in order to get started, running two or three interviews as if conducting them with a stranger. Tape-record the discussion, then get the recording transcribed as a written record of everything that was said, laid out like the dialogue of a play. Although more expensive than relying on an interviewer's or observer's notes or memory, verbatim transcripts are the only way to note against the vagaries of memory and to capture the nuances of speech and content.[1]

Review the transcripts with a few colleagues. Is the interviewer following the script? Were all opportunities for follow-up identified and used? When the subject asked for information, did the interviewer stick to the protocol, either ignoring the query or saying something like, "I'm not allowed to answer questions yet" or "I'd be happy to answer that later"? Did the interviewer inadvertently supply information (perhaps unable to overcome a natural inclination to help)?

---

[1]You might experiment with voice recognition software to produce the transcripts, with a speaker echoing what he or she hears on the tape. For most of our mental models studies we have used professional transcription. Quality control is important for this, too. Take care to avoid a work schedule that creates the risk of typing or voice injury (National Research Council, 2001).

Even when an interview seems to have gone well, we often identify problems in the transcript. For example, the draft protocol might flow poorly or lack natural ways to explore certain issues. In that case, the protocol must be reworded and tried again. It usually takes several rounds of such pilots before we get a design that covers the right topics and makes our interviewers comfortable. Once that point has been reached, a few more trial runs should be conducted with strangers, in order to make sure everything is working.

Always close the interview by thanking subjects for their participation. We typically ask a few evaluative questions about the experience. For example, at the end of the interviews on climate change, we asked:

How was it to participate in this interview?

Were any questions too hard, unclear, or unpleasant to answer?

Were there any issues related to climate, weather, or the greenhouse effect that you thought of but didn't get a chance to talk about? (If so) What issues?

A natural question is how many interviewers to have. The answer depends on the degree of consistency that interviewer training can achieve. A single interviewer will provide the greatest consistency. Having multiple interviewers, trained to a common standard, reduces the risk of having an entire data set compromised by some feature of a single interviewer. For example, people may respond more frankly, or more extremely, with interviewers who share a feature that appears relevant to the topic (e.g., gender on gender-related topics). Unless a particular combination is defined (e.g., wanting to know what men tell men rather than what men tell women), then a more diverse set of interviewers will provide a more balanced set of interviewer effects. People are often surprised (both pleasantly and unpleasantly) by how well they do as interviewers. If several people are available for the project, consider having each run a few practice interviews, then decide which ones provide the best balance of consistency and diversity.

Appendix D reproduces three complete transcripts from the first two stages of radon interviews in order to provide a more complete idea of how these may proceed and how the interviewer follows up on subjects' openings. In these transcripts, you can also see where the interviewer has completed the first-phase follow-ups and gone on to the second stage. You might want to copy the interviewer work sheet reproduced in Figure 4.1 and try using it to keep track of the topics covered in these examples. Note that when subjects ask the interviewer questions designed to obtain information, the interviewer answers by simply repeating something that she has already said.

4.2.2   Quality Control

An interview typically lasts between 20 minutes and an hour. Conducting them is hard work. It is unrealistic to expect to complete more than four to six a day and remain alert. Thus, a set of 20 to 30 interviews will require a week or more.

After a few interviews, transcribe some tape recordings. Reviewing these with the research team can prevent drift in the protocol's administration, as well as resolve design issues that did not arise in the pretests.

4.2.3   Sample Participants

The participants for mental models interviews should be from the target audience. If the communication is designed for a well-characterized population, you might even want to select subjects from it randomly. Byram (1998) did this in her study of women's understanding of mammography and its role in managing the risks of breast cancer. She sought a national sample of women, stratified by age, ethnicity, and educational attainment. Using a commercially available database with some 80% of U.S. women, she had little difficulty filling her quota of white and Asian women with at least a high school education, but great difficulty in recruiting African American women at any educational level. The latter seemed just less interested in participating. As a result, although the quota was eventually filled, we were left with questions about the representativeness of this portion of the eventual "random" sample (i.e., who is the person who says "yes," after nine previous individuals sampled from the same category have said "no"?). The structured survey derived from these interviews was mailed to a random national sample as well and achieved a much higher (71%) response rate, despite having some demanding quantitative questions. Here, too, although not as badly as with the open-ended interviews, the response rate for African American women was lower.

A common target audience in much of our work has been reasonably well-educated members of the general public (e.g., having at least a high school education), who might be relatively interested in risk topics and in a position to become lay opinion leaders. In sampling such individuals, we have generally avoided people who might have specialized knowledge about the risk, such as engineers or doctors. A sample here might include a sales representative, a restaurant manager, a nurse, a state police officer, and a town manager. Occasionally, we have recruited subjects with cold calls, using a procedure such as selecting pages and line numbers at random from the telephone book.[2] More often, though, we have approached groups with no obvious connection to the risk, and diverse membership. For example, we have used the members of a neighborhood bowling club, the parents of a youth hockey club, civic groups, and church auxiliary groups. Usually, we have used subjects from several groups in any project. Subjects are told that their responses will be kept anonymous. We collect basic demographic information and keep track of it as we accumulate subjects in order to make sure that our group is appropriately diverse.

When drawing subjects from a group, we typically offer a contribution to its treasury for each member who completes an interview. We have also set up a booth at a public site, such as a home, boat, or car show, and offered money to people willing to complete an interview. In all cases, we have offered compensation in the range of $10 to $25 per hour, so as to make it clear that we take the task seriously and value what each individual has to say. The time that we save in scheduling and the improvement in the quality of the interviews are well worth the cost.

In a study that required actual opinion leaders, we used a "reference sample" procedure. With the help of personal contacts in the community, we identified a diverse initial sample. At the conclusion of the interviews, we asked participants whether it was a sufficiently satisfactory (or perhaps even enjoyable) experience that they would be willing to recommend it to others. We then described the kinds of "others" we were looking for

[2]Details on how to do this can be found in Section 5.3.

(e.g., "someone in the clergy whose opinion you might seek on this topic but could not predict now with confidence").

4.2.4 Sample Size

As in other domains, the size of the sample depends on the level of precision desired. If the aim is to estimate the frequency with which a belief is held in a population, then one could conduct the statistical power analyses needed to estimate the sample size providing the required precision (Cohen, 1992, offers a simple, authoritative guide). For those accustomed to the ±3% of national surveys, the required numbers are very large – and typically better achieved with structured surveys. If, however, the goal is to find out which beliefs are "out there" with some reasonable frequency, then much smaller samples become reasonable. If, for example, one's communication is intended to address any misconception held by 10% of the population, then one has, roughly speaking, a 50:50 chance of doing so with a sample of 10. Typically, we have conducted 20–30 interviews within a population group believed to have relatively similar beliefs.

One way to see the role of sample size is depicted in Figure 4.3, which plots the number of different concepts encountered in a set of interviews. Note that each of the first few interviews yielded quite a few new concepts. However, after about 20 interviews, the curves begin to approach an asymptote, as very few new concepts arise. Rather, one hears mostly familiar beliefs, while the new concepts are increasingly idiosyncratic ones. Of course, the exact shape of these curves depends on the order in which the interviews were conducted, but the pattern will be similar.

For our cryptosporidium project, we developed the following sampling plan: This waterborne parasite causes discomfort to healthy adults but poses a major health threat to immunocompromised individuals. As a result, we decided to sample equally from eight different risk groups. Because cryptosporidium is little known to the general public (except where there has been an outbreak), we decided that educational level and gender were the primary variables for which to seek commonality. Better-educated people might, coincidentally, have heard more about the problem or be better able to make inferences when the possibility is raised

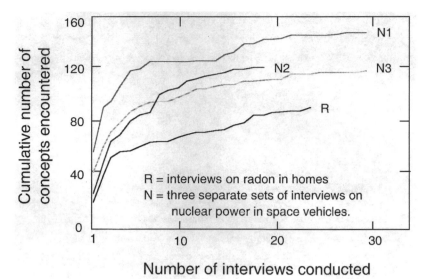

Figure 4.3. The number of new concepts encountered in mental models interviews often increases rapidly for the first 10 to 15 interviews conducted but then drops off, approaching an asymptote somewhere around 20 to 30 interviews. These curves for interviews on nuclear energy sources in space vehicles were conducted with populations having potentially diverse beliefs. *Source:* Maharik and Fischhoff (1993).

(suggesting the need for some market segmentation in communications). Men and women might be attuned to different issues or use different language. We also identified four groups with particular interests in cryptosporidium: (a) communities that had had an outbreak, (b) people with HIV/AIDS, (c) the elderly, and (d) pregnant women and families with infants. Considering our resources, we decided to sample 20 members of the general public, divided among those with relatively high and relatively low educational levels, as well as 5 from each of the four special interest groups.

Of course, these are very small samples from many subgroups. If one had reason to believe that elderly men and women had markedly different perspectives on cryptosporidium, comparing the two men and three women in the eventual sample would allow no responsible conclusions.

However, people have many attributes, so that there would be much larger samples for some features. For example, having 22 men and 18 women overall would allow for modest statements about overall gender differences.

4.3 Picture Sorting

When we include a picture-sorting task, we start the process by saying something like this:

> Now we are going to ask you to sort this stack of pictures into two different piles. In each case, we'd like you to look at the picture and tell us what it is. If, in your mind, the picture has something to do with radon, we'd like you to tell us the connection and then put it over here in a pile to the right. On the other hand, if you don't see any obvious connection to radon, say so, then put the picture over here in a pile to the left.
>
> I'll do the first two to get you started. This first picture is a picture of Mickey Mouse. Now if you were really creative, you might be able to invent some story that connects Mickey Mouse to radon, but there probably isn't any obvious connection that comes quickly to mind. So we'll say that there isn't any obvious connection to radon, and we'll put the picture here to start the pile on the left.
>
> This next one is a picture of a brochure that says it's EPA's *Citizen's Guide to Radon.* I guess it's pretty obvious that that has something to do with radon, so we'll put it over here to start the pile on the right.
>
> OK, you get the idea. Now please go ahead and do the rest of them.

The reason we ask subjects to tell us what they see in each picture is that otherwise we cannot be confident about what triggered their sorting decision. After a few pictures, many people forget to keep telling the interviewer what each picture depicts; if so, gentle reminders are in order.

4.4   Summarizing, Analyzing, and Interpreting the Results

Once the interviews have been completed and the tape recordings transcribed, the interviewer should check each transcript for accuracy and make any necessary corrections. Some transcribers have particular difficulty with technical words and concepts. Once transcriptions are complete, it is time to analyze the results, both for their intrinsic interest and as a step toward developing the structured questionnaire and the risk communication. We describe here a general approach to coding, which can be pursued with a level of vigor suited to the specific project. We strongly advise against skipping the formal coding. It is just too easy to read transcripts impressionistically and miss much of their content. Performing the coding often requires several iterations, in order to ensure that the scheme is understood and used consistently by the coders.

The template for the coding is the expert model. Each statement in the transcript is assigned to a node or link in the expert model, if possible. Those risk-related concepts that cannot be coded into the expert model are assigned new categories (see following). The simplest analysis asks how frequently people talk about each topic. More complex analyses look at patterns in these frequencies, as well as at the content and accuracy of what is said about each. One's interest in the different topics may vary considerably. As a result, one might look in depth at the statements assigned to some nodes, while hardly attending to others. Having everything coded, with the accompanying text stored electronically, enables us to examine new portions of the data when the need arises.

For developing a risk communication, identifying and counting key concepts may reveal the major patterns in the data. At other times, more elaborate coding schemes are needed. For example, in the case of radon, we grouped concepts into four categories: exposure, effects, identification, and valuations. The exposure and effects categories involved substantive knowledge, subdivided as in the influence diagram. Eventually, we coded into 14 first-level concepts (10 involving exposure and 4 involving effects), as well as 48 more specific concepts. Identification concepts involved general knowledge about a risk, such as "radon is a gas"; valuation concepts involved summary judgments, such as "radon is scary."

Beyond this, we characterized each link between concepts in terms of five different characteristics (see Bostrom, 1990, and Bostrom, Fischhoff, and Morgan, 1992, for details).

Of course, not everything that people say will find a clear place in the expert model. Sometimes, people speak too imprecisely for us to know exactly what they are saying. Sometimes, their ideas bridge nodes that are not connected in the model. Sometimes, their beliefs are unrelated to those that the experts saw as relevant to the problem. It is important to capture such beliefs, which show laypeople to be solving different problems than experts. At times, lay respondents provide concepts that are appropriately added to the expert model. For example, they may know about exposure routes unfamiliar to experts or care about neglected outcomes (e.g., stress).

We have found it useful to sort nonexpert concepts into four categories: (1) misconceptions; (2) peripheral beliefs, correct but not particularly relevant to the risk (although people believe that they are); (3) indiscriminate beliefs, correct as far as they go, but not specific enough to be very useful (e.g., "radon makes people ill," without naming the illness); and (4) background beliefs, so basic that they do not explicitly show up in the expert model, even if they represent facts important to determining its operation (e.g., "radon is a gas" and "radon is radioactive").

If the influence diagram does not explicitly represent risk mitigation processes, then they are coded according to the underlying concept in the influence diagram (i.e., the process they are intended to affect).

Once a coding scheme has been developed, it should be tested to make sure that it yields reproducible results. The best way to do this is to have two or three people follow the same written coding instructions and independently code the same two or three transcripts. Given the complexity of the task, it is unrealistic to expect perfect agreement, but it is realistic to expect different coders to agree at least two-thirds of the time. In the case of our radon study, three independent coders agreed about 75% of the time – not perfect, but much better than could be expected by chance, especially considering the large number of categories. This process is facilitated by having someone (or the group as a whole) divide the transcript into distinct statements, prior to the coding. That way, the coders can focus on what each statement means, without having to worry about whether it is a statement.

The results from a mental models study can be very rich and feel quite overwhelming. We have found the following to be a helpful order for presenting the data:

Exhibit 1 The expert model, reminding the work team and any audience of the formal structure of the problem. Where this model is complicated, it might be presented in stages, starting with the basic structure, then adding detail. (Chapter 8 does this in two stages for an expert model of HIV/AIDS).

Exhibit 2 The mental models for a few individual subjects, shown by highlighting the nodes of the expert model into which their statements have been coded and the nonexpert nodes that the subject added. Provide a list with the statements corresponding to each node. This exhibit will show the reality of these few individuals, while reemphasizing the expert model and raising the question of how critical the specific consistencies and discrepancies are.

Exhibit 3 The expert model with added nonexpert nodes, along with the frequency with which each node (or link) is mentioned. Frequency can be shown both with numbers and by visually highlighting the most heavily cited elements (e.g., by thicker outlines around the most cited nodes). Frequency can be calculated as the average number of mentions per node or as the number of people who mention each node at least once (to reduce the impact of particularly verbose – or well-informed – individuals). This exhibit shows where people's beliefs are concentrated.

Exhibit 4 The expert model with added nonexpert nodes, along with the frequency with which each node was raised by the interviewer in a typical interview. This display provides a feeling for the extent to which respondents have addressed a topic only because they were prompted to do so. (Exhibits 3 and 4 can be done separately for the separate interview phases.)

Exhibit 5   Collections of the statements associated with critical nodes in the expert model. If needed, develop a secondary coding scheme, organizing the beliefs regarding each such node. That organization could reflect the accuracy of those beliefs (correct, misconceptions, indiscriminate, or peripheral) or whatever structure emerges from examining them more closely.

These exhibits are relatively straightforward to produce if the codes are appended to the associated statements in the computer files. Doing so also makes it easier to come back to them when new topics arise ("what was it that they said about . . . ?"). Although we have experimented with special computer programs for analyzing qualitative data, it has proven easiest just to enter each distinct statement and code into a spreadsheet. Then it is easy to retrieve whatever anyone on the team wants.

Once the analysis of the mental models interviews is complete, it is time to move on to design a confirmatory questionnaire that can be administered to large numbers of people. That allows estimating how widely the concepts found in the mental models interviews are found in different segments of the general public (and without the special focusing of such interviews). Structured tests also provide an efficient way of evaluating the impact of interventions.

References

Atran, S. (1990). *Cognitive Foundations of the Natural World.* Cambridge University Press, London.

Bartlett, R. C. (1932). *Remembering.* Cambridge University Press, London.

Bostrom, A. (1990). "A Mental Models Approach to Exploring Perceptions of Hazardous Processes." Ph.D. dissertation, School of Urban and Public Affairs, Carnegie Mellon University.

Bostrom, A., Fischhoff, B., and Morgan, M. G. (1992). "Characterizing Mental Models of Hazardous Processes: A Methodology and an Application to Radon," *Journal of Social Issues,* 48(4):85–100.

Byram, S. (1998). "Breast Cancer and Mammogram Screening: Mental Models and Quantitative Assessments of Beliefs." Ph.D. dissertation, Carnegie Mellon University.

Chi, M., Hutchinson, J., and Rotin, A. (1989). "How Inferences about Novel Domain Specific Concepts Can Be Constrained by Structured Knowledge," *Merrill-Palmer Quarterly,* 35:27–62.

Cohen, J. S. (1992). "A Power Primer," *Psychological Bulletin,* 112(1):155–159.

diSessa, H. (1988). "Knowledge in Pieces," in G. Fosman and P. Putall, eds., *Construction in the Computer Age.* Lawrence Erlbaum Associates, London.

Ericsson, A., and Simon, H. A. (1994). *Protocol Analysis,* 2nd ed. MIT Press, Cambridge, Mass.

Fowler, F. J., Jr., and Mangione, F. W. (1990). *Standardized Survey Interviewing: Minimizing Interviewer-Related Error.* Sage Publications, Newbury Park, Calif.

Furnham, A. (1990). *Lay Theories.* Oxford University Press, London.

Gentner, D., and Stevens, A. L., eds. (1983). *Mental Models.* Lawrence Erlbaum Associates, Hillsdale, N.J.

Johnson-Laird, P. N. (1983). *Mental Models.* Harvard University Press, Cambridge, Mass.

Leventhal, H., and Cameron, L. (1987). "Behavioral Theories and the Problem of Compliance," *Patient Education and Counseling,* 10:117–138.

Maharik, M., and Fischhoff, B. (1993). "Contrasting Perceptions of Using Nuclear Energy Sources in Space," *Journal of Environmental Psychology,* 13:243–250.

McIntyre, S., and West, P. (1992). "What Does the Phrase 'Safe Sex' Mean to You? Understanding among Glaswegian 18 Year Olds in 1990," *AIDS,* 7:121–126.

National Research Council. (2001). *Work-Related Musculoskeletal Disorders.* National Academy Press, Washington, D.C.

Newell, A., and Simon, H. A. (1972). *Human Problem Solving.* Prentice-Hall, Englewood Cliffs, N.J.

Rouse, W. B., and Morris, N. M. (1986). "On Looking into the Black Box: Prospects and Limits in the Search for Mental Models," *Psychological Bulletin,* 100:349–363.

Tolman, E. C. (1932). *Purposive Behavior in Animals and Men.* Appleton-Century-Crofts, New York.

5

CONFIRMATORY QUESTIONNAIRES

Mental models interviews usually produce a rich array of lay beliefs about a risk. If one could afford to do a hundred or more of these interviews, the results should also provide relatively accurate estimates of how common various beliefs are in the population being studied. However, the expense of these interviews typically precludes doing more than a modest number. In order to estimate prevalence, we rely on closed-form questions, which can be much more efficiently administered to large numbers of respondents.[1]

5.1   Objectives of Questionnaire Studies

Knowing the frequency of concepts in the target population allows communicators to identify both widely shared correct concepts upon which a message can be built and widespread misconceptions that need to be addressed. Questionnaires can also be used to explore specific issues sug-

---

[1]Much has been written on the art and science of designing questionnaires and questions (e.g., Converse and Presser, 1996; Fowler, 1992; Krosnick, 1999; and Sirken et al., 1999). We won't cover this literature here, but we encourage you to consult it if you have questions regarding general guidelines or recent failings.

gested in the mental models interviews but not adequately resolved. For example, our mental models interviews about climate change suggested that many people confused the terms "climate" and "weather." Both refer to the condition of the atmosphere, measured in terms of wind, temperature, humidity, atmospheric pressure, precipitation, and so on. In most places, weather can change from hour-to-hour, day-to-day, and season-to-season. In contrast, climate is the average or overall pattern of weather in a place. For example, San Diego has a "Mediterranean climate," meaning that temperatures are generally moderate year-round, there is limited rainfall, and humidity is typically low.

In order to explore how well people understand the difference between weather and climate, we included the following six true-false questions in our structured questionnaire (Read et al., 1994):

Climate means average weather.
Weather means average climate.
Climate often changes from year to year.
Weather often changes from year to year.
Climate means pretty much the same thing as weather.
The earth's climate has been pretty much the same for millions of years.

The results confirmed what we had suspected: at least a quarter of our respondents confused the two concepts.[2] As a result, an effective communication about climate change would have to help respondents make that distinction. This result also suggests caution in interpreting results from national opinion polls about climate change. Respondents answering questions about climate may have been thinking about weather.

Sometimes a concept is so complicated that it cannot be adequately addressed with simple questions. For example, after a set of mental models interviews about the power-frequency electric and magnetic fields associated with power lines and electrical devices, we began to suspect that people have serious misconceptions about how the strength of such fields

---

[2] See Section 7.1 for additional details on work we have done on the weather-climate distinction.

changes with distance from the object. Because such quantitative relationships lend themselves poorly to multiple-choice questions, we designed a
special set of questions to explore this one, critical issue (see Sections 5.4
and 7.2).

5.2   Designing and Testing Confirmatory Questionnaires

Questionnaire design begins with constructing a list of concepts to be covered. That list begins with the nodes of the expert model and the concepts
that respondents raised in the open-ended interviews. It is trimmed by
considering the criticality of each concept in the expert model, lay models,
and in the decisions that people are likely to face. This process may lead to
several questions on some critical nodes (where there are several important
facts and misconceptions) and none on others (where understanding matters much less). With clear questions and format, respondents can typically
answer between 50 and 100 questions, once they get started. Maintaining a
constant question format reduces respondents' cognitive load.

Designing good questions is not easy. Even after we have done our
best, we sometimes find that a draft question is not interpreted as we
intended. Sometimes, there is no consensual interpretation of a concept,
creating the need for several questions addressing important concepts.
That allows one to look for a *pattern* of responses across questions and to
avoid basing important conclusions on any single question.

The order in which questions appear need not correspond to the priority list. Sometimes, it is natural to group questions that address a concept; at other times, it is wise to spread them around the questionnaire,
getting respondents to revisit the issue and reduce the risk of inducing
inferences and artificial consistency. For example, after a few initial summary questions, our climate change questionnaire had sections on climate
science, the causes of global warming, the consequences of global warming, and intervention or mitigation strategies. We closed with a few
demographic questions. Similarly, our questionnaire about the physics of
power-frequency fields contained sections about general properties of
fields, electric fields, and magnetic fields. Once again, the questionnaire
ended with a few questions asking for demographic information.

It is a good idea to begin with a simple explanation of why the study is being conducted. Here, for example, is the introduction from our climate study:

> This questionnaire is part of a general study being done in the Department of Engineering and Public Policy at Carnegie Mellon University in order to learn what people think and know about the subject of possible climate change. When you aren't sure of an answer, just give it your best shot. It is how you think about these issues that interests us. Your responses will remain anonymous. Please go through the questionnaire a page at a time. *Once you have completed a page, please do not return to previous pages.*

The final request, not to go back, was included because some of our later questions addressed issues that might have influenced answers to earlier questions. Because respondents typically want to get on with the work, we keep the introduction short. That also reduces the risks of inadvertently communicating expectations or content.

If the questionnaire is more than a few pages long, we may tell respondents in the introduction how the questionnaire is organized ("Part 1 asks about . . . Part 2 focuses on . . . , etc."). We then label the sections of the questionnaire to help people keep track of where they are. For ease in recording and analyzing the results, it is best to number all the questions consecutively from beginning to end.

Once drafted, the questionnaire goes through several rounds of testing and refinement. During this process, it is important to have some way to keep track of which questions cover which concepts, in order to make certain that the revision process does not lose important issues. One might do this with a spreadsheet program or with "sort" commands in a table. Or one can simply sort questions on file cards.

We have used a variety of question formats. True-false questions are often useful. They are compact, they supply the respondent with less information than multiple-choice questions, and they easily lend themselves to posing the same question in several different forms to allow cross-checks. In addition to the usual two-choice (T/F) response mode, sometimes we use a five-option scale requesting respondents' degree of confidence in answers. The questionnaire's introductory instructions define the meanings of the response scale. For example:

> This questionnaire includes 58 statements about radon. For each statement please circle the spot on the following scale that reflects your opinion about that statement. The scale should be interpreted as follows:

True – Maybe True – Don't Know – Maybe False – False

True: To the best of my knowledge, this is true.
Maybe True: I think this might be true.
Don't Know: I don't know if this is true or false.
Maybe False: I think this might be false.
False: To the best of my knowledge, this is false.

For example, if this statement were given:

> Cows have wings.

your response would look like this:

> True – Maybe True – Don't Know – Maybe False – (False)

Figures 5.1 and 5.2 reproduce typical pages from the true-false questionnaires in our studies of radon and of electric and magnetic fields.

In some cases, we have asked respondents (a) to give the probability (from 0% to 100%) that a statement is true or (b) to mark a statement as true or false, then give the probability (from 50% to 100%) of having chosen correctly. Doing so allows us to evaluate the appropriateness of their confidence in their beliefs as well as the extent of their knowledge.[3]

For some populations, we have found that a more standard likert scale (strongly agree, agree, neither agree nor disagree, disagree, strongly disagree) is more acceptable.

All questions should be formulated clearly enough to allow comparison with the scientific consensus. This is often easier said than done, given

[3]For a discussion of these options and further evidence, see Krosnick and Fabrigar's chapter in Lyberg et al., 1997.

True:	To the best of my knowledge, this is true.
Maybe True:	I think this might be true.
Don't Know:	I don't know if this is true or false.
Maybe False:	I think this might be false.
False:	To the best of my knowledge, this is false.

43. Radon-contaminated vegetables and food are a significant source of people's exposure to radon.

True – Maybe True – Don't Know – Maybe False – False

44. As long as radon is coming into a house, the concentration of radon in the house will continue to increase to higher and higher levels.

True – Maybe True – Don't Know – Maybe False – False

45. Exposure to radon significantly increases the chance that houseplants will die.

True – Maybe True – Don't Know – Maybe False – False

46. If a lot of radon (100 pCi/L) is detected in a house, then the only way to reduce the inhabitants' risk is to move.

True – Maybe True – Don't Know – Maybe False – False

47. Most of the radon to which people are exposed is found indoors.

True – Maybe True – Don't Know – Maybe False – False

48. As the concentration of radon is increased the risks from radon increase.

True – Maybe True – Don't Know – Maybe False – False

49. Exposure to radon increases the chance that a person will develop lung cancer.

True – Maybe True – Don't Know – Maybe False – False

50. If a lot of radon (100 pCi/L) is detected in a house, usually opening a window will eliminate most of the risk.

True – Maybe True – Don't Know – Maybe False – False

Figure 5.1. One page of true-false questions from the structured questionnaire in our study of radon. The first page instructed respondents to circle the response that best reflected their opinion about the statement.

For each question, please check the box which comes closest to describing your thinking about the answer.

We have done two things to simplify the wording of the questions:

1. When we say a field is "weak" or "strong" we mean weak or strong compared with the average fields people encounter in their day-to-day lives.

2. When we say something "makes a field" we mean makes a field where people usually would be. Thus, for example, if we are talking about an appliance like a dishwasher, we aren't talking about fields down inside the electric motor, we're talking about fields out in the kitchen where people would be.

PART 1: General Questions about Fields.

1. Some things which use or carry lots of electric power do not make strong fields.

❑ ❑ ❑ ❑ ❑ ❑ ❑ ❑ ❑
not true ... probably not true ... do not know ... probably true ... true

2. Most fields make an audible buzzing or vibrating sound.

❑ ❑ ❑ ❑ ❑ ❑ ❑ ❑ ❑
not true ... probably not true ... do not know ... probably true ... true

3. Fields can deflect or push away other fields.

❑ ❑ ❑ ❑ ❑ ❑ ❑ ❑ ❑
not true ... probably not true ... do not know ... probably true ... true

4. Fields can add to or subtract from other fields.

❑ ❑ ❑ ❑ ❑ ❑ ❑ ❑ ❑
not true ... probably not true ... do not know ... probably true ... true

5. Among common materials water is uniquely good at attracting fields.

❑ ❑ ❑ ❑ ❑ ❑ ❑ ❑ ❑
not true ... probably not true ... do not know ... probably true ... true

Figure 5.2. One page of true-false questions from our study of the intuitive physics of power-frequency electric and magnetic fields. In this case, a particular design challenge was creating questions for which experts agreed on the correct answers.

the need to avoid specialized technical language and complex statements. Once the questions have been pretested, we try to administer them to technical experts in order to see if they give the answers we expect. Getting questions to work for both laypeople and experts can require several iterations, involving both subject matter and communication specialists. Sometimes, we need to provide definitions. For example, in our study of power-frequency electric and magnetic fields, we wrote:

We have done two things to simplify the wording of questions:

1. When we say a field is "weak" or "strong," we mean weak or strong compared with the average fields people encounter in their day-to-day lives.
2. When we say something "makes a field," we mean makes a field where people usually would be. Thus, for example, if we are talking about an appliance like a dishwasher, we aren't talking about fields down inside the electric motor, we're talking about fields out in the kitchen where people would be.

The demographic questions at the end of the survey elicit information that allows analyzing answers by group. We restrict this section to questions whose answers could affect communication design. We begin by reiterating our assurance that "all answers will be kept confidential"; we look for formulations that will feel as unobtrusive as possible. Age, gender, race and ethnicity are often related to risk beliefs. Education can affect beliefs and learning. For continuous variables, we offer categories, for example, six to eight income categories and four to six education categories (e.g., some high school; completed high school; some college or trade school; completed undergraduate college; graduate school). Zip code can provide useful geographic information. Occupation and "highest level of science or math course completed" can reveal technical expertise. For some risks, health status is important (e.g., "How would you describe your health over the past few years? excellent; good; fair; poor"). For dissemination planning, we may ask where people get their information (e.g., "How often do you read newspapers?" "How often do you watch TV news, newsmagazine, science, or health shows?" – with answers like daily, over 30 minutes; daily, under 30 minutes; occasionally; rarely). Figure 5.3 shows a typical demographic form.

Testing and refining a draft questionnaire begins by having some technically oriented colleagues complete the questionnaire and provide feedback. The revision that follows helps to ensure that we are asking scientifically sound questions. We then run a pilot study, administering it to about a dozen people from the population that will be used in the actual study. We time how long it takes these people to complete the questionnaire and ask them for a critical evaluation once they are done. We make appropriate changes in wording and length. We also conduct think-aloud protocols, asking respondents to read and think "out loud" as they answer the questions.

We analyze the results of the pilot study as though they were from an actual study, entering them into a computer spreadsheet or statistical package, then running some simple analyses. For example, we look at simple histograms and crosstabs, as well as at the consistency of answers on key concepts. Although we recognize that small-sample results are unstable, this exercise forces us to think more concretely about the story we will be able to tell with our questions. It also allows us to work out any problems in data analysis. This exercise provides a final chance to reflect on the choice and wording of our questions. Often 20% of the questions need changes, ranging from simple editing to replacement. Sometimes, we discover unexpected gaps in our coverage. If needed, we conduct additional trials.

Often, several iterations are required before all the kinks are worked out. It is important to resist the temptation to rush at this stage. One will be living with the results for a long time; it is worth doing all one can to get them right.

5.3   Conducting and Analyzing the Study

Once the questionnaire has been finalized, it can be administered to a large sample. That process depends on one's objectives and resources. Unless one needs to know the prevalence of views in specific population groups, a diverse sample may be sufficient to reveal common patterns of belief and inference. We have often used people recruited from clubs and other civic organizations whose membership reflects the target audience. If the communication is for the general public, we might choose several

---

1. Highest level of education: ❑ some high school   ❑ completed undergraduate college
   ❑ completed high school   ❑ graduate school
   ❑ some college or trade school

   Did your education involve significant technical or scientific training?   ❑ Yes   ❑ no

2. ❑ Homeowner   ❑ Renter   ❑ Live with family or friends, without rent.
   Zipcode where you live: _____

3. Your approximate age: ❑ under 20   ❑ 20-40   ❑ 40-60   ❑ over 60

4. How would you describe your health over the past few years?
   ❑ Excellent   ❑ good   ❑ fair   ❑ poor

5. Your sex: ❑ male   ❑ female

6. What is your present status:
   ❑ employed   ❑ unemployed   ❑ student   ❑ retired
   Do you work: ❑ full-time   ❑ part-time

7. How would you describe your career:
   ❑ Homemaker   ❑ "blue collar" ❑ "white collar"   ❑ service/sales/clerical/secretarial

8. Do you consider yourself: ❑ technically or mechanically inclined (e.g., have hobbies like
                                    woodworking, fix things around home, read something like
                                    Popular Mechanics, etc.)
                                ❑ Not technically or mechanically inclined

9. How often do you read newspapers?
   ❑ daily, over 30 minutes   ❑ daily, under 30 minutes   ❑ occasionally   ❑ rarely

10. How often do you watch TV news, news magazine, science or health shows?
    ❑ daily, over 30 minutes   ❑ daily, under 30 minutes   ❑ occasionally   ❑ rarely

---

Figure 5.3. Typical demographic form.

groups whose members span a range of socioeconomic, educational, and political backgrounds. As mentioned, we have used bowling and other recreational groups, including parents supporting youth sports leagues, church groups, PTAs, library members, social clubs, members of a nature reserve, and similar groups.

When we use members of a group, we offer a donation to the organization's treasury for each complete, usable questionnaire. Sometimes, the organization provides a mailing list or labels. We then send an introductory letter explaining our plans and include a postcard, so that people can respond easily if they would like to participate. Alternatively, we may supply the organization with the materials and reimburse them for the cost of the mailing. Sometimes, a group leader will write to the membership on our behalf. With prior agreement, we have sometimes attended a group function, explaining what we were doing and asking for volunteers.

Another strategy is to set up a booth in a shopping center or at a major public event, such as a home or auto show. We once ran a study with a booth at Point State Park in downtown Pittsburgh on Fourth of July afternoon! In such cases, we put out a sign explaining that we are running a research project on what the public thinks about risk and offering cash to adults for answering a few questions. The sign does not say what the specific topic is, because we don't want to encourage or discourage people who have particular views or knowledge about it.

Whatever the recruiting procedure, the demographic questions provide important help in determining how far results can be generalized. Population demographic information, for comparison purposes, is available for various places.[4] If the sample does not fit the desired profile, it may be necessary to find other sources of respondents.

If a true random sample of a specific population subgroup is desired, survey research firms can obtain such a sample; then, with varying degrees of precision (and cost), they can also administer the questionnaire. Their work can be approximated with random digit dialing – which gets at all phone numbers but draws many inappropriate ones (faxes, businesses, unused numbers). One can also sample randomly from the listed numbers in the telephone directory, chosen to cover a large enough geographic region to ensure broad socioeconomic diversity. A random number function can generate page numbers for the book. Then for each page, select two more random numbers, one to choose the column and one to choose the line. Comparing demographic information for the sample and the population can show how representative the resulting sample is.

How big a sample is needed? The answer depends on the precision needed. For most purposes, 100–300 should suffice. Remember, the principal objective is to get a reliable notion of the rough prevalence of key beliefs in the target audience. One is not trying to predict the outcome of the next election with an accuracy of a few percentage points!

Once the questionnaires have been returned, the data analysis begins.

[4]In the case of the United States, see http://www.census.gov and http://www.dhhs.gov.

Results should be tabulated for each question, and each set of questions, addressing a particular concept. Results should also be broken down by key demographic variables, especially for audiences that could be targeted specially. For example, are there important differences in the answers of women and men? Do well-educated people have different misconceptions than less well-educated people?[5] For practical purposes, simple analyses are often adequate. The basic objective is to learn how well the key concepts are understood. Which of the important misconceptions uncovered in the open-ended interviews appear to be widely shared? Which ones appear not to be common and, hence, can be safely ignored? Deciding in advance which differences to examine reduces the risk of discovering something significant just by chance; so does insisting that the absolute differences between groups be fairly large before taking them seriously.

5.4   Special Questionnaires to Explore Key Points

Some topics lend themselves poorly to true-false questions and require other formats. For example, in studying how people think about power-frequency fields, we asked respondents to estimate field strengths at various locations in pictures showing exposure situations (see Section 7.2). We found that few people understand how rapidly the strength of a field decreases as one moves away from the source. That misconception could lead to ineffective field-management strategies, such as unduly increasing the width of a power-line right-of-way. We needed the special study to ascertain the magnitude and prevalence of this misconception. The more innovative the measurement procedure, the more pretesting is needed.

References

Converse, J. M., and Presser, S. (1996). *Survey Questions: Handcrafting the Standardized Questionnaire.* Sage Publications, Beverly Hills.

[5]In many of the studies we have done, the answer to this question has often been "no."

Fowler, F. J., Jr. (1992). "How Unclear Terms Affect Survey Data," *Public Opinion Quarterly*, 56(2):218–231.

Krosnick, J. A. (1999). "Survey Research," *Annual Review of Psychology*, 50:537–567.

Lyberg, L., Biemer, P., Collins, M., deLeeuw, E., Dippo, C., Schwarz, N., and Terwin, D., eds. (1997). *Survey Measurement and Process Quality.* John Wiley and Sons, New York

Read, D., Bostrom, A., Morgan, M. G., Fischhoff, B., and Smuts, T. (1994). "What Do People Know about Global Climate Change? Part 2: Survey Studies of Educated Laypeople," *Risk Analysis,* 14(6):971–982.

Sirken, M. G. et al. (1999). *Cognition and Survey Research.* John Wiley and Sons, New York.

6

DEVELOPMENT AND EVALUATION OF COMMUNICATIONS

6.1 Principles

The mental models interviews and follow-up questionnaires typically identify many more misconceptions and gaps in lay knowledge than one can hope to address or fill with a risk communication of modest length. As a result, the first stage in developing a communication is to set priorities. If one had a fully computational expert model and a full set of parameter estimates, then one could compute the impact of providing different pieces of missing information. Specifically, one could compute the percentage of people whose decisions would change as a result of providing each piece of information (Fischhoff, Bostrom, and Quadrel, 1997; Fischhoff, Downs, and Bruine de Bruin, 1998; Merz et al., 1993; Riley, 1998).

Here, we will focus on more heuristic methods. However, the logic is the same. Communications should focus on the facts that will have the greatest impact on the greatest portion of the audience. There is little point in emphasizing a central fact in the expert model if audience members know it already – unless repeating that fact helps to tell a more coherent, memorable, and understandable story. Nor is there much point in filling a common gap if knowing that fact would not change people's overall judgments or actions.

This chapter begins by describing the choices we made in designing our communications regarding radon (Section 6.1.2). It proceeds to general procedures for building messages (6.2). It then offers methods for the evaluation that should be part of any developmental process (6.3), including technical review (6.4), text-based evaluation (6.5), and reader-based evaluation (6.6). Each is illustrated with examples from the development of a radon communication.

6.1.2   Choosing Message Content: A Radon Example

As mentioned, our study of radon identified various misconceptions. Some, like the idea that radon can permanently contaminate a house, are clearly critical. People holding that belief could forgo testing the radon concentration in their homes, believing that they could do nothing about any problem they found; as a result, they may be better off not knowing. Because it could undermine the value of much correct knowledge, this misconception must be set right – by explaining that radon problems will vanish once the influx is stopped.

Another, less common misconception is the belief that radon comes from decaying garbage in the ground – rather than when the element radium, present in rocks and soil, undergoes radioactive decay. Presumably, this misconception arose as a result of hearing the word "decay" used in discussions of radon. However, we decided not to confront and correct it in one of our communications because we concluded both that there were other, more important topics and that this one was unlikely to lead people seriously astray. A "garbage decay" mental model leads to conclusions similar to those of a "radioactive decay" mental model, unless smell is taken as a necessary indicator and quick depletion is expected. On the positive side, the garbage mental model might reduce the expectation of permanent contamination. In any case, explaining how radon problems can be solved should indirectly dispel the "decaying garbage" model.

When the communication opportunity is limited, one may choose to address central concepts more than once, even if that means skipping less central ones. Using different language, drawing implications, providing supporting illustrations, and simply repeating oneself can all improve understanding. Readers may not "get things" the first time they see them, or they may skip around and not read all the text. For example, our climate change research found that many people hold the nonspecific belief that many forms of atmospheric pollution contribute to climate change, while "green" practices reduce it. In fact, though, contributions to climate change are dominated by emissions of carbon dioxide from burning fossil fuels. The "all pollution" mental model is too general to show the importance of energy conservation (which reduces fuel use and the associated carbon dioxide emissions) and conversion to renewable energy sources. This overly general model may have contributed to some people's erroneous belief that nuclear power contributes to climate change. Thus, we decided to focus our communication on the fossil fuel–carbon dioxide connection, using different wording and several contexts (see Section 7.1 for details).

Once the key concepts have been selected, a logical organizing principle is needed to help people make sense of what they are learning and integrate it with their existing mental models. How text is organized can enhance or hinder readers' ability to understand and remember what they read. The best presentation structure matches readers' internal representation of the subject matter (Fletcher and Chrysler, 1990; Garnham, 1987; van Dijk and Kintsch, 1983). Facts placed at the highest level in the hierarchy of information have the greatest chance of being recalled (Kintsch and van Dijk, 1978; Eylon and Reif, 1984; Meyer and Rice, 1984; Reder, 1985; Trabasso and Sperry, 1985; Trabasso and van den Broek, 1985) and are also more likely to be integrated, compared to information placed lower in the hierarchical structure (Walker and Meyer, 1980).

Communications should also use comprehension aids, such as section headings, "advance organizers" (outlining what is in the text) and summaries (Schriver, 1997). Headings help readers to recall information more easily (Krug et al., 1989) and find it more rapidly (Kobasigawa, Lacasse, and MacDonald, 1988). Outlines also increase recall (Ausubel, 1960; Reder, 1985; Mannes and Kintsch, 1987; Krug et al., 1989). Summaries can be more effective than connected text in facilitating recall (Reder, 1982, 1985; Reder and Anderson, 1982).

In our radon studies, we developed two separate brochures, described in greater detail later. One was structured around the influence diagram, the other around people's radon-related decisions. Both versions did comparably well in conveying information and significantly better than the first edition of the EPA's *Citizen's Guide to Radon,* whose organizational principle was far less apparent (perhaps because it was the compromise product of committee work).

A follow-up study compared two brochures about global climate change with identical content, chosen through mental models studies. One used an influence diagram as the organizing principle, going from cause to effect to mitigation decisions. The second went from effect to cause to mitigation decisions. Although readers of both brochures recalled similar amounts of factual information, the influence diagram version facilitated remembering mitigation information.

We believe that, to a first approximation, the critical thing is to have *some* organizing principle and to execute it well. A decision analytic structure, such as an influence diagram, is a logical candidate structure for risk-related information.

As noted, our research has focused on written messages. However, the same choices – selecting key concepts and organizing them logically – arise in preparing a message for radio, television, or a museum display and might benefit from following the same steps (Atman et al., 1994).

6.2   Building Messages from Users' Decision Needs and Mental Models Results

With a list of key concepts and organizing principles in hand, it is time to produce a first draft of the communication. The primary author of our communications has always had a detailed understanding of the technical issues, applied within the constraints determined by the mental models research. If a technical expert with a gift for writing for the lay public is not available, it may be necessary to team an expert with a writer. In our experience, it is easier to improve the style of technically accurate writing than to correct factual errors in nicely styled prose. A communication must be clear, interesting, and useful to lay readers, as well as balanced, correct, and understandable to technical experts. Finding the right wording is usually an iterative process. This may be particularly challenging in the beginning of a communication, where important new concepts are being introduced.

One common wording problem arises with issues involving scientific controversy or uncertainty. Treating readers with respect means leveling with them. Present a balanced explanation of where things stand, allowing readers to draw their own conclusions. When the scientific community is divided, explain the different views, asking members of opposing camps to approve the summaries of their positions.

As mentioned, readers need help to find their way around the message, including opening and closing summaries, subheadings, and advance organizers. Even the questions in a question-and-answer format provide some structure, relative to uninterrupted text. Multiple methods are needed to serve readers with diverse reading styles. Some will read the communication from start to finish in one sitting, while others will take it in pieces; some will want a few basic points, while others will want many details. Even those who want a lot may not want equivalent detail about each topic.

A hierarchical organization can help readers to achieve this goal. For simple messages, a conventional brochure can easily do that. With more complicated topics, effective organization is more challenging. Hypertext allows flexible hierarchical organization in a computer. Where computers are unavailable, we have developed a form of "paper hypertext." As illustrated in Figure 7.6 in the next chapter, it provides two levels of detail in a conventional brochure, then adds additional levels in booklets that pull out from pouches.

People cannot always infer errors in their mental models from factual statements that implicitly contradict them. In order to increase the chances of correcting key misunderstandings, we often include a "myth-fact" section, stating each incorrect belief, followed by the correct one, along with an explanation designed to help readers to revise and integrate their mental models. Examples can be found in the appendices. In experimental tests, we have found that stating both the misconception and correction explicitly is critical. Integrating the explanation with the overall mental model should improve retention.

In order to break up the text, we try to use devices such as diagrams, drawings, and special boxed sections. Sometimes, they highlight a key point (like misconceptions). At other times, they elaborate on a point that does not fit smoothly into the main message. All can make the brochure more appealing visually.

Some people think better with pictures, while others prefer verbal explanations. Having the same material appear in both formats increases the chances that both verbal and visual people will see it in the best way at least once. However, if during the review process, we repeatedly hear, "You know, I looked at that illustration for the longest time, because I figured it was important, but I could never figure it out," we rework (or drop) it. Chapter 7 shows how we corrected one such picture. In a series of studies comparing an illustration, an influence diagram, a bulletized summary, and text as ways to present the same information on global climate change, we found that readers overwhelmingly preferred the illustration (Atman and Puerzer, 1995).

Layout and design are important. If no one on your team has appropriate experience, you may want help from a professional designer. However, the designer needs clear instructions about the kind of impression you want the document to create. For example, a designer may assume that a technical topic warrants a high-tech look, with glossy paper, bright colors, crisp photographs, and sharp diagrams. However, you may decide that such a style will alienate those readers who are skeptical about technology to begin with. Many of our brochures have been produced on an antique cream buff paper, using hand-drawn illustrations in a reddish brown ink, reminiscent of the Leonardo da Vinci sketchbooks. We hoped that this design would create a friendly, humanistic feel.

The same warning applies to illustrations. Some designers view graphics as decoration. Although it should be aesthetically appealing, artwork should have some substantive content. It should help to communicate part of the message, not just provide a designer with personal expression.

Another common stylistic choice is dealing with readers' desire to know what you would do if the risk involved *you* or *your* family. Where addressing this concern seems unavoidable, we try to draw a sharp distinction between the general discussion and any personal conclusions, so as to make clear the role of personal values in such choices. We hope, thereby, to recognize readers' concerns without interjecting our values. The brochures on power-frequency electric and magnetic fields in the appendices address these issues.

6.3   Evaluation

If there is one thing that we have learned in our studies of risk communication, it is that no one gets the design of risk messages entirely right the first time. Drafts always need testing with people drawn from the target audience (Bostrom et al., 1994). Even with apparently simple issues, such as comparisons among risks, one can get only so far with general guidelines and personal experience (Chapter 8; Roth et al., 1990). For example, a pretest showed that an early version of our climate change brochure started at too high a level for some readers. Adding a simpler introductory section made the remaining material more accessible.

Affective responses to communications, like the impressions created by style, need empirical evaluation. For example, in a brochure on the risks of spacecraft with nuclear energy sources, we mentioned the *Challenger* explosion in order to illustrate a technical point. Some pretest readers jumped all over us: "How could you cold, heartless people talk about *Challenger* in that way?" After some probing exploration, we found that it was not the comparison that caused this reaction but the neutral way in which we made it. Once we changed the text to refer to the "tragic explosion that caused the *Challenger* accident," the objections disappeared. Such mistakes can undermine the credibility of otherwise sound communications.

The cover of a brochure on power-frequency magnetic fields featured a montage of images related to its three major sections: (a) What are fields? (b) What is known about possible health risks from fields? and (c) What can be done? Because many experimental studies of possible health risks used rats, the second section of the montage included a sketch of a lab rat in a field exposure system. We found that some pretest subjects were extremely averse to reading something with a rat on it. Because the rat was not essential to any point that we were trying to make, we replaced it with a woman in a lab coat using a microscope.

Well-articulated objectives are a prerequisite for any evaluation. Ours assume that risk communications should support decision making. To that end, risk communications should improve mental models by adding missing knowledge, by restructuring overly general knowledge, by reducing any focus on peripheral information, and by dispelling misconceptions – all ways to reduce the discrepancies between mental models and expert models.

The next few sections describe how and why you might want to use each of three evaluation methods: review by technical experts, formal text evaluation, and empirical tests of reader impact.

6.4   Technical Review

Even if the authors and their colleagues are very expert in the subject matter, external technical review is still essential. Other specialists, viewing the topic from other perspectives and less involved in the communication design, may identify missing topics or alternative interpretations of included material. Because the document as a whole can convey messages, reviewers should see it all. If need be, paste up a draft copy for their review, with rough sketches of illustrations and editorial notes on how the final version would look.

6.4.1   Choosing Experts

How you choose experts for the technical review should be guided by the goals for your communication. Informing people to enable them to reduce their risk requires experts specializing in each step in the hazardous process creating the risk and in offering opportunities for risk reduction. Expertise can be identified by reputation, organizational affiliation, publications, or other public actions. A crude rule of thumb for scientific expertise is that those who have published the most peer-reviewed articles (especially in high-prestige publications) and are most widely cited by other scientists are the most expert. Experts can be found through citation searches, using the *Science* or *Social Sciences Citation Indices,* one or more of the expertise databases now online, such as the Web of Science, directories such as *American Men and Women of Science,* university faculty directories, and the memberships of scholarly and professional organizations. There are also specific search engines online that you can use to look for specific kinds of experts. One of these is academicinfo.net. For example, by looking for math resources via academicinfo.net you can find a searchable directory of women in mathematics (http://www.agnesscott.edu/lriddle/women/search.html; 6/28/00).

The politics of expertise can be hard for an outsider to follow. Even experts' interpretations of scientific results can be colored by whether the research reaches a conclusion that agrees with the reviewer's own ideas – when in theory it should be reviewed on the basis of its scientific quality (a review of biases in the interpretation of research results is provided by MacCoun, 1998). Scientists' judgments may differ depending on their institutional affiliation, as well as their training (Barke and Jenkins-Smith, 1993). For these and other reasons, it is a good idea to try to solicit reviews from a balanced panel of experts, as far as your resources permit – balanced in terms of affiliation (e.g., university, government, industry, other nonprofit), training (e.g., biology, physics, law), and subject matter (e.g., radiation health effects, property law).

Experts think differently about problems than do nonexperts (e.g., Larkin et al., 1980). This means that you will likely have to do some translation in order to turn your expert reviews into useful edits and additions. It also means that it is critical that your expert reviewers understand your goal for the communication so that they don't go off on tangents or suggest including expert details that won't help your eventual readers.

With the technical review complete, your team should sit down together and work systematically through the document. If there are fundamental criticisms, you may have to throw out some or even all of the first draft and redo the work. If the criticisms are more modest, then you need to go through them, page by page, and line by line, discussing each and deciding what changes to make. Often, reviewers will give contradictory advice, and you will have to exercise judgment. Sometimes, reviewers will give advice that violates your design objectives or invokes details that you have decided to omit. In such cases, you may decide to ignore some or all of their advice. The mental models research should drive the communication, not the reviewers' intuitions about the public. Writing down your choices can help you later to remember or defend all the little decisions that are part of effective communication.

6.5   Text-Based Evaluation Methods

The technical review helps to ensure that what you have said is accurate. Text-based evaluations help to ensure that you have said it the right way. Both should be conducted before testing the communication on members of your intended audience. The simplest text-based evaluation method is to assess the reading level of the document, which can be done using common word-processing software. Other routine assessments include checking the structure and format for organizing features (such as headers or summaries), counting words, and performing a content analysis on the document.

One form of content analysis that emerges from the mental models approach is comparing the document to the expert model. This can be done in three steps. First, have two people code the content of the text using the mental models coding scheme (checking the coding reliability and reconciling disagreements). Second, map these results into the expert model. Although this is just a mechanical translation, it shows graphically how well the text covers the expert model. Third, check the nonexpert concepts coded in the text, making sure that you have contradicted the major misconceptions and not inadvertently reinforced any. This three-step process can also be performed for structured survey instruments (Chapter 5).

6.5.1   A Radon Example of Text-Based Evaluation

Two brochures about indoor radon were written at Carnegie Mellon University (CMU) using a mental models approach. Each used a different structure. They will be referred to as CMUN (for the Directed Network brochure) and CMUD (for the Decision Tree brochure). Each was authored by a single individual and extensively critiqued by reviewers. Each attempted to cover the basic nodes in the influence diagram and the detailed concepts that the author had decided were important in conveying the significance of the basic level concepts.

Table 6.1 presents the results of a content analysis for the two CMU brochures and the 1986 EPA *Citizen's Guide to Radon.* The reliability

Table 6.1   The contents of the two Carnegie Mellon brochures and the 1986 EPA *A Citizen's Guide to Radon.*

	CMU Directed Network	CMU Decision Tree	1986 EPA Citizen's Guide
Basic concepts			
Exposure	9	8	7
Effects	4	4	4
Identification	4	4	4
Specific concepts			
Exposure	23	14	15
Effects	1	1	3
Identification	2	2	2
Number of words	~2350	~2750	~3170

Source: Atman et al. (1994) (abridged).

revealed in comparing the codes assigned by the two coders ranged from 92% to 98%. All differences were resolved and are reflected in the reported frequencies. The numbers of expert concepts covered at the basic and the specific level are presented as well. The counts are broken down by exposure (e.g., radon from soil gas), effects (e.g., lung cancer), and identification concepts (e.g., radon is a gas).

All three brochures covered almost all of the basic-level concepts and approximately half of the specific-level concepts. Figure 6.1 maps the exposure and effects concepts onto an unlabeled version of the expert influence diagram (Figure 3.4 on page 49 presents the full diagram). Filled nodes are covered in the text, with solid nodes indicating basic-level concepts and crosshatched nodes indicating specific-level concepts.

Visual inspection shows that while all three communications covered somewhat different specific concepts, each went into the greatest detail for those in the lower-left-hand box: "radon from soil gas," the most likely exposure route. The CMU Directed Network brochure is the most complete in this sense, in part because it is based directly on the influence diagram.

The number of nonexpert concepts mentioned was 46 for CMUN, 51 for CMUD, and 40 for EPA. Although the numbers were similar, their

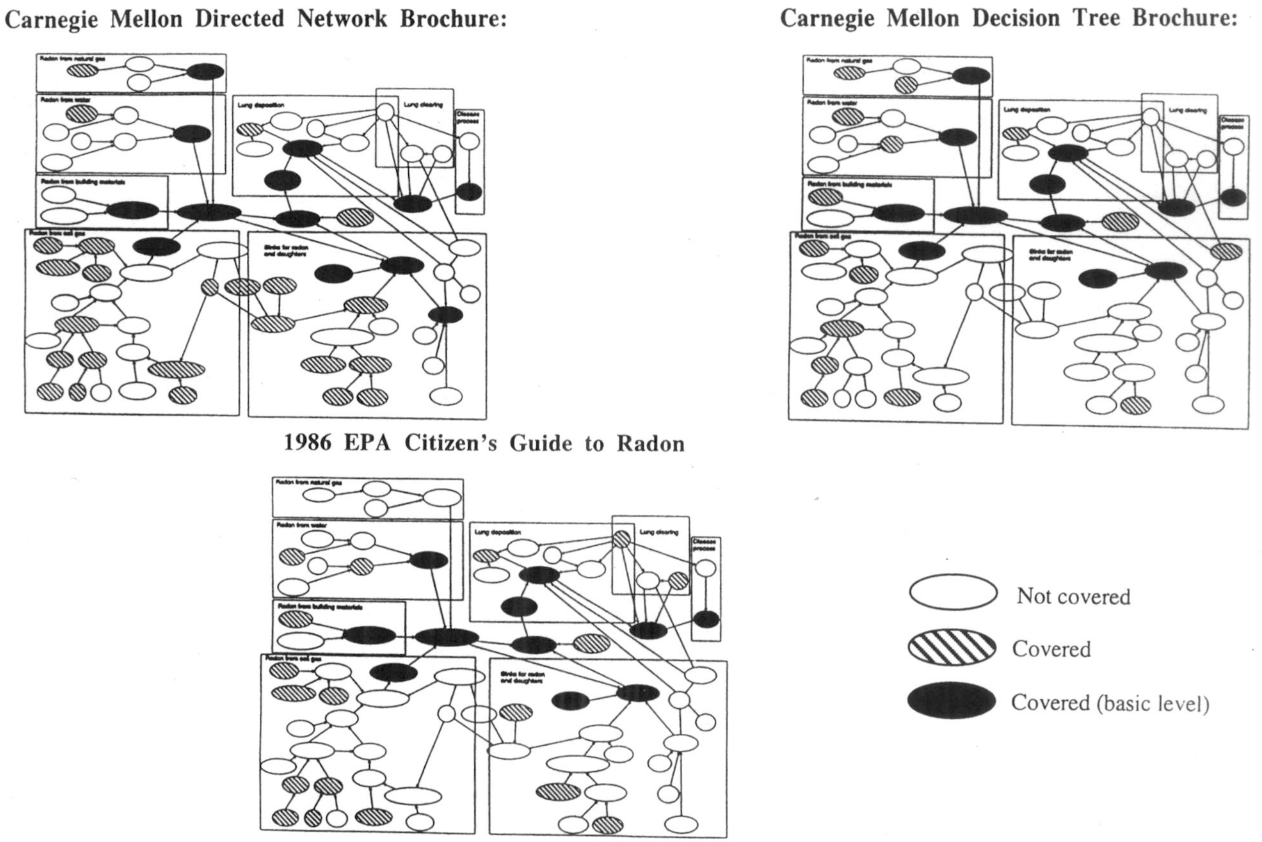

Figure 6.1. Comparison of concepts covered in two Carnegie Mellon brochures and the 1986 EPA *Citizen's Guide to Radon*. See Figure 3.4 for the original influence diagram.

Table 6.2   Abbreviated list of nonexpert concepts mentioned in the two Carnegie Mellon brochures and the 1986 EPA *A Citizen's Guide to Radon*.

	CMUN	CMUD	EPA		CMUN	CMUD	EPA
Exposure concepts				Effects concepts *(continued)*			
Radon in industrial waste	*	*	*	Allergies	*	*	
Radon in environment				Inhibits growth (children)			
Radon in radioactive waste	*			Radon contaminates	*	*	
Radon attaches to dust				Health problems	*	*	
Radon from garbage	*			Contaminates water	*		
Radon from tank leak	*			Skin lesions	*	*	
Radon from mines			*	Absorption through skin	*		
Pollutes the air				Health effects			
Radon from gas supply				Contaminates blood			
Radon from underground/soil				Identification concepts			
More higher in house				Radon is a form of energy			
More lower in house	*	*	*	Radon is poisonous			
Fans (ventilation)	*		*	Radon is "nuclear"			
Elevation				Radon is manufactured	*		
Lead or concrete				Extracted from soil			
foundation/barrier				Odor	*	*	*
Effects concepts				Heavy gas			
Cancer		*		Radon is an element			
Genetic mutation	*			Radon occurs naturally	*	*	
Corrosion				Not volatile			
Affects plants		*	*	Valuation			
Illness and death				Radon is risky, dangerous		*	
Breast cancer	*	*		Costly to society			
Leukemia	*	*		Harmful		*	
Affects animals	*			Scary			
Lung problems	*	*		Mitigation is expensive			
Gas explosion				Unreliable measurement		*	
Contaminates food			*				

identity was different. Table 6.2 displays an abbreviated list of nonexpert concepts mentioned in the lay interviews, with an asterisk indicating whether it was covered in each brochure.

CMUN directly contradicts several misconceptions: (a) radon comes from garbage, chemical tank leaks, and toxic waste dumps; (b) radon affects plants and animals; (c) radon can build up on surfaces in the home and contaminate them; and (d) radon causes leukemia, breast cancer, skin problems, or birth defects. The CMUD brochure directly contradicts the concepts (a) that radon affects plants and animals and (b) that radon can build up on surfaces in the home and contaminate them. It indirectly contradicts the idea that radon causes a variety of health problems by stating that it causes *only* lung cancer. The EPA brochure does not directly address any of these wrong concepts, although it also states that the only known health effect is lung cancer.

Thus, all three brochures have similar coverage for the expert concepts, particularly at the basic level. The brochures also cover a roughly equivalent number of nonexpert concepts; the CMU brochures focus on the problems with peripheral and wrong concepts.

Text structure   The expert model shows the processes determining the most common route of exposure to radon. The Directed Network brochure (CMUN) uses Figure 6.2 as an organizing hierarchy, with the nodes in the directed network appearing as subsection titles. A final section provides information about actions that an individual can take. Following this structure ensures that the critical physical processes and decisions appear at the highest level in the communication's hierarchy, where they have the greatest chance of being remembered.

The EPA brochure also presents its information in a loose exposure-to-effects order. It defines radon, then discusses, in turn, exposure processes, effects processes, detection procedures, and control techniques, as seen in the section headings in Figure 6.2c. The crosshatched rectangles in Figure 6.2c show, however, that it jumps around from topic to topic. Based on text-structure research, one would expect readers of CMUN to remember more about radon processes than would readers of the EPA brochure.

Text comprehension aids   As seen in Table 6.3, the CMU brochures have all three kinds of aids. The sections, determined by the decision analysis, are reinforced by titles that separate them. Advance organizers are provided by a table of contents, a summary, and a short introductory paragraph informing the reader about what to expect. There is also a concluding summary.

Information in the 1986 EPA brochure is also segmented. Section headings are presented as questions, which are then answered in the text that follows. Neither advance organizers nor summaries are provided. The 1992 version of the EPA *Citizen's Guide* provides a summary of its most important information at the beginning of the brochure. The other brochures in the table also used section headings but did not use summaries or advance organizers, potentially undermining the value of the good writing in them.

(a)

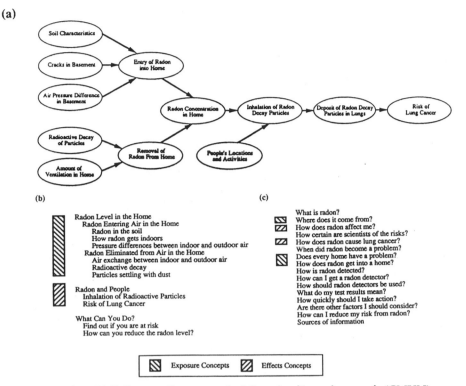

(b)

Radon Level in the Home
  Radon Entering Air in the Home
    Radon in the soil
    How radon gets indoors
    Pressure differences between indoor and outdoor air
  Radon Eliminated from Air in the Home
    Air exchange between indoor and outdoor air
    Radioactive decay
    Particles settling with dust

Radon and People
  Inhalation of Radioactive Particles
  Risk of Lung Cancer

What Can You Do?
  Find out if you are at risk
  How can you reduce the radon level?

(c)

What is radon?
Where does it come from?
How does radon affect me?
How certain are scientists of the risks?
How does radon cause lung cancer?
When did radon become a problem?
Does every home have a problem?
How does radon get into a home?
How is radon detected?
How can I get a radon detector?
How should radon detectors be used?
What do my test results mean?
How quickly should I take action?
Are there other factors I should consider?
How can I reduce my risk from radon?
Sources of information

	Exposure Concepts		Effects Concepts

Figure 6.2. (a) Influence diagram underlying the directed network (CMUN) brochure structure. (b) Section headings in order of appearance for CMUN brochure. (c) Section headings in order of appearance for 1986 EPA *A Citizen's Guide to Radon. Source:* Atman et al. (1994).

6.6   Reader-Based Evaluation Methods

Reader-based evaluations can be both open-ended, such as think-aloud protocols and focus groups, and structured, like surveys.

Open-ended procedures reduce the risk of underestimating readers' knowledge if their frame of reference differs from that of the evaluator, by allowing them to speak their own minds. Open-ended procedures also reduce the risk of overestimating readers' knowledge when they harbor unsuspected understandings that structured tests might miss altogether. However, because open-ended, reader-based evaluations are more expensive, they may be most useful as a stepping stone toward structured procedures. Closed-

Table 6.3 Text comprehension aids included in radon communications.

	Text Comprehension Aids			
Brochure	Summary at End	Summary at Beginning	Advanced Organizer	Section Headings
This study				
CMU Directed Network	√	√	√	√
CMU Decision Tree	√	√	√	√
1986 EPA *Citizen's Guide*				√
1992 EPA *Citizen's Guide*		√		√
Other radon brochures				
NYSERDA/EPA study				√
NJ/EPA study				√
NY State Health Dept.				√
NJ Dept. of Environ.				√
Bonneville Power				√

Source: Atman et al. (1994).

ended tests, such as multiple-choice or true-false tests, are vulnerable to (a) *reactivity,* changing people's beliefs through the cues offered by questions or answer options; (b) *illusory expertise,* restricting the expression of nonexpert beliefs; and (c) *illusory discrimination,* suppressing inconsistent beliefs.

6.6.1 Open-Ended Methods

In a think-aloud, or "read-aloud," protocol, individual participants are asked to say everything that passes through their mind as they read the text, such as, "Geez, that's pretty dumb," "OK, I guess I understand that," and "Why are they telling me this?" Learning how to do this takes a bit of practice, and the interviewer may have to prompt test readers periodically in order to keep the comments coming. However, with a little effort, most people can do this quite well. The interview should be tape-recorded for later reference and analysis. The interviewer will probably also want to take notes on a copy of the communication as things go along.

There is no single way to analyze a read-aloud protocol. One procedure is to count the positive and negative evaluative comments, as well as the number of unanswered questions that the document raised while the individual was reading it. These are counted by two people, who code the interviews independently and then compare their results, in order to ensure reliability. One could also try to assess the kinds of thinking, such as interpreting, drawing inferences, or commenting on the text. Often, a lot can be garnered with no formal analysis at all.

Illustrations need to be reviewed as well as text. The interviewer should ask readers to describe each picture, explain what it conveys, discuss why they think it was included, and evaluate its effectiveness.

It is important that the person who conducts the interviews not have an emotional stake in the design or wording of the communication being evaluated. If the interviewer has any obvious pride of authorship, or is the least bit defensive, readers may hold back in their comments. References to the authors should use the neutral third person: "What do you think they are trying to say here?" If a reader comments negatively on a design feature, the interviewer should simply explore the complaint and resist the temptation to explain the original rationale.

If these evaluations prompt major changes, additional interviews will be needed. Ericsson and Simon (1994) and Schriver (1989) provide guidance on conducting verbal protocols. (Examples can be found in Anderson, 1987; Carley, 1990; Krippendorff, 1980; Nazaroff and Nero, 1988; USEPA and USDHHS, 1986.)

Turning now to group processes, our focus groups have typically involved 8 to 12 people each. Participants are asked to prepare for their meeting by reading the draft communication carefully, marking with a pencil anything that they dislike or find unclear. When the group meets, the facilitator begins by asking for general comments or reactions. The meeting proceeds by working through the communication, asking for comments, suggestions, and advice. Because anything in a communication can affect its clarity and credibility, the review begins with the cover and introductory materials, then moves systematically through each section, including illustrations, tables, boxed items, glossary, and suggested readings (if present). For each part, the facilitator asks for general comments, then has the group discuss things paragraph-by-paragraph and, when necessary, line-by-line. Here, too, the facilitator should not be emotionally involved with the communication. Merton (1987) and Stewart and Shamdasani (1990) provide perspectives on focus groups.

Our facilitators usually take notes as the session goes along, both to help keep track of it and to show interest in participants' comments. When possible, we videotape (or at least audiotape) the sessions so that the team can review them. Typically, participants forget about the tape once the conversation gets going. Because focus groups can be affected by group dynamics, more than one is needed. People say new things when stimulated by others but also suppress views that they might otherwise express. As with one-on-one interviews, focus groups can be analyzed formally or impressionistically. Nevertheless, a couple of focus groups, or a handful of think-aloud protocols, is better than no empirical evaluation at all.

As with the revisions made in response to expert reviews, it is important to list explicitly all the issues raised by pretest subjects. Some problems may be fixed with simple word changes. Others may be more fundamental, requiring a communication to be redesigned or the explanation of a concept to be reworked. On the other hand, some advice is silly, scientifically inaccurate, or contrary to design objectives. The review format can pull participants into a hypercritical mood, finding problems where none really exist. They may provide speculations regarding others' reaction to the material rather than direct evidence of their own. As elsewhere, the more substantial the changes, the greater the need to test the revised communication.

The choice between individual and group evaluations is a common one in the social sciences. If people will receive and process the actual communication individually, then think-aloud protocols will more closely simulate their eventual experience. Individual interviews also offer greater opportunity to explore the interpretations of individuals in greater depth while reducing the inhibitions on public expression of uncertainty or confusion. Focus groups might be better predictors of the impact of messages that will be read together by groups with a composition like that of the focus groups' membership. Group interactions can draw out ideas that might not otherwise arise, as well as keep individuals from being unduly captured by a particular frame of reference. Interpersonal interactions will differ in groups organized by neutral investigators and by individuals promoting a particular perspective. The interdependence of views in a group setting means that the effective sample size is smaller than when the same number of people are interviewed individually.

A radon example   Subjects completed think-aloud protocols as they read one of the three radon brochures: CMUN, CMUD, or EPA. A fourth, control group, CTRL, solved puzzles. Comments by subjects in the three experimental groups were coded (a) as *content* or *presentation* and (b) as *negative, positive,* or *neutral.* Content comments referred to what was said, presentation comments to how it was said. Negative content comments include confusion about things being said and questions about things unsaid (e.g., "I think that's kind of, I don't know, fuzzy"). Positive content comments include associations with prior knowledge and (correct) spontaneous inferences (e.g., "I think they make that really clear"). Better-written material should generate fewer comments, because it is easily understood.

The subjects were 15 undergraduates from a university social science communications class who volunteered in return for extra class credit. Each brochure was randomly assigned to 5 of these subjects. Each experimental session lasted approximately 90 minutes. It began with mental models interviews conducted by a single experimenter. Then a second experimenter administered a think-aloud protocol for a brochure. Following a five-minute break, the first experimenter returned to administer a second mental models interview (without being told which brochure the subject had read). Finally, each subject completed a true-false test and some demographic questions.

Comments made by subjects as they read the brochures were coded by two individuals independently. The reliability of these codings was 62% at the detailed level and 72% at the general level. Differences were resolved by discussion. The codings are summarized in Table 6.4. Each brochure evoked an average of two positive comments per subject, one each referring to its content and its presentation. The EPA brochure produced more than twice as many negative comments (Mann-Whitney test, p = .01). Three-quarters of these dealt with its contents, expressing confusion about specific wording or irritation about particular omissions. The details of these comments (and the comparable ones for the CMU brochures) are given in Atman (1990). Most of the negative comments concentrated on the brochure pages that described how to use radon detectors and interpret test results. These pages also include risk comparisons.

Although we were interested in evaluation rather than further design, these think-aloud protocols highlighted some residual problems with the

Table 6.4   Comments by brochure condition ($N = 5$ per condition).

Comments	Brochure		
	CMUN	CMUD	EPA
Positive			
On content	4	7	8
On presentation	6	5	4
Total	10	12	12
Mean per subject	2.0	2.4	2.4
Negative			
On content	10	24	48
On presentation	9	4	18
Total	19	28	66
Mean per subject	3.8	5.6	13.2
All			
On content	40	73	112
On presentation	23	17	30
Total	63	90	142
Mean per subject	12.6	18.0	28.4

Source: Bostrom et al. (1994).

texts' structure and organization. So, even with brochures that performed fairly well, not every reader understood everything. Other evaluation techniques involve physical measurements, such as eye movements or response latencies for problem solving and information search in a communication. Such tests can provide information such as which graphics and text strings readers are actually processing, how fast they can find information in a brochure, and how easily they can interpret a narrative (Schriver, 1997). However, they are even more expensive than open-ended interviews. Whether they justify the cost depends on the stakes riding on successful communication – and on the chances of learning something useful.

6.6.2   Structured Evaluations/Surveys

Once a final draft of the message has been prepared, its effectiveness can be evaluated by surveying a sample of people using confirmatory questionnaires developed along the lines discussed in Chapter 5. Surveys require a much greater investment up front than do interviews or focus groups, and much less effort to analyze. As a result, it is best to do them as late as possible in a project, in order to take advantage of all possible insight from the mental models interviews. These surveys, too, must be evaluated with read-aloud protocols or focus groups before being administered. The test sample should represent the eventual audience. Section 4.2.3 describes possible sampling procedures.

A brochure's effects can be evaluated either by comparing those who have read it with those who have not (or, perhaps, with those who have read a competing brochure) or by having respondents answer the survey before and after reading the brochure. A before-and-after design is more efficient, because it can control for individual differences and obtain two sets of observations from each participant. However, the second set of answers will reflect having completed the survey before, as well as the impact of reading the brochure. Actual readers will not have the priming that comes with completing the initial test.

For the sake of realism, you might impose a time constraint on your respondents, similar to that anticipated with actual readers. If that time is unsure, you might want to allow some readers to spend as long as they like while limiting the time spent by others.

Because structured questionnaires can be administered relatively efficiently, such an evaluation can provide an inexpensive way to assess how well the final draft communication achieves its objectives. Considering the stakes riding on many communications, the price is small relative to its potential value in identifying and resolving residual problems.

A radon example   Our structured survey for evaluating the radon brochures had 58 statements. For each, respondents circled one of five responses: true, maybe true, don't know, maybe false, or false. (See Section 5.2.) About half of the items addressed misconceptions observed in the mental models interviews; the remainder dealt with basic concepts in the expert model. We tried to avoid the common design problems described earlier (reactivity, illusory expertise, and illusory discrimination). For comparison purposes, we administered a seven-item multiple-choice test designed for the EPA (Desvousges, Smith, and Rink, 1989). Subjects were 54 female and 39 male undergraduate students from a social science communications class who volunteered for the 50-minute experimental session in return for extra class credit. Of these, 75% described themselves as "not technically inclined." Subjects were randomly assigned to one of the three brochures or a filler task (for the control group).

They were given 15 minutes to read and study the brochure. In pretests, the slowest subject took 13 minutes to read the EPA brochure, the longest of the three. After each 5 minutes, the time remaining was announced. Subjects who finished early were instructed to put the brochure away and proceed to the test materials.

EPA test Overall, the three brochure groups performed equally well, and much better than the control group ($F3,88 = 21.03$, $p < .001$) on the EPA's seven-item multiple-choice knowledge test (which, presumably, focused on the information that the EPA thought most important). Differences emerged on two of the seven questions.

> When radon is measured in a home, which of the following will affect the level most?
>
> (a) The time of year it's measured;
> (b) The amount of industrial pollution around the home;
> (c) The number of appliances in the home;
> (d) Don't know

Fifty percent of the EPA group chose the first response (a), while the modal responses for CMUN (61%) and CTRL (57%) were "Don't know"; for CMUD, it was (b) (39%). Theoretically, the amount of radon in a home could be influenced by (a), (b), or (c), depending on respondents' default assumptions about measurement conditions. The results may indicate, however, that CMUD did not successfully dispel the peripheral belief that industrial waste is a primary source of indoor radon.

The final EPA test question asks, "What can homeowners do to reduce high radon levels in their home?" Virtually all CMUN and CMUD respondents (100% and 96%, respectively) chose the correct response (b) hire a contractor to fix the problem (a move that EPA suggests). Forty-three percent of the EPA respondents chose "don't know" and 9% chose "there is no way to fix the problem." Most of the control group (78%) responded "don't know," while the rest of their responses were divided between (a) remove the appliances causing the problem and (b) hire a contractor. Because the goal of each brochure is to motivate reasoned action, in this sense, the EPA brochure was less effective than the CMU brochures.

True-false test results Our scoring reflects distance from the expert answer: 0 indicates that the respondent agrees with the expert response; 1 indicates that the respondent answered "Maybe True" when the expert response was "True" or "Maybe False" when the expert response was "False"; 4 indicates saying "False" instead of "True" or vice versa.

Consistent with results on the EPA test, a one-way ANOVA on these distance scores showed that all three brochures improved subjects' performance relative to the control group ($F_{3,89} = 64.6, p < .001$). The 95% confidence intervals for group means show no performance differences between the respondents who read one of the two CMU brochures but significantly lower performance for those who read the EPA brochure.

We compared the CMU (CMUN and CMUD combined) and EPA brochure subjects, using Bonferroni adjusted t-tests to avoid overstating significance levels. By this criterion, CMU respondents outperformed EPA respondents on questions regarding contamination ($p < .0001$), decay ($p < .0001$), pet death from radon ($p = .0001$), radon from mines ($p < .0001$), and the health effects of waiting a few weeks before mitigating a radon problem ($p = .0002$). Repeating the analysis, after coding the "don't know" responses as missing values, left the same pattern.

Enough questions were asked on five topics to assess the frequency with which subjects produced correct answers consistently. As seen in Table 6.5, fewer EPA than CMU brochure subjects consistently provided expert beliefs; very few control-group subjects gave complete and consistent responses on any topic. Compared to CMU brochure subjects, EPA brochure subjects had more trouble with decay and contamination questions ($p < .001$), detection questions ($p < .001$), and mitigation questions ($p = .013$). Each brochure improved correctness, completeness, and individual consistency, both across individual test items and across tests; however, the CMU brochures did this better.

For example, almost all respondents who read any brochure correctly answered the EPA test item on health effects and the true-false test items on cancer and lung cancer (93% of CMU, 96% of EPA subjects). However, a larger proportion of EPA subjects (57%) than CMU subjects (22%)

Table 6.5   Frequencies of consistently expert beliefs ("maybes" included).

Topic	Decay	Mitigation	Detection	Odor	Source	Effects
CMUN (N = 24)	10	7	7	22	15	16
CMUD (N = 23)	11	8	17	23	13	14
EPA (N = 23)	0**	2*	2**	21	9	9*
Control (N = 23)	–	1	0	10	1	0

*Significant difference between the CMU (combined) and EPA brochures (x^2 test), $p < 0.05$.
**Significant difference between the CMU (combined) and EPA brochures (x^2 test), $p < 0.001$.
Source: Bostrom et al. (1994).

said that radon causes breathing difficulties. In the control group, the true-false cancer question produced 78% correct answers and the EPA health effects question 43% correct. Most respondents in the control group (87%) missed the true-false breathing difficulties question. Thus, responses to items asking for equivalent information are consistent, but the true-false test picks up differences in knowledge not captured by the EPA test. These differences appear to favor the CMU brochures. In this case, the EPA test underestimates respondents' general knowledge and overestimates their specific knowledge.

The CMU brochures appear to surpass the EPA brochure in filling knowledge gaps, restructuring knowledge for decision making, and contradicting misconceptions, all steps in completing and correcting individuals' mental models. However, these effects could reflect noncontent differences, such as using comprehension aids (e.g., advance organizers), having a single lead author rather than committee authorship, and having the test brochures and evaluation procedure designed by the same research team.

6.7   Conclusion

The most demanding kind of evaluation is whether readers do what the communication recommends (Walker and Meyer, 1980; Meyer, 1985). However, such action requires readers not only to understand the message but also to see it as relevant to their personal circumstances. For example, a radon communication intended to motivate testing might not prompt action for readers who lack the resources to fix any problems that they find (Kobasigawa, Lacasse, and MacDonald, 1988). A communication might be considered a failure, or even unethical, if it motivated action that was personally ill-advised (Krug et al., 1989).

Our more modest and more neutral goal is to ensure that readers understand the message, remember it when they have finished, and make appropriate inferences from it. These steps show that they have a coherent mental model of the topic.

The most revealing evaluation is an open-ended interview, allowing respondents to express their beliefs in their own terms (albeit directed at topics of the investigators' choosing). Collected either concurrently or retrospectively, open-ended interviews can be used to evaluate many attributes of text, including both content and organization. However, they are too resource intensive for studying large samples quickly. As a result, they are best used in developmental work, such as improving the initial design of communications and knowledge surveys (USEPA, USDHHS, and USPHS, 1992; van Dijk and Kintsch, 1983; Ausubel, 1960).

Poorly structured or superfluous risk information may bore recipients or frustrate their attempts to understand what is really important. Unless the decision relevance of information is made explicit, people may not extract it or trust their own inferences based on it. Misconceptions may coexist with more accurate beliefs, unless challenged. The mental models approach provides a systematic way to identify, avoid, and evaluate these pitfalls. It also provides a way to evaluate risk communications derived from other perspectives. The design and evaluation steps discussed in this chapter combine the mental models approach with findings and methods from other literatures.

References

Anderson, M. K. (1987). *Environmental Diseases*. Franklin Watts, New York.

Atman, C. J. (1989). *A Citizen's Guide to Radon: What It Is and What to Do about It*. Department of Engineering and Public Policy, Carnegie Mellon University, Pittsburgh.

———— (1990). "Network Structures as a Foundation for Risk Communication: An

Investigation of Structure and Formal Differences." Ph.D. dissertation, Department of Engineering and Public Policy, Carnegie Mellon University.

Atman, C. J., Bostrom, A., Fischhoff, B., and Morgan, M. G. (1994). "Designing Risk Communications: Completing and Correcting Mental Models of Hazardous Processes, Part I," *Risk Analysis,* 14(5):779–788.

Atman, C. J., and Puerzer, R. (1995). *Reader Preference and Comprehension of Risk Diagrams* (Technical Report 95–8). Department of Industrial Engineering, University of Pittsburgh.

Ausubel, D. P. (1960). "The Use of Advance Organizers in the Learning and Retention of Meaningful Verbal Material," *Journal of Educational Psychology,* 51(5):267–272.

Barke, R. P., and Jenkins-Smith, H. C. (1993). "Politics and Scientific Expertise: Scientists, Risk Perception, and Nuclear Waste Policy," *Risk Analysis,* 13:425–429.

Bostrom, A., Atman, C. J., Fischhoff, B., and Morgan, M. G. (1994). "Evaluating Risk Communications: Completing and Correcting Mental Models of Hazardous Processes, Part II," *Risk Analysis,* 14(5):789–798.

Carley, K. (1990). "Content Analysis," in *The Encyclopedia of Language and Linguistics.* Pergamon Press, Edinburgh.

Desvousges, W. H., Smith, V. K., and Rink, H. H., III (1989). "Communicating Radon Risk Effectively: Radon Testing in Maryland" (EPA-230-03-89-408). U.S. Environmental Protection Agency, Office of Policy, Planning, and Evaluation, Washington, D.C.

Ericsson, A., and Simon, H. A. (1994). *Verbal Protocol Analysis.* MIT Press, Cambridge, Mass.

Eylon, B., and Reif, F. (1984). "Effects of Knowledge Organization on Task Performance," *Cognition and Instruction,* 1(1):5–44.

Fischhoff, B., Bostrom, A., and Quadrel, M. J. (1997). "Risk Perception and Communication," in R. Detels, J. McEwen, and G. Omenn, eds., *Oxford Textbook of Public Health.* Oxford University Press, London, pp. 987–1002.

Fischhoff, B., Downs, J., and Bruine de Briun, W. (1998). "Adolescent Vulnerability: A Framework for Behavioral Interventions," *Applied and Preventive Psychology,* 7:77–94.

Fletcher, C. R., and Chrysler, S. T. (1990). "Surface Forms, Textbases, and Situation Models: Recognition Memory for Three Types of Textual Information," *Discourse Processes,* 13:175–190.

Garnham, A. (1987). *Mental Models as Representations of Discourse and Text.* Halsted, New York.

Kintsch, W., and van Dijk, T. A. (1978). "Toward a Model of Text Comprehension and Production," *Psychological Review,* 85(5):363–393.

Kobasigawa, A., Lacasse, M. A., and MacDonald, V. A. (1988). "Use of Headings by Children for Text Search," *Canadian Journal of Behavioral Science,* 20(1):50–63.

Krippendorff, K. (1980). *Content Analysis: An Introduction to Its Methodology.* Sage Publications, Beverly Hills.

Krug, D., George, B., Hannon, S. A., and Glover, J. A. (1989). "The Effect of Outlines and Headings on Readers' Recall of Text," *Contemporary Educational Psychology,* 14:111–123.

Larkin, J., McDermott, J., Simon, D. P., and Simon, H. A. (1980). "Expert and Novice Performance in Solving Physics Problems," *Science,* 208(4450):1335–1342.

MacCoun, R. J. (1998). "Biases in the Interpretation and the Use of Research Results," *Annual Review of Psychology,* 49:259–287.

Mannes, S. M., and Kintsch, W. (1987). "Knowledge Organization and Text Organization," *Cognition and Instruction,* 4(2):91–115.

Merton, R. K. (1987). "The Focussed Interview and Focus Groups," *Public Opinion Quarterly,* 51:541–557.

Merz, J., Fischhoff, B., Mazur, D. J., and Fischbeck, P. S. (1993). "Decision-Analytic Approach to Developing Standards of Disclosure for Medical Informed Consent," *Journal of Toxics and Liability,* 15:191–215.

Meyer, B. J. F. (1985). "Prose Analysis: Purposes, Procedures, and Problems," in Bruce K. Britton and John B. Black, eds., *Understanding Expository Text: A Theoretical and Practical Handbook for Analyzing Explanatory Text.* Lawrence Erlbaum Associates, Hillsdale, N.J.

Meyer, B. J. F., and Rice, G. E. (1984). "The Structure of Text," in P. D. Pearson, R. Barr, M. L. Kamil, and P. Mosenthal, eds., *Handbook of Reading Research.* Longman, New York and London, pp. 319–351.

Morgan, M. G. (1989). *A Citizen's Guide to Radon: What It Is and What to Do about It.* Department of Engineering and Public Policy, Carnegie Mellon University, Pittsburgh.

Nazaroff, W. W., and Nero, A. V., eds. (1988). *Radon and Its Decay Products in Indoor Air.* John Wiley & Sons, New York.

Reder, L. M. (1982). "Elaborations: When Do They Help and When Do They Hurt?" *Text,* 2(1–3):211–224.

(1985). "Techniques Available to Author, Teacher, and Reader to Improve Retention of Main Ideas of a Chapter," in S. F. Chipman, J. W. Segal, and J.

R. Glaser, eds., *Thinking and Learning Skills: Vol. 2. Research and Open Questions.* Lawrence Erlbaum Associates, Hillsdale, N.J., pp. 37–64.

Reder, L. M., and Anderson, J. R. (1982). "Effects of Spacing and Embellishment on Memory for the Main Points of a Text," *Memory and Cognition,* 10(2):97–102.

Riley, D. (1998). "Human Factors in Exposure Analysis for Consumer Paint Stripper Use." Ph.D. dissertation, Department of Engineering and Public Policy, Carnegie Mellon University.

Roth, E., Morgan, M. G., Fischhoff, B., Lave, L. B., and Bostrom, A. (1990). "What Do We Know about Making Risk Comparisons?" *Risk Analysis,* 10(3):375–392.

Schriver, K. A. (1989). "Evaluating Text Quality: The Continuum from Text-Focused to Reader-Focused Methods," *IEEE Transactions on Professional Communication,* 32(4):238–255.

(1997). *Dynamics in Document Design.* John Wiley & Sons, New York.

Stewart, D. W., and Shamdasani, P. N. (1990). *Focus Groups: Theory and Practice.* Sage Publications, Newbury Park, Calif.

Trabasso, T., and Sperry, L. L. (1985). "Causal Relatedness and Importance of Story Events," *Journal of Memory and Language,* 24:595–611.

Trabasso, T., and van den Broek, P. (1985). "Causal Thinking and the Representation of Narrative Events," *Journal of Memory and Language,* 24:612–630.

U.S. Environmental Protection Agency and U.S. Department of Health and Human Services. (1986). *A Citizen's Guide to Radon* (EPA-86–004). U.S. Government Printing Office, Washington, D.C.

U.S. Environmental Protection Agency, U.S. Department of Health and Human Services, U.S. Public Health Service. (1992). *A Citizen's Guide to Radon: The Guide to Protecting Yourself and Your Family from Radon* (ANR-464, 402-K92–001). U.S. Government Printing Office, Washington, D.C.

van Dijk, T. A., and Kintsch, W. (1983). *Strategies of Discourse Comprehension.* Academic Press, New York.

Walker, C. H., and Meyer, B. J. F. (1980). "Integrating Different Types of Information in Text," *Journal of Verbal Learning and Verbal Behavior,* 19:263–275.

7

CASE STUDIES: APPLICATIONS TO ENVIRONMENTAL RISKS

This chapter applies the general methods of the previous chapters to develop risk communications in four specific areas: climate change, power-frequency electric and magnetic fields, radon in homes, and nuclear energy sources on spacecraft.

7.1 Climate Change

The possibility that human activities are changing our climate[1] has emerged as one of the primary environmental concerns of our era. Water vapor and carbon dioxide, which occur naturally in the earth's atmosphere, trap heat, giving the earth a temperature that supports life. This natural process is called the "greenhouse effect." Burning fossil fuels releases additional carbon dioxide into the atmosphere. Some is taken up by plants or dissolved in the ocean, but about half remains in the atmosphere. Since the beginning of the industrial revolution, the concentration of carbon dioxide has increased by about 30%. Without dramatic changes in how

[1]Readers may find it useful to read some or all of the brochure *Global Warming and Climate Change,* reproduced in Appendix A, before reading this section.

we produce or use energy, that concentration will continue to rise. The amount of heat that is trapped will also increase, probably making the earth's climate warmer, modifying patterns of atmospheric and ocean circulation, changing patterns of precipitation, and causing changes in the human and ecological systems that depend on climate.

We began our studies of public understanding of global climate change by constructing a series of influence diagrams similar to the one reproduced in Figure 3.11. We used it to guide pilot mental models interviews with seven staff and graduate students at Carnegie Mellon University. We found that even these rather well-educated people conceptualized climate change very differently than do climate experts. Their mental models highlighted depletion of the stratospheric ozone layer by chlorofluorocarbons (CFCs) and often omitted the principal contributor to global warming: carbon dioxide buildup caused by burning fossil fuels.

The pilot interviews also revealed considerable confusion about the meaning of basic terms and disagreement with expert usage (Section 5.1). Before refining the interview protocol and administering it to a larger sample of the general population, we decided to conduct a separate study of definitions. In it, we asked laypeople (20 teenagers and 31 adult parents) to write out definitions of one of six key concepts: *climate, climate change, the greenhouse effect, weather, air pollution problems,* and *ozone problems.* A panel of six experts at Carnegie Mellon matched these lay definitions to expert definitions of the same concepts. The best match was for *air pollution problems* (93%). *Weather* was matched successfully 74% of the time and most often confused with *climate. Climate* and *climate change* were successfully matched only 45% and 44% of the time, and most often confused with *weather. Greenhouse effect* and *ozone problems* were correctly matched 58% and 57% of the time, and most often confused with one another.[2] The revised protocol instructed interviewers to request clarification of these frequently confused terms in order to ensure that we knew what respondents meant.

After refining the protocol, we conducted mental models interviews with 37 adults recruited at a booth set up at the Pittsburgh automobile show. Figure 7.1 shows the interviewer work sheet. In addition to conventional mental models questions, we also asked respondents to provide a number

[2]See Section 5.1 for discussion of additional work we have done on the weather/climate distinction, with a set of questions in the confirmatory questionnaire.

Date: *Time:*
Subject: *Interviewer:*

This interview is part of our research on risk perception and communication at Carnegie Mellon University. We are interested in how you think about these issues. Don't worry about whether your ideas are right or wrong. We are interested in everything you think about this and want you to say everything you think about these issues.

Climate Change Interview

Tell me all about the issue of global climate change . . .

Neutral prompts:

> ☛ Can you tell me more about _____?
> ☛ Can you explain how_____?
> ☛ Does _____bring anything else to mind?
> ☛ If you were going to explain climate change to someone else, is there anything you would say differently or add to what you have said?

Now I am going to ask you several questions. Some of these may seem to repeat things you have already said. Please bear with me. I have to ask all of the questions to make sure I have covered everything. You may refer to your previous answers if you feel you have already answered a question and have nothing more to say about it.

Exposure
☐ What factors might be changing our climate?
☐ What sorts of climate change might there be?
☐ How fast will climate change take place?

Effects
☐ What effects will climate change have?
      ☐ Will climate change affect other things?
☐ Will the effects of climate change be the same everywhere?
☐ Will climate change affect everyone/everything similarly?

Benefits/costs
☐ What might be bad about sea level rise?
☐ What might be good about sea level rise?

Risk Management
☐ What can be done about climate change?
☐ Who should be responsible for dealing with climate change?

Figure 7.1. Copy of the interviewer work sheet used in interviews about climate change.

(continued)

Figure 7.1. *(continued)*

Scientific uncertainty

❐ What do scientists think about whether there will be
      global climate change?
❐ Is there any chance that climate change won't happen?

Now I am going to ask you for several definitions. These too may seem repetitive. Please bear with me. I'm going to ask for definitions of climate, climate change, global warming, the greenhouse effect, weather, ozone, and air pollution. Don't worry about how much you know. We're interested in what you think about these things. Ok, now I'm going to ask you for the definitions, one at a time.

Climate change
❐ What is "climate"?
❐ What is "climate change"?
❐ What is "global warming"?
❐ What is the "greenhouse effect"?

Weather
❐ What is "weather"?
❐ What is "weather change"?

Ozone
❐ What is "ozone"?
❐ What ozone problems are there?
❐ What effects does ozone have?

Pollution
❐ What is "air pollution"?

Can you tell me if (and if so how) air pollution has anything to do with
      ❐ climate change
      ❐ global warming
      ❐ the greenhouse effect
      ❐ weather change
      ❐ ozone

Please list all of the causes of global warming that you can think of
(**write on cards**):

_____

_____

_____

_____

Figure 7.1. *(continued)*

Do you believe that there is or will be a greenhouse effect?

Do you believe that all of the factors you mentioned will contribute to
that greenhouse effect?
(If not, which will - *hand subject cards*)

Now, please order these factors by importance (First = most important,
Second = next most important, etc.) and explain why you are ordering
them this way. So, to start with, please tell me why _____ is the
most important cause of the greenhouse effect.

Do you think a greenhouse effect would be good, bad, or neutral? Why?

Do you think a greenhouse effect would be good, bad, or neutral for you
personally?

Do you think that the United States should do anything about this?
(If yes) What?

Who or what did you think I meant by "the United States"?

How was it to participate in this interview?

Were any questions too hard, unclear, or unpleasant to answer?

Were there any issues related to climate, weather, sea level rise or the
greenhouse effect that you thought of but didn't get a chance to talk
about? (If so) What issues?

October 26, 1990

of definitions and explain some possible causal linkages that pretests had suggested might be important sources of confusion. Finally, we asked respondents to list possible causes of global warming on file cards, then to sort the
cards according to their relative importance. Details of this study, and of the
two studies described earlier, can be found in Bostrom et al. (1994).

The results indicated that lay mental models of global climate change
suffer from several basic misconceptions: Explanations of the physical
mechanisms underlying global climate change were inconsistent and
incomplete, typically including the erroneous belief that climate change is
caused by increased ultraviolet light entering the atmosphere due to
stratospheric ozone depletion caused by CFCs. Table 7.1 presents the

Table 7.1 Causes of global warming mentioned by respondents during the initial open-ended phase of the mental models interviews.

Cause of Global Warming	Percentage of 37 Respondents Who Mentioned This Cause
Stratospheric ozone depletion	95
Pollution and air pollution	86
Aerosol cans	70
Automobile use, exhaust, or pollution	70
Industrial emissions	68
Deforestation	43
Acid rain	30
Chemicals	30
Fossil fuels	30
Energy use in buildings	24
Carbon monoxide	22
Carbon dioxide	19
Space exploration	16
Nuclear power	11

causal factors mentioned in the open-ended portion of the interview. In both cases, ozone depletion and pollution-related terms are mentioned frequently. Deforestation was also widely invoked. Fossil fuels and carbon dioxide received few mentions. Many respondents held other fundamental misconceptions, such as a belief that the greenhouse effect would lead to increased "steaminess" of the earth (as in a horticultural greenhouse) or that a cap on the atmosphere prevents noxious gases from escaping. Often, misconceptions coexist with correct beliefs, such as citing both ozone depletion and automobile emissions. However, few respondents offered an appropriate account of the role of carbon dioxide or mentioned any greenhouse gases apart from CFCs. Those who cited deforestation attributed its effects to the loss of plants' ability to clean air rather than to a change in the earth's surface reflectivity (planetary albedo) or the destruction of carbon sinks. The few respondents who connected energy use and climate change rarely mentioned the key role of carbon dioxide.

Respondents had a more accurate sense of the likely effects of climate change, although they cited an increased incidence of skin cancer, consistent with their confusion over stratospheric ozone depletion. Table 7.2 presents likely effects mentioned by 10% or more of respondents. Despite

Table 7.2   Effects of global warming mentioned by respondents during the initial open-ended phase of the mental models interviews.

Effect of Global Warming	Percentage of 37 Respondents Who Mentioned This Effect
Increases in temperature	89
Changes in precipitation patterns	86
Human health effects (e.g., skin cancer, sunburn, psychological changes)	83
Ecosystem impacts	81
Changed agricultural yields	59
Melting of polar ice caps	54
Chronic flooding	46
Financial and economic changes	41
Reduced photosynthesis	35
Changes in seasons (e.g., longer summers, short winter)	32
Sea-level rise	30
Changes in local weather	30
Changing demand on heating and cooling	30

significant press coverage, none mentioned sea-level rise nor its associated impacts. Although most respondents believed that climate change is a threat and favored actions to address the problem, their flawed mental models restricted their ability to distinguish between effective and ineffective strategies. Such misconceptions could lead people to waste their energies on ineffective actions, such as conscientiously refusing to use spray cans, while neglecting critical strategies, such as energy conservation.

In order to obtain a larger sample, and confirm these findings, we constructed a questionnaire based on the mental models interviews. Details of this second set of studies can be found in Read et al. (1994). Its questions addressed four broad topics: basic facts and definitions involving weather and climate (19 items), causes of climate change (15 items), effects of climate change (15 items), and the effectiveness of various policy options (21 items).

Our respondents were an opportunity sample of 177 adults, most recruited at a booth during afternoon Fourth of July celebrations at Point State Park in downtown Pittsburgh.

After a brief introduction, the questionnaire asked respondents, "How likely do you think it is that human actions have changed global climate?" Thirty-seven percent said that such change was "certain" and an

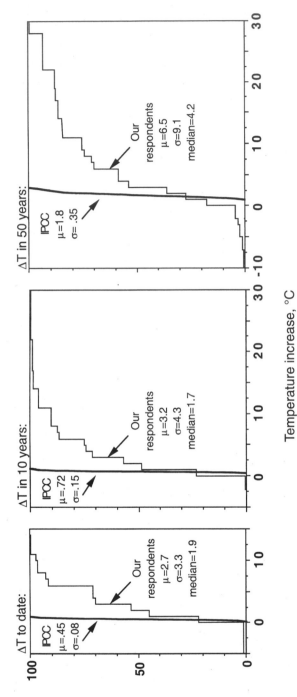

Figure 7.2. Cumulative distributions of respondents' point estimates of the amount of warming that has occurred to date (left), will occur in 10 years (center), or will occur in 50 years (right), compared with a distribution that we derived by making plausible assumptions about the IPCC consensus estimates (IPCC, 1992), namely, that estimates of change-to-date are normally distributed (μ = .45, σ = .075) and that the additional change in 10 years and in 50 years will be the average of IPCC scenarios IS92a, IS92b, and IS92d, whose uncertainties are taken to be lognormally distributed, with geometric standard deviations of 1.5.

additional 61% said it was at least "somewhat likely." Figure 7.2 presents cumulative frequency distributions of subjects' estimates of the amount of warming that has already occurred and will occur in the next 10 and 50 years. These results are compared with distributions we constructed by making plausible assumptions about the consensus judgments of climate experts published in 1990 by the Intergovernmental Panel on Climate Change (IPCC, 1992). The scientists saw little chance that warming to that date had exceeded 0.5°C. If greenhouse gas emissions continued along the IPCC "business as usual" scenario, warming was expected to be between 0.2 and 0.5°C per decade. As indicated in Figure 7.2, our subjects' estimates were much larger.

Responses to the questionnaire also confirmed the confusion between *climate* and *weather* and between *global warming* and *stratospheric ozone depletion,* as seen in the mental models interviews.

Respondents were asked to "list all the things that you think of that could cause global warming." Then they were asked 12 multiple-choice questions about causes. Results are summarized in Table 7.3 and Figure 7.3. Note the considerable overlap with the results from the mental models interviews reported in Table 7.1.

Table 7.3   Most frequently mentioned "things" that "could cause global warming" listed by respondents in the confirmatory questionnaire. Respondents were given an open-ended question and asked to produce a list.

Cause of Global Warming	Percentage of 177 Respondents Who Mentioned This Cause
Reduction of biomass	57
Automobiles	41
Industry	32
Pollution	30
Depletion of ozone layer	27
Aerosol cans	26
CFC emissions	20
Burning fossil fuels	18
Gases/chemicals	18
Nuclear power/weapons	15
CO_2	14
Natural causes	14
Overpopulation	11

Cause	Mean DA +2 to -2	Distribution T, ≈T, ?, ≈ F, F
Clearing tropical rainforest	1.42	
Deforestation	1.37	
Aerosol spray cans	1.16	
Burning fossil fuels (e.g., coal and oil)	1.12	
Ozone in cities (e.g., smog in Los Angeles)	1.10	
The hole in the Antarctic ozone layer	0.80	
Toxic wastes (e.g., hazardous chemicals in dumps)	0.77	
Ocean dumping	0.17	
Use of nuclear power	0.14	
Acid rain	0.14	
Cows, rice paddies, termites and swamps	- 0.04	
The space program	- 0.69	

Figure 7.3. Responses to statements citing possible causes of global warming, rank-ordered by mean degree of agreement (DA), ranging from +2 (complete agreement) to −2 (complete disagreement). The full distribution of responses is displayed in the right-hand column. T means true; ≈T means probably true; ? means don't know; ≈F means probably false; F means false.

Figure 7.4 reports responses to 12 questions related to the effects of climate change. Comparing them with Table 7.2 shows the same general patterns.

When we asked about personal actions that could increase or reduce global warming, driving and using aerosol spray cans headed the lists. When we asked about possible government policies, the most frequently cited were preventing deforestation (34%), limiting pollution (31%), and protecting the ozone layer (28%). Figure 7.5 summarizes evaluations of these policies.

Cause	Mean DA +2 to -2	Distribution T, ≈T, ?, ≈ F, F
Agricultural problems and starvation in many places	1.28	
Increase skin cancer	1.00	
Ecological disasters all over the world	0.97	
Shorter, milder winters all over the world	0.95	
Cause sea level to rise	0.83	
More and larger storms all over the world	0.80	
Shortage of oxygen in the atmosphere	0.78	
Make the climate "steamier"	0.68	
Increase precipitation and humidity all over world	0.49	
Reduce photosynthesis	0.41	
War and large immigration problems	0.25	
The main cause of species extinction today	- 0.35	

Figure 7.4. Responses to statements citing possible effects of global warming, rank-ordered by mean DA index (+2 complete agreement, −2 complete disagreement).

Overall, questionnaire results confirmed patterns from the open-ended interviews: laypeople (a) do not understand the central role played by carbon dioxide produced by burning fossil fuels and (b) confuse global warming with the stratospheric and tropospheric ozone problems. There seems to be a general blurring of climate change with other environmental problems, resulting in a mental model insufficiently precise to produce correct inferences about policy options.

The world's economically developed countries are currently considering responses to climate change that could entail expenditures in the trillions of dollars. We cannot have intelligent democratic debate on these choices unless lay mental models are better informed, especially if they are shared by legislators and the public to whom they report. Our climate brochure attempts to provide the basic understanding that citizens need in order to be informed participants in these deliberations. Its development followed the procedures outlined in Chapter 6.

The brochure structure is shown in Figure 7.6; it is reproduced in Appendix A. We summarized the three sections of the brochure, both pictorially and in text, on the front cover. These are "What is climate change?" "If climate changes, what might happen?" and "What can be done about climate change?" This organization is illustrated with a three-part pictorial montage in which climate feeds to impacts, which feed to policy, which, in turn, feeds back to climate.

The initial draft had three two-page spreads covering each part, followed by a details booklet that pulled out of a pouch. This format worked well with motivated and well-educated readers. However, pretests with less well-educated readers showed that our treatment jumped to the details too quickly. As a result, we created a two-page introduction, "The issue at a glance . . ." We also moved a list of five of the most common misconceptions into a box in this section.

Following the interview and questionnaire results, we emphasized the central role of carbon dioxide produced from the combustion of fossil fuel, discussing it in the first bullet of the overview, the first misconception, and the opening discussion of "Part 1: What Is Climate Change?" Interview results determined other content: (a) the amount of warming that has occurred and is projected to occur; (b) the role of other gases, dust, deforestation, and other factors affecting the earth's radiative balance; and (c) the distinction between the problem of stratospheric ozone depletion and the issue of global warming. Finally, a separate boxed section, "Climate Is Not Weather," differentiated the two terms.

Most physical scientists would naturally begin to explain issues of climate and weather by talking first about planetary heat balance and global circulation. Although we started an explanation this way, it took up so much space that we eventually moved it into the Part 1 details booklet.

As noted in Chapter 6, we attempt to serve the needs of readers oriented to using pictures, statistics, or words. If something works for some readers but others skip it, we don't worry, as long as that topic is covered elsewhere. However, a display that frustrates readers who attempt to

Strategy	Mean BA +2 to -2	Distribution $\Downarrow$, ≈$\Downarrow$, 0,?, ≈$\Uparrow$, $\Uparrow$
Using all known energy conservation measures	1.41	
Planting trees	1.29	
Stopping use of fossil fuels	1.16	
Stopping pollution from chemical plants	1.11	
Stopping use of aerosol spray cans in the U.S.	1.09	
Making national parks out of remaining trop. rain forests	1.08	
Recycling most consumer goods	1.05	
Stopping release of coolant from refrig.s and ACs.	1.03	
Ban chloroflourocarbons	1.02	
Meet clean air act standards	1.02	
Convert to electric cars	0.98	
Reduce population growth	0.95	
Switching from styrofoam to paper cups	0.78	
Switching to florescent or other efficient lights	0.67	
High tax on all fossil fuels	0.67	
Switching from coal to natural gas	0.66	
Switching from fossil fuels to nuclear power	0.44	
Fertilize ocean to make algae grow faster	0.38	
Stop the space program	0.28	
Make more clouds high in the atmosphere	0.24	
Put dust in the stratosphere	-0.39	

Figure 7.5. Responses to statements citing the likely impacts of various strategies on global warming, rank-ordered by mean belief in abatement (BA), ranging from +2 (strong belief that strategy will abate climate change) to −2 (strong belief that strategy will aggravate climate change). The full distribution of responses is displayed in the right-hand column. ↓ means will slow global warming; ≈↓ means will probably slow global warming; o (white bar) means no effect; ? (black bar) means effect unclear; ≈↑ means will probably speed global warming; ↑ means will speed global warming.

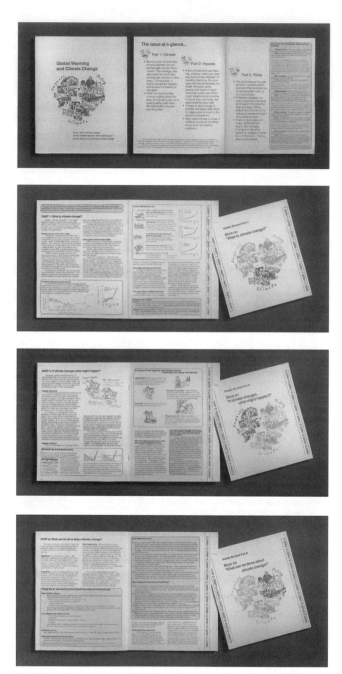

Figure 7.6. General structure of the brochure developed on global warming and climate change, illustrating the hierarchical organization (paper hypertext) including a third level of detail provided in pull-out details booklets. Full text of the brochure is reproduced in Appendix A.

138

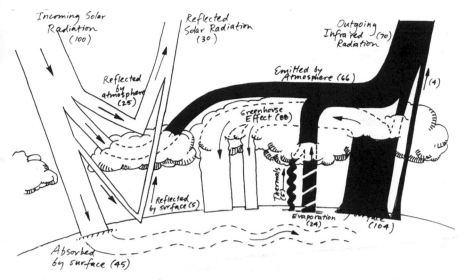

Figure 7.7. Diagram of atmospheric energy flows originally developed for the climate change brochure, based on similar diagrams appearing in the technical literature (e.g., NRC, 1975; Budyko, 1982; Schneider and Louder, 1984; IPCC, 1990). In pretests, many lay respondents indicated that they could not understand this figure.

understand it needs to be fixed. For example, we originally used a sketch like Figure 7.7, based on similar diagrams routinely used in the technical and semitechnical literature. After discovering that many readers tried but failed to understand the drawing, we replaced it with the more explicit step-by-step drawing shown in Figure 7.8. We found that most pretest readers understood it, if they chose to spend time looking at it.

Because our studies revealed that most people have a fairly realistic notion of the potential impacts of climate change, we devoted less space to correcting misconceptions in Part 2. We discussed separately impacts on people and on nature. Boxed sections addressed such complicating factors as sea-level rise, rapid climate change, and carbon dioxide fertilization of plants, with elaboration in the details booklet. The details booklet also included material on agricultural impacts, evidence from paleoclimatic studies, and the four specific impacts highlighted in a boxed section in Part 2 of the main brochure (plant migration, insect pests, coral reefs, and mangrove swamps).

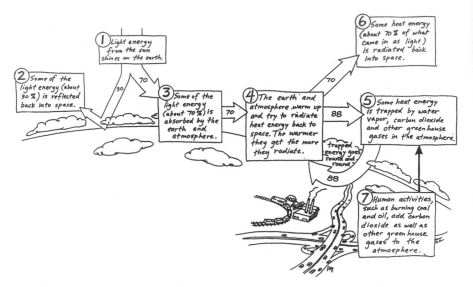

Figure 7.8. Reworked step-by-step diagram of atmospheric energy flows, developed after pretests showing lay confusion with diagram in Figure 7.7.

Part 3 attempted to help readers form their own judgments about policy issues. It discussed the three broad policy options of abatement, adaptation, and geo-engineering, with elaboration in the details booklet. Separate boxed sections discussed options open to individuals and to nations. Emissions from the developing world received special attention.

In order to avoid telling readers what to choose, we sketched a general approach to making decisions about climate policy. Pages 10 and 11 of the details booklet illustrated how three women, Ann, Sue, and Pat, with different beliefs and different values, reach different policy conclusions. To make this more interesting, we included portraits of the women. However, in order to minimize the risk that readers would infer that particular individual traits might be related to particular beliefs or conclusions, we used the same female face for all three and simply varied the hairstyle.

The final pages of the Part 3 details booklet provided a glossary and a list of additional readings. Their availability was noted at the bottom of the first page of the introductory overview. Finally, the back cover of the brochure provided information on who wrote it, how it was reviewed and paid for, as well as institutional information.

7.2   Power-Frequency Fields

Wherever there is electric power, there are electric and magnetic fields.[3] The possibility that exposure to these fields may produce adverse health effects has been a subject of considerable scientific and policy attention (OTA, 1989; NRC, 1996, 1999). In the early 1980s, as part of policy studies on this issue (Morgan, Florig, et al., 1985; Hester et al., 1990; Morgan, 1992), we began studies of public understanding. Our first study, using Carnegie Mellon alumni as respondents, compared risk perceptions for fields and a variety of other risks (Morgan, Slovic, et al., 1985). Using methods previously reported in Fischhoff et al. (1978) and Slovic, Fischhoff, and Lichtenstein (1980, 1985), we found that fields from large power lines lay in the upper-right quadrant of the risk-factor space, along with such risks as X-rays, pesticides, and nuclear power (Figure 7.9). In contrast, fields from electric blankets fell in the upper-left quadrant, along with such items as caffeine, plastic food containers, and microwave ovens. On the basis of these findings, and previous work by Slovic, Fischhoff, and Lichtenstein (1982, 1985), we conjectured that well-educated laypeople were "likely to want little or no regulatory response to electric blankets and a significant, but not severe, regulatory response to transmission line fields." We suggested further that if "events" that involved possible health effects from power-line fields were to occur, they were likely to be seen as having a fairly high "signal potential." As a result, we argued, "they will probably receive considerable media publicity and generate a great deal of concern. The indirect or higher order costs of such events are likely to be quite high." In contrast, we suggested that "events" involving electric blankets "will probably be seen as having only modest 'signal potential.'" This is, in fact, the way that things appear to have worked out over the ensuing decade and a half.

Responses to several risk evaluation tasks led us to conclude that, on

[3]In North America "power-frequency" refers to 60 Hz fields and their harmonics. In Europe and some other parts of the world, the phrase refers to 50 Hz fields and their harmonics. It has become common in recent years to refer to power-frequency electric and magnetic fields as "EMF." However, because those same initials have long stood for "electromotive force" in electrical engineering, we do not use that abbreviation.

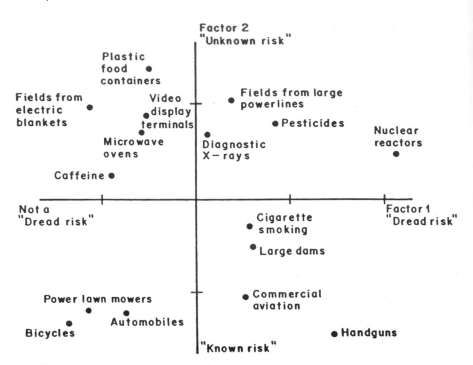

Figure 7.9. Risk-factor space similar to that in Figure 1.1, derived from a study including "fields from large power lines" and "fields from electric blankets."

average, our well-educated respondents "did not view either transmission lines or electric blankets as particularly risky technologies." When we provided respondents with information about fields and the possible associated risks, their assessments did not change dramatically but did move somewhat in the direction of greater concern (Morgan, Slovic, et al., 1985).

Because of the many inquires that we received from concerned citizens, we decided to produce that brochure in a form suitable for distribution to the general public. At that time, we were just beginning to develop the mental models methodology. As a result, our first brochure *Electric and Magnetic Fields from 60 Hz Electric Power: What Do We Know about Possible Health Risks?* (Morgan, 1989) used only a portion of the methods described in this book. It provided the first test bed for iteratively refining a message, with reviews by experts, focus groups, and read-aloud protocols. A shortened version was used in a set of evaluation studies (MacGregor, Slovic, and Morgan, 1994). Between 1989 and 1995, approximately 150,000 copies of this brochure were distributed by public health agencies, power companies, and similar organizations, to whom we made them available at cost. The brochure is 45 pages long, because we had found that people interested enough to order it typically want detailed discussions (e.g., because a power line is being built nearby, or they are trying to decide whether to buy a house near a line). We have had discussions with many readers who had carefully read all of the brochure and were looking for more!

At the same time, we received complaints from public health officials and utility representatives that the brochure was too elaborate for people with a more casual interest. As a result, we developed a hierarchically organized brochure using the format of the climate brochure, allowing people to obtain as much information as they wish.

After conducting some lay mental models interviews, we developed a structured questionnaire with a true-false–don't know response mode (Morgan et al., 1990). We paid particular attention to ensuring that the technical experts agreed on unambiguously correct answers. Success required several iterations. The questionnaire was administered to four different groups: a random sample of Pittsburghers (N = 46); an opportunity sample of blue-collar Pittsburghers (N = 41); a group of engineering students who had just completed a course in electromagnetic field theory (N = 38); and a group of power company public affairs representatives (N = 40). Overall scores were 48%, 42%, 71%, and 69% correct, respectively. Noting that (% correct + % incorrect + % don't know) = 100 allowed the use of the triangular display in Figure 7.10. Grouping the 54 questions into 20 basic concepts, Table 7.4 shows that respondents in our random sample correctly knew only about half of the 20 basic concepts while the blue-collar group knew only a few. Although there is substantial confusion about many concepts, between 75% (blue-collar) and 80% (random sample) of responses lie on the left-hand side of the display, indicating beliefs that lean toward the correct interpretation. Thus, systematically incorrect mental models should not pose a major obstacle to educating lay groups about most of the basic ideas of fields. Concepts 15–20 in Table 7.4 are obviously those with the greatest tendency to misinterpretation.

In order to explore beliefs about the magnitude of fields, we devel-

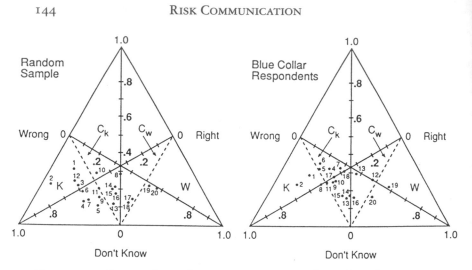

Figure 7.10. Centers of mass for responses to 20 sets of questions about power-frequency fields. **K** indicates correct knowledge. **W** indicates wrong beliefs. C_k indicates confused, but leaning toward correct knowledge. C_w indicates confused, but leaning toward being wrong. Results on the left are for a random sample of 46 Pittsburgh residents and on the right for an opportunity sample of 41 blue-collar respondents. Numbers on points correspond to rows in Table 7.4.

oped a second questionnaire that relied heavily on pictorial sketches. Respondents in this study were adult Pittsburgh residents, recruited among volunteers at Children's Hospital ($N = 32$), power company public affairs representatives ($N = 42$), and MBA students at the Wharton School of Business ($N = 17$).

Respondents received a deck of six cards with illustrations of common exposure situations. Figure 7.11 shows two, as examples. Respondents were asked to order the cards in terms of field strength, to write a 1 in the box on the card with the weakest field and proportionally higher numbers on the other cards. The same task was performed separately for electric and magnetic fields (using pencils of two different colors).

The six exposure situations involve a wide range of electric and magnetic fields. Respondents correctly judged that fields from transmission lines are, on average, stronger than fields from distribution lines, and that both are stronger than fields in a typical living room. However, while the actual range of field strengths across the depicted settings varied by more than a factor of 1,000, half or more of the respondents judged the range to

Table 7.4 Summary of the location of the "center of mass" of responses to sets of questions about understanding of basic field-related concepts as displayed in triangular graphical displays such as those shown in Figure 7.10. **K** indicates correct knowledge. **W** indicates wrong beliefs. C_k indicates confused, but leaning toward correct knowledge. C_w indicates confused, but leaning toward being wrong. **E** = electric fields. **B** = magnetic fields.

	Respondent Group			
Concept	*Random Pittsburgh Sample*	*Blue-collar Respondents*	*EE Students*	*Utility Representatives*
1. Relation between charge and voltage	K	K	K	K
2. Moving charges make currents	K	K	K	K
3. Charges (not current) make E	K	C_k	K	K
4. Relation of voltage to E and B	K	C_k	K	K
5. E exerts force on charges	K	C_k	K	K
6. Currents make B	K	C_k	K	K
7. B exerts force on current	K	C_k	K	C_k
8. Fields can induce currents in the body	C_k	K	K	K
9. Field strength falls off with distance K	C_k	K	K	
10. Field strength falls off slower from exerted objects	C_k	C_k	K	K
11. E can be shielded	K	C_k	K	K
12. B can't be shielded	K	C_w	W	K
13. Relative strength of fields from transmission lines, distribution lines, and appliances	C_k	C_w	C_w	K
14. Fields from electric blankets	C_k	C_k	W	K
15. Relationship of voltage and current to power	C_k	C_k	K	K
16. Relationship of power to field strength	C_k	C_w	C_w	C_k
17. Ability of fields to "deflect objects in flight"	C_w	C_k	K	K
18. Field-field interactions	C_w	C_k	K	C_k
19. Relation of fields to water	W	W	K	C_k
20. Field detection by human senses	W	W	K	K

be less than a factor of 100. That is, people systematically underestimate the very wide range of field strengths encountered in day-to-day life. Judgments for electric fields and for magnetic fields were essentially identical.

The six exposure settings included fields from three appliances: an electric blanket, an electric shaver, and a toaster. The electric shaver produces magnetic fields that are at least ten times larger than those associated with the transmission line. The electric blanket produces electric fields comparable to those of the transmission line. However, our respondents judged all three appliances to produce similar fields, and less than that of the transmission or distribution lines. Figure 7.12 summarizes the results.

In another task, respondents indicated how field strength varied with distance from the sources in a series of sketches. Actual field strength falls off very rapidly with distance (roughly as $1/r^2$ for power lines and as $1/r^3$ or faster for some appliances). However, most of our respondents believed that field strength falls off much more slowly, if at all, over the distances involved. Figure 7.13 shows results for the 32 Pittsburgh lay respondents. Follow-up studies have confirmed this finding (Read and Morgan, 1998). It means that people overestimate the magnitudes of fields and underestimate the effectiveness of the common exposure control strategy of increasing the width of transmission line rights-of-way.

As discussed in Chapter 2, in early mental models interviews we encountered a subject who had apparently confused power-frequency fields with ionizing radiation. In fact, the two are very different physical agents. However, if such a mental model were widely held, it would be very important to know about it in designing risk communications. In order to explore the prevalence of this belief, we developed a questionnaire that posed 26 questions about basic physics, bioeffects, sensory perception, and other topics, such as food contamination. Respondents answered each question for five different agents: X rays; microwaves; radiation, of the kind associated with nuclear waste; ultrasonic sound; and fields, like those from electric power (Morgan et al., 1990).

Beliefs about 60 Hz fields differed from those for the other agents. For example, respondents believe that people can sense the presence of fields (they typically can not). Changes in mood, thought, behavior, and "electrical aura" were all seen as plausible results of field exposure, but not for other agents. Few believed that fields could contaminate food or had a lingering presence. Other studies explored the kinds of field-control actions that people consider appropriate, the levels of intervention that they advocate, and the expenditures that they consider appropriate for exposure control (Adams et al., 1995; Bostrom et al., 1994).

Please judge the electric field

This is a drawing of a typical American living room. It is early afternoon. The room is not being used. There are fields present in the middle of the room that come from electric appliances and lighting fixtures around the house, from the electric wiring in the house, and from the normal local power distribution lines that run on wooden poles outside the house.

Please judge the electric field

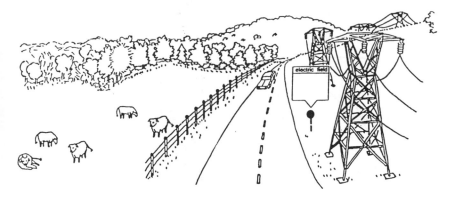

This is a drawing of a country road mid-afternoon on a summer day. Along the road is a high voltage transmission line running on tall steel towers. This line carries electric power to serve the entire region including a nearby city.

Figure 7.11. Two of the six cards used in the card-sorting tasks. The location of interest in each drawing is indicated by a marked point and associated response box. Respondents first sorted the cards in order of field strength from weakest to strongest. Then they wrote a 1 in the box on the card with the weakest field and appropriately higher numbers in the other boxes.

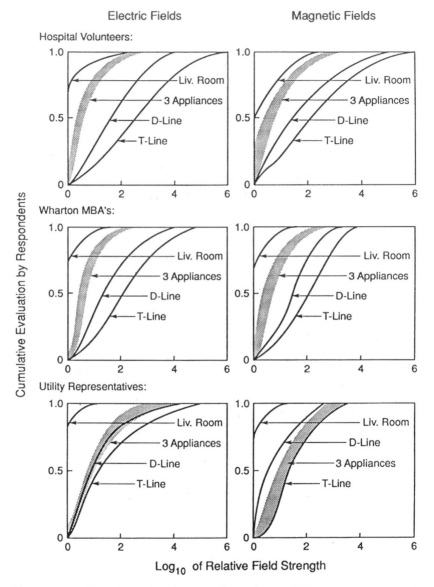

Figure 7.12. Cumulative distributions of the relative field strengths estimated by the three groups of respondents for the six exposure situations for electric field *(left)* and magnetic field *(right)*. Because differences between respondents' estimates of the fields associated with the three-appliance exposure were smaller than the associated uncertainties, the three-appliance curves have been replaced by a single shaded band.

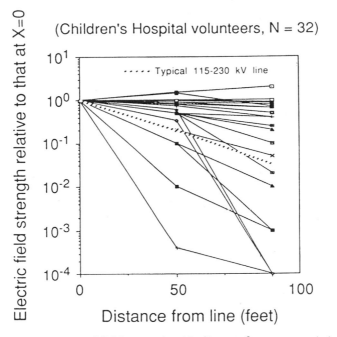

Figure 7.13. Estimates of field strength with distance from a transmission line provided by 32 hospital volunteers. Eighty percent of the responses indicate a belief that fields decrease with distance more slowly than they actually do.

With these results in hand, we used a hierarchical (paper hypertext) design and developed a new brochure entitled *Fields from Electric Power,* employing the same general structure illustrated in Figure 7.6. The brochure has three subheadings: "What are they?" "What do we know about possible health risks?" and "What can be done?" At the bottom of the cover, we added text summarizing the message and providing a brief description of its contents.

We had observed that people using the climate brochure often inadvertently opened it to pages 3 and 4 and the pouch between them, missing the overview on single pages 1 and 2. To avoid this problem, we cut the cover page 0.4 inches narrower than the rest of the brochure and added a strip of text reading SUMMARY • SUMMARY • SUMMARY along the right side of page 2, so that readers would see it and turn there first.

Because of its importance, the relationship between field strength and distance from the source is explained several times, with both text and graphical displays. The summary on page 1 includes the following text:

> Just like heat from a campfire, or the light from a candle, the strength of most electric and magnetic fields decreases rapidly as you move away from their sources. For example, while a power line may make a strong field on the ground directly beneath the wire, a few hundred feet away, the field is usually very weak.

Part 1, "What are fields?" begins with basic definitions, followed by a large graphic, showing how rapidly field strength decreases as one moves away from a source. Meter readings were used because some readers ignored a simple graph or found it difficult to read.

The second page of Part 1 has two boxed sections. One compares the unfamiliar concepts of electric and magnetic fields with the more familiar one of gravitational fields. The other box briefly discusses measurement, noting that although average field strength may be easiest to measure, it is not the most relevant to possible health risks.

The Part 1 details booklet provides an extended tutorial about fields, again stressing decreasing field strength with distance. This time, a two-page graphic uses a common motor-driven electric bedside clock. Boxed sections describe the structure of the electric power system, the average field strength of various common devices, and how fields vary with time of day and location.

Part 2 of the brochure discusses the kinds of evidence available on possible health risks. Switching to first person in a box, the author gives his personal judgments about the nature and the extent of the risk. A box elaborates on the relevance of average field strength. The Part 2 details booklet discusses biological and epidemiological evidence. Margin drawings clarify the ideas of "hot spots," the difference between correlation and causation, and "resonant systems." A section of the text addresses the question, "With all this evidence, why do some scientists still doubt that weak fields can produce any biological effects?" The final page discusses agricultural and ecological impacts.

Part 3 lays out the pros and cons of three policy options and discusses personal strategies that people can adopt if they want to limit their exposure to some fields. One boxed section addresses the issue of fields when buying a house. A second uses first person to describe what the author had done regarding field exposures in his own home. In addition to elaborating the three options, the Part 3 details booklet discusses the issue of standards, includes a table comparing various risks, discusses the principal contributors to cancer risk, and deals with field measurements. The booklet ends with a glossary and an annotated bibliography of further reading (both noted on the front cover). Again, the back cover of the brochure provides information on who wrote it, how it was reviewed and paid for, as well as institutional information.

Prior to developing the brochure on power-frequency fields discussed here and reproduced in Appendix B, we developed three other brochures titled *Electric and Magnetic Fields from 60 Hertz Electric Power: What Do We Know about Possible Health Risks? Part 1: Measuring Power-Frequency Fields,* and *Part 2: What Can We Conclude from Measurements of Power-Frequency Fields?* The latter two were developed for use by utilities and independent contractors offering in-home field measurement programs. Much of the textual content is similar to our other brochures, with more emphasis on measurement. Copies of all three are available for sale, at cost, through the Department of Engineering and Public Policy at Carnegie Mellon University.

7.3   Radon in Homes

As discussed earlier, radon in homes provided a test bed for much of our work in developing mental models methods. Radon is a colorless, odorless gas created when the element radium, a natural constituent in most rocks and soils, undergoes radioactive decay. Radon can enter homes directly from the soil, from building materials, or from water. Radon is radioactive. It decays first into particles and then, within a few days, into an inert substance that is not dangerous. If the radioactive particles lodge in the lungs, exposure to their radiation can increase the probability of lung cancer. Radon can be removed from most homes by sealing off sources and improving ventilation. Once that has been done, there are no lingering effects.

Most respondents in these mental models interviews mentioned radon flowing into living spaces and concentrating there. About half mentioned radon flowing out of living spaces, although these mentions typically came only in the photo-sorting task (see Section 4.3). Few respondents mentioned the basic sources of radon, with about one in four mentioning water and soil and only one in eight mentioning building materials. As a result, our communication addresses sources of radon and flows into, through, and out of a house.

Less than 10% of interview respondents mentioned that radon decays, much less how quickly it disappears once influx has been stopped. Radon's rapid decay is important for understanding both the damage that can be done by small concentrations and the possibility of resolving the problem by proper remediation.

A few exposure concepts in the expert model were common knowledge. Specifically, most respondents mentioned the influence of location in the house (70%), the geographic area (70%), the influx of radon into basements or crawl spaces (58%), and the role of pipes and ducts (67%), as well as of holes, cracks, and seams (58%) in that influx – although they needed the photos to prompt these latter comments. A few mentioned air-exchange methods, consistent with the few who mentioned the general concept of radon outflow.

Radon respondents showed less awareness of effects than of exposure processes. The most frequently cited expert concept, the inhalation of radon, was mentioned by only 54% of respondents and, by most of these, only after seeing the photos. Although 63% mentioned cancer, only 20% specifically mentioned lung cancer. The photos evoked a variety of peripheral and erroneous concepts. These included the beliefs that radon affects houseplants (58%) and animals (33%), that it causes breast cancer (29%) and contaminates blood (37%), water (20%), and food (17%). Quite a few respondents described radon as dangerous, harmful, and so on. Thus, while people know that radon is bad for them, they do not have a very clear idea of why that is.

These findings suggest that, at a minimum, a public communication about radon should explain: (a) that there is no sure way to tell if one has a radon problem without testing, (b) how to test, (c) how quickly radon decays, making remediation possible, and (d) how remediation is accomplished.

As described in Chapter 6, we developed two different brochures about radon with roughly the same substantive content. One had a "decision tree structure," the second a "directed network" structure. To conserve space, the brochures are not reproduced in this book but are available from the authors on request.

The first pages of both brochures have a table of contents and a summary or overview. The decision-tree brochure has two parts and a question-and-answer format. The first part discusses why it is important to test one's home for radon, by addressing four questions:

> What is radon and why is it dangerous?
>
> Where is radon found and where does it come from?
>
> Once it gets into a home, where does radon go?
>
> How can I tell if there is a dangerous concentration of radon in my house?

The second part explores solving a radon problem, by answering the question:

> What can I do if there is a dangerous concentration of radon in my house?

The brochure based on a directed-network structure uses a text format, organized as follows:

> Radon level in the home
>> Radon entering the air in the house
>>> Radon in the soil
>>> How radon gets indoors
>>> Pressure differences between in- and outdoors
>> Radon eliminated from air in the house
>>> Air exchange between indoor and outdoor air
>>> Radioactive decay
>>> Particles settling with dust
> Radon and people
>> Inhalation of radioactive particles
>> Risk of lung cancer
> What can you do?
>> Find out if you have a risk
>> How can you reduce the radon level?

Both brochures conclude with a summary and a section answering the question, "How can I learn more?"

The two brochures use identical covers, shown in Figure 7.14, illustrating the flow of radon through a house, using dots to show gas concentrations, but with no explanatory text. They contain identical illustrations within the body of the brochures. One diagrams and explains how radon can enter a home. The second illustrates how radioactive radon-decay particles can become lodged in the lung and cause exposure. The third illustrates common radon measurement kits. The fourth uses the same basement view as the first, in order to reinforce graphically the message that one should seek help from a qualified contractor if measurements show high concentrations of radon in the home.

Finally, both brochures contained identical boxed sections explaining the EPA "action level," which is a recommendation, not a standard. Both contain a glossary.

While the two brochures use different structures and language, their central message and basic content is quite similar. Thus, it is reassuring that our comparative tests revealed similar learning with each (Sections 6.5 and 6.6).

7.4   Nuclear Energy Sources for Space Missions

Spacecraft that go to the outer solar system or have very large power demands require nuclear energy sources when there is not enough sunlight or they cannot carry enough alternative fuels. A few missions have used nuclear reactors. More typically, the fuel sources consist of a radioactive isotope, which produces heat that generates electricity through a thermocouple.

Figures 3.5 and 3.6 show the expert models developed by Michael Maharik (1992) for this domain. His mental models interviews involved individuals drawn from three groups: environmental and peace activists (N = 30), engineering societies (N = 30), and the general public (N = 19). His closed-form questionnaire was administered to an opportunity sample of 263 Pittsburgh adults. He also developed and ran a structured survey, exploring public opinion of engineering design options and the feasibility of eliciting public input about macro-design choices.

Department of
Engineering and Public Policy

Carnegie Mellon University

A Citizen's Guide to Radon

**What It Is
and What to Do
About It**

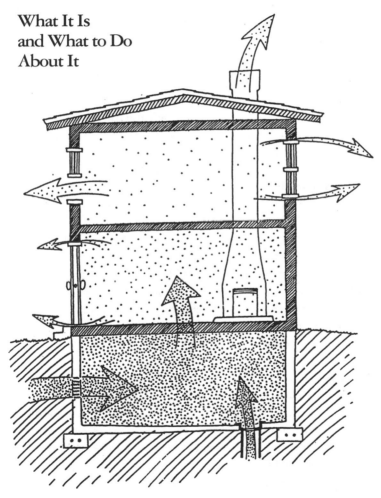

Figure 7.14. Cover for the two versions of brochures on radon in homes.

On the basis of his empirical findings and influence diagrams, he developed a 50-page risk communication brochure, which was subjected to expert and lay review. He developed a questionnaire to test its effectiveness and administered it to an opportunity sample of 144 adults. Its effectiveness was compared in a variety of ways with materials on the same topic being distributed by NASA.

Because of its length, the brochure is not reproduced in this book. However, it, along with a full discussion of all of the analyses and copies of the various questionnaires, can be found in his Ph.D. thesis (Maharik, 1992), as well as in Maharik and Fischhoff (1992, 1993a, 1993b) and Maharik, Fischhoff, and Morgan (1993).

Maharik (1992) summarized his research as follows:

> Overall, respondents in the open-ended study had quite a large body of knowledge about the risks of using nuclear energy in space, in the sense that their pooled repertoire of concepts covered large portions of the expert model. However, their . . . beliefs also had . . . weaknesses, which included gaps in knowledge and misconceptions. Respondents were often found to use scientific terms [such as "radiation" or "radioactive"] without a clear understanding of what they meant. Respondents' mental models were not always coherent: sometimes they contained scattered and inconsistent entries; occasionally concepts were combined inappropriately. . . . Activist respondents had more complete knowledge than technology-oriented respondents on health effects . . . while technology-oriented respondents had higher accuracy scores on the whole physical process. Members of the general public knew less, were less accurate, had less specific knowledge, and produced more misconceptions, than the other two groups. Females in the general public knew less [about this topic] than males. . . .
>
> People generally accepted space technology when its contribution to life on earth was obvious but were much less favorable to its use when they viewed its contribution as questionable. . . . Respondents generally agreed with the experts on the acceptability and desirability of using nuclear energy sources in space. The two primary reasons for disagreeing with experts were a) doubting the experts' assessment of the consequences of possible accidents, and b) doubting the experts' ability to estimate the probability of failures. . . .
>
> In addition to confirming the public's willingness to take part in the process of choosing among engineering options, the [final] study indi-

cated that the public expressed coherent opinions even without having detailed expertise on the technical aspects of risky technologies. Respondents made reasonable judgments among the options and identified central issues.

The communication effectiveness test found that the CMU brochure, derived from the study of readers' existing mental models, provided a better communication tool than NASA's material derived (apparently) from experts' perspective. It included material that readers judged more relevant and which added more to their knowledge. Both communications improved knowledge relative to a control group.

The better performance of experimental subjects was generally due to adding knowledge on issues that they had not known, rather than correcting wrong beliefs. This finding confirms previous research showing that people's existing beliefs are very difficult to change.

These studies found that nuclear energy technology for spacecraft became more attractive when people learned more about it, whether through natural processes or with a risk communication developed with a mental models procedure (Maharik, Fischhoff, and Morgan, 1993). The research also found that good communications could allow laypeople to become sufficiently knowledgeable to be reasonable and informed participants in the process of making macro-engineering design choices (Maharik and Fischhoff, 1993b).

References

Adams, J. G., Zhang, J., Morgan, M. G., and Nair, I. (1995). "A Method for Evaluating Transmission Line Magnetic Field Mitigation Strategies That Incorporates Biological Uncertainty," *Risk Analysis,* 15(3):313–318.

Bostrom, A., Morgan, M. G., Adams, J., and Nair, I. (1994). "Preferences for Exposure Control of Power-Frequency Fields among Lay Opinion Leaders," *Risk: Health, Safety and Environment,* 5(4):295–318.

Budyko, M. I. (1982). *The Earth's Climate: Past and Future.* Academic Press, New York.

Fischhoff, B., Slovic, P., Lichtenstein, S., Read, S., and Combs, B. (1978). "How Safe Is Safe Enough? A Psychometric Study of Attitudes towards Technological Risks and Benefits," *Policy Sciences,* 9:127–152.

Hester, G., Morgan, M. G., Nair, I., and Florig, H. (1990). "Small Group Studies of Regulatory Decision Making for Power-Frequency Electric and Magnetic Fields," *Risk Analysis,* 10:213–228.

Intergovernmental Panel on Climate Change. (1990). *Climate Change: The IPCC Scientific Assessment,* J. T. Houghton, G. J. Jenkins, and J. J. Ephraums, eds. Cambridge University Press, New York.

(1992). *Climate Change 1992: The Supplementary Report to the IPCC Scientific Assessment,* J. T. Houghton, B. A. Callander, and S. K. Varney, eds. Cambridge University Press, Cambridge.

MacGregor, D. G., Slovic, P., and Morgan, M. G. (1994). "Perception of Risks from Electromagnetic Fields: Psychometric Evaluation of a Risk-Communication Approach," *Risk Analysis,* 14:815–831.

Maharik, M. (1992). "Public Perceptions of the Risks of an Unfamiliar Technology: The Case of Using Nuclear Energy Sources for Space Missions," Ph.D. dissertation, Department of Engineering and Public Policy, Carnegie Mellon University.

Maharik, M., and Fischhoff, B. (1992). "The Risks of Nuclear Energy Sources in Space: Some Activists' Perceptions," *Risk Analysis,* 12:383–392.

(1993a). "Contrasting Perceptions of Risks of Using Nuclear Energy Sources in Space," *Journal of Environmental Psychology,* 13:243–250.

(1993b). "Public Views of Using Nuclear Energy Sources in Space Missions," *Space Policy,* 9:99–108.

Maharik, M., Fischhoff, B., and Morgan, M. G. (1993). "Risk Knowledge and Risk Attitudes Regarding Nuclear Energy Sources in Space," *Risk Analysis,* 13:345–353.

Morgan, M. G. (1989). *Electric and Magnetic Fields from 60Hz Electric Power: What Do We Know about Possible Health Risks?* Department of Engineering and Public Policy, Carnegie Mellon University.

(1992). "Prudent Avoidance," *Public Utilities Fortnightly,* (March 15):26–29.

Morgan, M. G., Florig, H. K., Lincoln, D., and Nair, I. (1985). "Power-Line Fields and Human Health," *IEEE Spectrum,* 22(February):62–68.

Morgan, M. G., Florig, H. K., Nair, I., Cortés, C., Marsh, K., and Pavlosky, K. (1990). "Lay Understanding of Low-Frequency Electric and Magnetic Fields," *Bioelectromagnetics,* 11:313–335.

Morgan, M. G., Slovic, P., Nair, I., Geisler, D., MacGregor, D., Fischhoff, B., Lincoln, D., and Keith, D. (1985). "Powerline Frequency Electric and Magnetic Fields: A Pilot Study of Risk Perception," *Risk Analysis,* 5:139–149.

National Research Council. (1975). *Understanding Climatic Change.* National Academy Press, Washington, D.C.

(1996). *Possible Health Effects of Exposure to Residential Electric and Magnetic Fields.* National Academy Press, Washington, D.C.

(1999). *Research on Power Frequency Fields Completed under the Energy Policy Act of 1992.* Board of Radiation Effects Research, Commission on Life Sciences, National Academy Press, Washington, D.C.

Office of Technology Assessment. (1989). *Biological Effects of Power Frequency Electric and Magnetic Fields.* Background paper prepared by I. Nair, M. G. Morgan, and H. K. Florig (OTA-BP-E-53), U.S. Government Printing Office, Washington, D.C.

Read, D., Bostrom, A., Morgan, M. G., Fischhoff, B., and Smuts, T. (1994). "What Do People Know about Global Climate Change? Part 2. Survey Studies of Educated Laypeople," *Risk Analysis,* 14:971–982.

Read, D., and Morgan, M. G. (1998). "The Efficacy of Different Methods for Informing the Public about the Range Dependency of Magnetic Fields from High Voltage Power Lines," *Risk Analysis,* 18(5):603–610.

Schneider, S. H., and Louder, R. (1984). *The Coevolution of Climate and Life.* Sierra Club Books, San Francisco.

Slovic, P., Fischhoff, B., and Lichtenstein, S. (1980). "Facts and Fears: Understanding Perceived Risk," in R. C. Schwing and W. A. Albers, Jr., eds., *Societal Risk Assessment: How Safe is Safe Enough?* Plenum, New York.

(1982). "Why Study Risk Perception?" *Risk Analysis,* 2:83–93.

(1985). "Characterizing Perceived Risk," in R. W. Kates, C. Hohenesmer, and J. Kasperson, eds., *Perilous Progress: Technology as Hazard.* Westview, Boulder, Colo.

8

A MENTAL MODELS
APPROACH TO HIV/AIDS

Since early in the HIV/AIDS epidemic, it has been apparent that people's understanding of its risks are a primary public health concern. People must learn to avoid some behaviors (e.g., unsafe sex, sharing IV drug needles) while not avoiding others (e.g., giving blood, living and learning with infected individuals). As with many other risks, the information that people need is both quantitative and qualitative. For example, they require both a credible estimate of the prevalence of contaminated blood and a feeling for signs that their blood bank or drug partner is above (or below) that average. Moreover, an understanding of how the risks are created and controlled may be essential for making quantitative estimates intuitively plausible (e.g., "how could it be that condoms only reduce risks by a factor of 10?"). That understanding may also provide the feelings of self-efficacy needed to deal with an issue, and to lead others toward appropriate behavior.

Recognizing these factors, public health officials have invested extensive resources into getting the message out about HIV/AIDS (CDC, 1994; Institute of Medicine, 1996). These efforts have included TV spots and specials, school posters and pamphlets, as well as courses and curricula. Considering the magnitude of this effort and the stakes riding on its success, it is essential that the content of the messages be appropriate. This chapter reports an application of the mental models approach to this task. Section 8.1 presents the expert model underlying the effort, and the issues faced in its creation. Section 8.2 describes mental models interviews conducted with a diverse set of 60 adolescents. Section 8.3 presents a structured survey, derived from the comparison between the expert model and the lay interviews; it can be used both to confirm the results from those interviews and to evaluate the impact of informational interventions. Section 8.4 performs such an evaluation, contrasting a communication derived from our approach and another in circulation. Section 8.5 reflects on these results and on their relationship to a subsequent project, examining teens' mental models of the risks of other sexually transmitted diseases.

8.1   An Expert Model of HIV/AIDS

The spread, control, and consequences of HIV/AIDS involve complex processes that are still being studied by specialists from many disciplines. In creating an expert model of these processes, we sought the factors most relevant to predicting (a) the probability of virus transmission to uninfected individuals, (b) the associated health (and other) consequences, and (c) the feedback processes that affect the likelihood of infected individuals passing on the virus. Figure 8.1 shows the basic structure of the model for the first two of these foci. Figure 8.2 completes the model, adding both additional factors and the possibility of feedback (which, in effect, begins a new iteration of the model, with the parameters reset to accommodate any changes caused by the infections and other effects arising from the preceding round).[1]

A strategic choice in designing this expert model was to create a single representation for all modes of HIV transmission (sex, mother-to-fetus, blood transfusion, IV sharing).[2] Although the relevant science and parameter estimates are often very different for these different routes, the progress of the disease and its sequences are essentially identical, once the virus has been transmitted.[3] Moreover, some of the same kinds of processes emerge

[1]The line shading will be explained in the next section.

[2]It could also apply to people's mental models of transmission routes that research has proven to be nonexistent.

[3]One possible difference is in the nonhealth effects for people identified as having acquired the disease through different routes.

with each route, meaning that they pose similar intellectual challenges for people hoping to understand the epidemic and their exposure to it.

For example, risk depends on the *prevalence* of the disease, which affects, in turn, the chances that the virus will be in a *source* to which an individual might be exposed. The size of that dependency might depend on whether the *source* provides blood, needles, or sex. However, in each case, people must be able to take base-rate probabilities into consideration. Many studies have shown the difficulty that people have in doing so, and the tendency for their estimates to be dominated by their impressions of the specific cases that they encounter (Kahneman, Slovic, and Tversky, 1982). As a result, one would expect people's mental models to exaggerate the effectiveness of *screening* in reducing their risk of coming into contact with a virus-bearing source (to the point where their mental model might omit the prevalence node altogether).

In the model of Figure 8.2, the critical decisions are how frequently to engage in a risk *behavior* (e.g., sex), whether to undertake *mitigation* actions (e.g., use condoms), and what screening to do in order to reduce exposure. These decisions are influenced by the *perceived risks and benefits* of these actions (making that node a complex one, including a wide variety of considerations). The *prevalence* of the disease in an area could affect these considerations, for example, if it leads people to talk about HIV/AIDS and, therefore, to change their sexual (or blood-donation) behavior. If people realized that this was happening, then the prevalence-belief link would appear in their mental models, as it does in the expert one.

Alcohol use (and, by implication, other substance use) appears because it can affect both people's beliefs and their ability to act on those beliefs when attempting to execute desired *screening, mitigation,* and *risk behaviors.* Alcohol use could increase risks (e.g., if people are too muddled to insist on condoms or to use them properly) or decrease their risk (e.g., if they are too sick to have sex or to be an appealing partner). Whether mental and expert models correspond depends on whether people are in denial (as substance abusers might be) or aware (e.g., as when people get drunk in order to have an excuse for subsequent risky behaviors).

The right-hand side of the expert model shows the progression of the disease to the often tragic cascade of health and other effects. These processes will influence the chances of infected individuals engaging in behaviors that could pass the virus on to others. Those beliefs can influ-

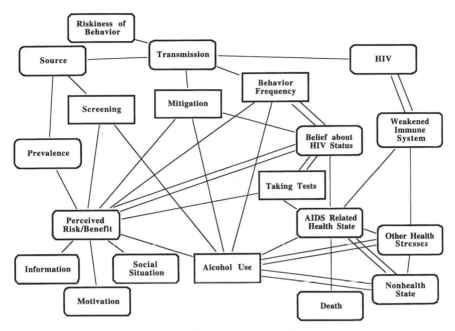

Figure 8.1. The basic structure of the expert model for HIV/AIDS.

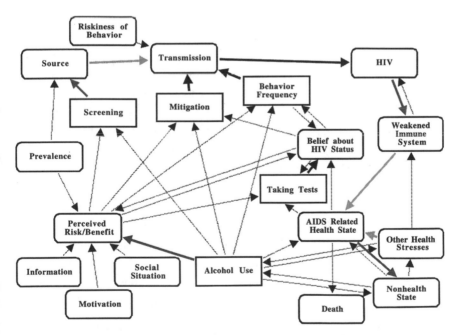

Figure 8.2. Complete expert model for HIV/AIDS. Shading reflects the frequency with which questions are asked about each link in mental models interviews.

ence whether people *take tests* to determine their status, as can the experience of *AIDS-related health states*. And so on.

Like other expert models, this one can be tested in two ways. One is
by scrutinizing its relationships for consistency with existing scientific
knowledge. The second is seeing whether real-life phenomena can be
interpreted in its terms. As with other expert models depicting situations
in which voluntary decisions play a significant role, the associated mental
models will show people's degree of self-awareness regarding their own
decision-making processes. Research into people's beliefs about their own
psychology should also shape the expert model (e.g., how accurately do
they estimate their ability to hold a drink?) (Furnham, 1987).

8.2   Mental Models Interviews

We chose to focus on adolescents because of the risks that they face, the
great volume of communications directed at them, and the opportunity to
provide relevant information at a formative stage, when lifelong behavior
patterns are being formed. In order to ensure the broadest possible applic-
ability of our methods and results, we recruited teens from diverse sources.
Our goal was to draw equal samples of teens who were male and female,
white and African American, and from high-risk settings (group homes,
detention centers) and low-risk ones (after-school clubs at suburban high
schools). The actual sample ranged in age from 13 to 18, with a mean of
16.1 (sd = 1.2). It had 32 females and 28 males, 31 blacks and 29 whites,
and 27 low-risk youths and 33 high-risk ones.[4] Samples of this size should
elicit beliefs held by any significant portion of the population, as well as
reveal major differences in belief prevalence across groups.

The interview protocol followed the usual format. It began with a very
general request to "tell me everything that you know about HIV/AIDS,"
then asked respondents to elaborate on whatever they said. As the interview proceeded, increasingly directive questions were posed, pointing to
the general areas of the expert model, then repeating those probes for each
of the major modes of transmission (if they had not been mentioned spon-

[4]Thirteen participants were interviewed twice, at roughly a two-week interval, in
order to check test-retest reliability of interview responses.

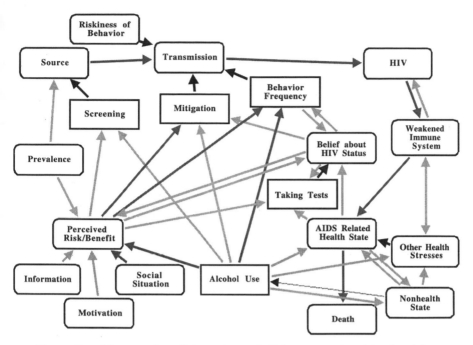

Figure 8.3. Mean number of times that each link was mentioned by 60 adolescent subjects in mental models interviews.

taneously). The interview concluded with fairly specific questions about some topics of special research interest (e.g., "Does the risk depend on how often someone has sex with other people who have the virus?"), providing that respondents had already touched on that general area.

The shading of the arrows in Figure 8.2 shows the number of questions asked about each link, hence the emphasis given to each topic. These frequencies reflect either the importance of the link in the expert model (and, hence, the importance of determining respondents' understanding), the number of different processes subsumed in each link (e.g., the several ways that a source could lead to transmission), our priors about beliefs lurking there (e.g., respondents exaggerating their screening ability), or our questions about just what respondents meant in unclear pretest comments. The frequency with which respondents mentioned a link (Figure 8.3) needs to be considered, of course, in light of how often it was raised as a topic.

As usual in such interviews, an effort was made to use each respondent's personal terminology. The only concession to the respondents' age was taking extra care to treat them as collaborators rather than as test subjects. Once teens felt confident that we really were interested in their view of the world, they typically became very cooperative participants. Especially for the high-risk teens, this seemed to be an unusual and positive interaction. Under these conditions, the teens talked a lot. The typical interview lasted about three-quarters of an hour; on average, teens provided 93.5 statements. Of these, 84.2 could be coded into specific links in the expert model, while the remainder were "shortcuts," descriptions of processes that omitted some intermediate links (e.g., "if you get the virus, then you will die before too long"). Our probing explored whether teens omitted these links because they did not know them or assumed that we did (so that the details went without saying). Often, teens offered multiple statements about a topic, either paraphrasing themselves or discussing different aspects. On average, teens discussed 21.8 different topics (17.2 links, 4.6 shortcuts).

All but one of the links was mentioned by at least one teen. Most teens spontaneously provided three of the potential risk behaviors: sex, drugs, and blood. Few mentioned fetal transmission, even when asked about additional pathways. Figure 8.3 shows the number of times that each link was mentioned. The most common links concerned how behavior affects transmission chances (21.6 per teen), how mitigation affects transmission (15.2), how screening affects the chances of exposure to a source (7.1), how other health stresses affect AIDS-related health problems (5.5), and how the riskiness of specific behaviors affects transmission chances (5.1).

Thus, singly and collectively, these teens were aware of a large portion of the topics in the expert model. Looking at the numbers of topics, links, shortcuts, and risk behaviors, we saw no significant race or risk-status differences (alpha = .05). There was, however, a main effect of gender: the girls talked more, producing more of each kind of material ($p < .05$ or .01). However, this was because they talked more about the links, shortcuts, and topics that they mentioned ($p < .01$), not because they mentioned more of them.

The next level of analysis asks what teens had to say about these top-

Table 8.1   Example quotes from mental models interviews with adolescents.

Links	Quotes
Behavior to Transmission	It's passed on by intercourse.
Mitigation to Transmission	I'd say wear a condom and protect yourself.
Screening to Source	They start looking real sickly.
Other Health Stresses to AIDS-Related Health State	Some of the littlest colds and coughs can kill you.
Riskiness to Transmission	It only takes once if the person is infected. It could, it could not. So I guess it's a fifty-fifty chance.
Shortcuts	
From HIV to AIDS-Related Health State	There's two steps, you can have HIV, then you have AIDS.
From Behavior to Taking Tests	If they had sex with someone and they suspected that person had AIDS, they can get tested.
From Social Situation to Behavior	If you don't do it, they probably just talk stuff on you. Then you go do it.

ics. Table 8.1 provides examples of these teens' language for discussing some links and some shortcuts. Although other mental models studies have created performance statistics comparing lay and expert models, we did not compute them in this case. Our teen respondents often spoke so imprecisely that it was hard to tell if they were right or wrong. For example, what should one conclude if a teen says (a) "It takes only one time to get the virus," when asked if the amount of sex matters; (b) "It is important to know your partner," in the context of a discussion of screening; or (c) "when you drink, you don't know what you're doing"? One purpose of the structured survey (discussed next) was to pose questions whose answers could be evaluated more confidently.

8.3   A Structured Survey

Questions were generated on the basis of the expert model, the mental models interviews, and the comparison between them. Specifically, each link in the expert model was the subject of at least one question. The con-

tent of those questions focused on topics that in the mental models interviews appeared as important correct beliefs, misconceptions, and areas of
ignorance, or "gaps" (where teens had nothing to say about a link). In the
formulation of these questions, we sought to ensure that each could be
understood by teens of varying literacy levels (so that it would be a test of
HIV/AIDS knowledge, and not of reading ability) and that there was a
clear correct answer. This necessitated many rounds of pretesting and
rewriting. The complexity of some of the concepts is sufficiently great
that it was a real challenge to produce the fourth-grade reading level that
we sought.

We used a true-false format, both because it is familiar to teens and
because it focuses their cognitive effort on understanding a single statement, posing less of a burden than multiple-choice questions, which
require the parallel processing of several answers (Bruine de Bruin and
Fischhoff, 2000). We also sought to discourage a common response bias,
expecting positively worded statements to be true (and negatively worded
ones to be false). As a result, we made positively and negatively worded
statements equally likely to be true and false (so that those cases in which
respondents were confident in their answers would not create a response
bias).[5] We also produced two versions of each question, one worded positively and one worded negatively, so that our evaluation of respondents'
understanding of a topic would not be confounded with question wording. Table 8.2 shows examples of the paired positive and negative versions
of questions. In all, there were 200 items, whose order was counterbal-
anced in two 100-item versions of the test.

For decision-making purposes, it is important not just to have as
much knowledge as possible but also to recognize the extent (and limitations) of what one has. Correct beliefs are less valuable if one is unsure
about them. Incorrect beliefs can be particularly damaging if held confidently. As a result, we structured the test to evaluate the appropriateness
of respondents' confidence in their beliefs, sometimes called "calibration."
After indicating whether they thought that each statement was true or
false, respondents were asked to "Think about how sure you are of your

[5]That is, respondents would not infer, say, "usually, when I'm sure that a question is
false, there's a 'not' in it."

Table 8.2 Structured test examples/questions.

Framing	Formulation	
	True	*False*
Version A		
Positive	A person can get the AIDS virus (HIV) from a virgin.	The AIDS virus (HIV) is found in sweat.
Negative	Having HIV isn't the same thing as having AIDS.	A man can't get the AIDS virus (HIV) from having sex with a woman who has it.
Version B		
Positive	A man can get the AIDS virus (HIV) from having sex with a woman who has it.	Having HIV is the same thing as having AIDS.
Negative	The AIDS virus (HIV) isn't found in sweat.	A person can't get the AIDS virus (HIV) from a virgin.

answer. What is the percent chance that you are right?" They responded on a scale marked with 50, 60, 70, 80, 90, and 100%, with the two ends labeled as "just guessing" and "absolutely sure." Several examples were provided to clarify scale use.

Because we were particularly concerned about the accessibility of the test for low-literacy individuals, we administered it in two ways: a conventional test-taking setting and one in which testees had the opportunity to listen to a tape (with headphones) in which each question was read to them. We expected low-literacy respondents to benefit especially from this opportunity. A standardized reading test, the Nelson-Denny (Brown, Fishco, and Hanna, 1993), was administered after the HIV/AIDS questionnaire as a way to evaluate this hypothesis, as well as to measure the residual relationship between literacy and test performance. Participants were drawn from the same high-risk and low-risk teen populations as the interviews, with the addition of 37 adults, yoked to teens in the low-risk group. The mean grade levels on the Nelson-Denny test were 7.7 for the high-risk teens and 14.2 for the low-risk teens. (The adults' reading levels were not tested.)

The test was scored by the percentage of correct answers. There was no difference between males and females, nor between the low-risk teens and yoked parents, in HIV/AIDS knowledge. The low-risk teens did, however, perform considerably better than their high-risk counterparts (72.5 vs. 66.5% correct; $p < .001$). Much to our surprise, using the audio-taped version of the questionnaire reduced performance of the high-risk teens and improved that of the low-risk teens ($p < .001$, for the interaction). Our post-hoc explanation is that receiving information through two channels (eyes and ears) further overloaded the high-risk (low-literacy) teens while it reduced the chances of low-risk teens missing details (and making silly mistakes).

The calibration of confidence judgments has provided remarkably constant results across varied groups and conditions (Yates, 1989): People tend to be overconfident for relatively hard questions ($< 70\%$ correct) and underconfident for relatively easy ones ($> 80\%$ correct). Overall, the confidence judgments of the low-risk teens and adults replicated this general pattern: They were somewhat overconfident, about to the degree seen in previous studies with subjects having similar knowledge levels. The high-risk teens were about as confident as the low-risk ones, despite having a considerably lower level of knowledge. As a result, they were very overconfident, much more so than is typical with these difficulty levels. This replicates the findings of an earlier study (Quadrel, Fischhoff, and Davis, 1993) and provides one of the few consistent differences that we have found associated with teens' risk level (Beyth-Marom and Fischhoff, 1997).

Looking at the yoked pairs of teens and adults, we found little correlation between their percentages of correct answers ($r = .22$) but a high correlation between their mean confidence judgments ($r = .56$). Thus, these teens' knowledge levels were not related to those of their parents, but their confidence was. Cynically, this suggests a tendency to acquire self-presentation, but not content, from one's parents. Other researchers have found that parents influence their children's health knowledge and attitudes only when they have (and use) extensive opportunities for education (DeLoye, Henggeler, and Daniels, 1993; Sigelman et al., 1995).

Further analyses of these test results examine the consistency of knowledge here with that in the mental models interviews, consistency across alternative versions of the same question (Table 8.2), differences in specific beliefs as a function of risk status, and the relationship between performance and literacy. They can be found in Parker et al. (2000).

8.4   A Mental Models Communication and Its Evaluation

The great volume and wide extent of teens' beliefs, as expressed in the mental models interviews, suggest that it would be a mistake for health-risk communications to provide the big picture of HIV/AIDS. Teens already have it. As a result, they might have little patience (or respect) for communicators who take up their time repeating familiar HIV/AIDS facts. The cumulative impact of existing communications has, apparently, succeeded in teaching teens a lot. What teens need now is to have a relatively small number of gaps filled and misconceptions corrected. A communication that focused effectively on these residual problems might not only provide needed information but also be seen as using teens' time and attention well. We sought to fill this niche with our communication, which is offered in full in an appendix to this volume.

Figure 8.4 shows the topics addressed by our communication, which comes in the form of a series of small brochures, suitable for reading in isolation or as a package. Table 8.3 shows the section headings, reflecting the specific aspects of these links that emerged in the research as needing attention. For example, we found that teens (like adults in other circumstances) have difficulty understanding how risks mount up through repeated exposure to an adverse event that either does or does not happen. People seem not to think about cumulative risk and to underaccumulate when they do.[6] Many view the risk from many exposures to be equal to that from a single one. Our brochure on this topic provided the broader perspective, explained why it might be counterintuitive, and computed the numbers for readers, presenting them in graphic form.

Participants in the evaluation were randomly assigned to one of three conditions: reading the CMU brochures, reading the best existing material

---

[6]For example, Linville, Fischer, and Fischhoff (1993) asked college students first to estimate the probability of HIV being transmitted in one case of unprotected sex with someone having it, then to estimate the probability with 10 and 100 exposures. Their estimates were higher than those of scientists for a single exposure (with a median of about 10%). However, for about 40% of respondents, the probability for multiple exposures was about that for single exposures. Among those whose estimates were monotonically increasing with exposure, the cumulative probability was much too low (about 50% for 100 exposures, when it should be a virtual certainty if the exposures are independent).

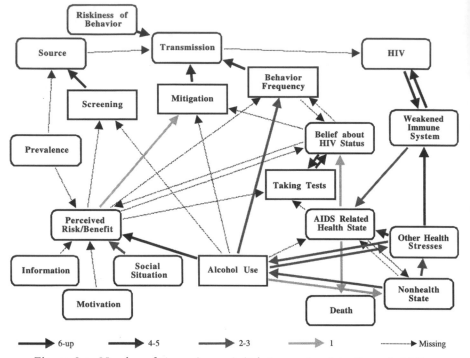

Figure 8.4. Number of times that each link is mentioned in Carnegie Mellon brochures derived from mental models interviews.

that we could find (a combination of three brochures from ETR Associates, 1996a, 1996b, 1996c), and reading nothing at all. There were 44 low-risk teens and 68 high-risk ones. After reading their communication (if any), participants completed the structured test. We expected our brochure to be superior to the alternative brochure and that, in turn, to be better than nothing. Respondents also completed a Nelson-Denny literacy test, the scores on which were used as covariates. Those receiving our communication performed best on the structured test (as measured by an a priori linear contrast, $p < .05$). Nonetheless, the high-risk teens still performed much worse than the low-risk ones ($p < .001$) in all three conditions. There was a strong correlation between literacy and knowledge, suggesting a limit to written communications ($r = .68, p < .0001$). The fuller analysis of these data asks about changes in performance on individual nodes (e.g., was it similar on the matched items dealing with each node? Was it greater on the nodes emphasized in the brochures?) (Downs, Bruine de Bruin, and Fischhoff, 1998).

Table 8.3   CMU brochure topics.

- Is knowing your partner enough?
- Why are some condoms lubricated?
- Does alcohol make you lose control?
- Do some kinds of sex have more risk for getting HIV?
- They say you can get AIDS the first time . . .
- Is AIDS the same as HIV?
- How can you tell if you have HIV?

8.5   Discussion

There is a certain circularity in the process for evaluating our AIDS brochure, as well as with the other communications produced with the mental models approach. Ours did better than the best alternative brochure, and better than no brochure at all. However, the performance standard was our own structured survey, developed from the same theoretical and empirical base as our brochure. That base specifies what is worth knowing (considering the expert model) and what is worth saying (considering the mental models revealed in the interviews and structured test). Had the competing brochure been accompanied by its own test, we would not have been particularly interested in results produced with it, except to the extent that we were convinced that its item selection followed the same logic as our own.[7] In this sense, the mental models approach is a paradigm, setting its own problems and standards.

Another way of seeing a communication's selection criteria is by characterizing it in terms of the expert model (as done in Figure 8.4 for our brochures). The figure for the ETR brochures (not shown) looks much like that for our own with a few exceptions, such as emphasizing the source-transmission-HIV links, which we had determined to be superfluous, and the importance of getting good information, which we had determined went without saying. On the other hand, we saw the

---

[7]We would also ask whether its items were developed through the same rigorous testing process as our own. In another study (Bruine de Bruin and Fischhoff, 2000), we have shown how a knowledge test used by an organization prominent in HIV/AIDS education (the Red Cross) had poorly worded questions, which differentially affected respondents from different groups (reducing performance for high-risk ones, improving it for low-risk ones).

need to emphasize the impacts of alcohol use and social situations on judgment (and ways to reduce them), as well as how testing positive (and having AIDS) can change one's entire life. The ETR brochure was more attractive than ours physically, but it also had a much higher reading level.

An example of a more dramatic difference in content can be seen in Figure 8.5, which characterizes a brochure that captures one publisher's conception of "What Women Need to Know." As judged by our research on teens, it focuses too strongly on basic exposure-transmission processes that recipients are likely to know already (unless teens know more than the women targeted by this communication), while ignoring such topics as decision-making processes and the impacts of the disease on one's life. By the standards of our approach, such a communication runs the risks of (a) alienating people, by repeating things that they have already heard many times, (b) denying them needed information, and (c) creating a false sense of understanding, by implying that there is little left to learn.

Overall, the picture of teens that emerges from this research is of individuals who have successfully mastered many aspects of risk-related HIV/AIDS knowledge but still have "bugs" in their mental models, of the sort that could undermine the value of what they do know. These residual problems are the focus of our communication, which acknowledges that teens know a great deal already. We sought to make these problems seem important, interesting, and thought-provoking, so that teen recipients would feel that we cared enough to use their time well. Generally speaking, the topics of our brochures fell into one of three categories: (a) cognitive structures that teens seemed to lack – reflecting difficulties seen in other research into human judgment (e.g., how risks mount up through repeated exposure); (b) aspects of risk behaviors that required more explicit language than the writers of other communications may have been comfortable using (e.g., what anal sex is and why it is particularly dangerous); and (c) features of teens' mental models that required open-ended interviews to emerge (e.g., how they use alcohol to legitimate risky behavior, feeling that getting drunk is more excusable than the unsafe sex that follows).

Nonetheless, we were disappointed by the relatively small improvement in knowledge associated with our brochure. We believe that it

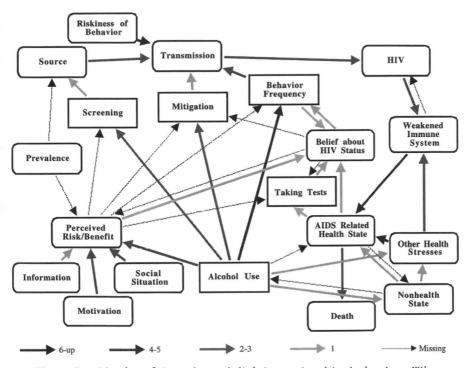

Figure 8.5. Number of times that each link is mentioned in the brochure *What Women Need to Know.*

reflects, in part, the limits to written communications, even (or especially) when they are read in a school-like setting. Teens may need greater control over their learning environment and opportunity to interact with it, in order to acquire knowledge. Moreover, a standard communication that addresses many recipients' information needs will still contain much information that each individual recipient already knows. Finally, our expert model focuses on individuals coping with the threat of HIV/AIDS. However, both sex and drug use are social activities, in which people must negotiate interpersonal contracts in order to act on their beliefs and desires.

As a result, we followed this project with another one, dealing with sexually transmitted diseases (STD) in general (and focused on young women). It took advantage of what we learned here about issues that also arise with other diseases (e.g., compromised immune systems increasing disease susceptibility). Indeed, we began that project by creating a general model of infectious disease, so as to identify recurrent issues that could be addressed with modular communications (and to ensure that we saw the problem as broadly as possible) (Fischhoff, Downs, and Bruine de Bruin, 1998). By relying on what we (and others) had learned already, we were able to focus our interviews on teens' mental models of the social relations affecting their control of their sexuality. We found that teens know very little about most STDs other than HIV/AIDS, consonant with the relative emphasis in communications directed at them. We also found that young women had difficulty seeing the decision-making opportunities in the sexual situations that they face (e.g., "If she went to a party like that, then she has agreed to have sex; there's nothing she can do about it.") (Fischhoff, 1996).

Our new intervention utilizes computer-interactive technology (a DVD platform) in order to allow teens to explore the contents of our communication, following their own priorities. Information about specific STDs takes advantage of the issues that are common to diseases (e.g., being caused by a virus, being hard to detect even by carriers). Decision-making processes are illustrated by following the stories of several young women, in which users are able to choose the direction taken at various decision points, then see what happens and engage in "cognitive role-playing" for how they would manage a similar situation. The intervention is designed to be suitable for use in medical offices, taking advantage of the spare time and relative privacy that teens may have there. A randomized clinical trial has just been completed, comparing it to a print version of the same material and the "standard care" of conventionally available brochures. The interactive video reduced chlamydia reinfection rates, while improving condom use (Downs et al., 2001)

As this project evolved, we gradually realized another dimension of experience that was omitted (or at least treated very lightly) in our comprehensive expert model of infectious disease. It is the stigma sometimes associated with having (or even discussing) some disease states. Stigma can override the sort of deliberative cost-benefit thinking that is assumed by informational approaches (Douglas, 1966; Goffman, 1967; Flynn, Kunreuther, and Slovic, 2001). In order to accommodate these concerns, we have developed a model of stigma that will serve as the basis for future research (Fischhoff, 1998b). In these ways, the mental models approach can encourage the joint development of analytical and descriptive approaches to understanding and improving human decision making (Fischhoff, 1998a).

References

Beyth-Marom, R., and Fischhoff, B. (1997). "Adolescent Decisions about Risk: A Cognitive Perspective," in J. Schulenberg, J. Maggs, and K. Hurnelmans, eds., *Health Risks and Developmental Transaction during Adolescence.* Cambridge University Press, New York, pp. 110–135.

Brown, J. I., Fishco, V. V., and Hanna, G. (1993). *Nelson-Denny Reading Test.* Riverside Publishing Company, Chicago.

Bruine de Bruin, W., and Fischhoff, B. (2000). "The Effect of Question Format on Measured HIV/AIDS Knowledge: Detention Center Teens, Health Science Students, and Adults," *AIDS Education and Prevention,* 12:187–198.

Centers for Disease Control. (1994). *External Review of CDC's HIV Prevention Strategies.* Department of Health and Human Services, Washington, D.C.

DeLoye, G. J., Henggeler, S. W., and Daniels, C. M. (1993). "Developmental and Family Correlates of Children's Knowledge and Attitudes Regarding AIDS," *Journal of Pediatric Psychology,* 18:209–219.

Douglas, M. (1966). *Purity and Danger.* Routledge and Kegan Paul, London.

Downs, J., Bruine de Bruin, W., and Fischhoff, B. (1998). "A Test for HIV/AIDS Knowledge." Unpublished manuscript, Carnegie Mellon University, Pittsburgh.

Downs, J. S., Fischhoff, B., Murray, P. J., White, J. P., Bruine de Bruin, W., and Palmgren, C. "Behavioral asnd Biological Outcomes of a Mental Models Intervention for Decreasing Sexually Transmitted Disease among Adolescent Females." Unpublished manuscript, Carnegie Mellon University, Pittsburgh.

ETR Associates (1996a). *HIV: Antibody Test.* Brochure, J. Schettler, Santa Cruz, Calif.

(1996b). *HIV: The Answers.* Brochure, J. Schettler, Santa Cruz, Calif.

(1996c). *HIV: The Immune System.* Brochure, J. Schettler, Santa Cruz, Calif.

Fischhoff, B. (1996). "The Real World: What Good Is It?" *Organizational Behavior and Human Decision Processes,* 65:232–248.

(1998a). "Communicate unto Others . . . ," *Reliability Engineering and System Safety,* 59:63–72.

(1998b). "Diagnosing Stigma," *Reliability Engineering and System Safety,* 59:47–48.

Fischhoff, B., Downs, J., and Bruine de Bruin, W. (1998). "Adolescent Vulnerability: A Framework for Behavioral Interventions," *Applied and Preventive Psychology,* 7:77–94.

Flynn, J., Kunreuther, H., and Slovic, P., eds. (2001). *Risk, Media, and Stigma.* Earthscan, London.

Furnham, A. (1987). *Lay Theories.* Oxford University Press, New York.

Goffman, E. (1967). *Stigma.* Harvard University Press, Cambridge, Mass.

Institute of Medicine. (1996). *AIDS and Behavior.* Institute of Medicine, Washington, D.C.

Kahneman, D., Slovic, P., and Tversky, A. (1982). *Judgment under Uncertainty: Heuristics and Biases.* Cambridge University Press, New York.

Linville, P. W., Fischer, G. W., and Fischhoff, B. (1993). "AIDS Risk Perceptions and Decision Biases," in J. B. Pryor and G. D. Reeder, eds., *The Social Psychology of HIV Infection.* Lawrence Erlbaum Associates, Hillsdale, N.J.

Parker, A., Downs, J., Bruine de Bruin, W., Fischhoff, B., and Dawes, R. M. (2000). "The Appropriateness of Adolescents' Confidence in Their Knowledge: AIDS-Related and General." Unpublished manuscript, Carnegie Mellon University, Pittsburgh.

Quadrel, M. J., Fischhoff, B., and Davis, W. (1993). "Adolescent (In)vulnerability," *American Psychologist,* 48:102–116.

Sigelman, C. K., Mukai, T., Woods, T., and Alfeld, C. (1995). "Parents' Contributions to Children's Knowledge and Attitudes Regarding AIDS: Another Look," *Journal of Pediatrics,* 20:61–77.

Yates, J. F. (1989). *Judgment and Decision Making.* Prentice Hall, Englewood Cliffs, N.J.

9

SOME CONCLUDING THOUGHTS

The preceding chapters have described the method and motivation for the Carnegie Mellon mental models approach to developing risk communications and attempted to provide enough worked examples to allow readers to implement each of its components on their own. We hope that readers will take our words as intended: as guidance on how to get started, not gospel to be followed slavishly in every detail. In addition to an empirical understanding of the science and perception of risk, good risk communications require imagination and creativity. Each application has presented us with new challenges and generated new methods. That, presumably, will be your experience as well. This guide is intended as a cookbook in the sense of a guide to planning nutritious meals rather than a set of recipes for specific dishes (although we have provided a few of our favorites).

9.1   The Cost of Risk Communication

The procedure that we have outlined takes time and effort. As noted in Chapter 2, while a rough version of the process might be accomplished with two or three person-months of effort, a thorough job may require between three to four times that. An organization preparing multiple communications might achieve economies of scale by reusing portions of protocols, interviewer training, results, and messages. Indeed, some of the specific pieces in our worked examples might be directly adapted to some settings (e.g., how to communicate cumulative risk (Chapter 8), air flows and radioactive decay (Chapter 6), fields (Chapter 7), the effect of drinking on judgment (Chapter 8), and the effect of values on policy choices (Chapter 7)). Similarly, there are expert models here that could be used as points of departure for ones on new topics.

Is it worth it? The answer depends on the specific communication context. We think that the stakes are often high enough to make the answer yes. Unfortunately, it may take some education (or some painful failures) to persuade senior managers of the importance of this kind of investment. Here are three arguments that might tip the scales: (a) You'd never design a new product on the basis of an engineer's best guess. You'd insist on careful empirical design and testing. The same standard should apply to a risk communication. Why rely on some expert's best guess, when such guesses are often wrong and empirical methods exist to get them right? (b) Why balk at spending an amount of money on getting the message right that is a tiny fraction of the stakes riding on correct public understanding? and (c) We wouldn't release a new drug without adequate testing. Considering the potential health (and economic) consequences of misunderstanding risks, we should be equally loath to release a new risk communication without knowing its impact.

9.2   Quality Assurance

This book has laid out a set of tools that can be used to develop more effective risk communications. Like all tools, these can be abused. We have argued that the developers of risk communications should do their best to present complete and balanced messages that provide recipients with the information they need to make informed, independent decisions (Fischhoff, 1998; Morgan and Lave, 1990). Unfortunately, not everyone who communicates about risk is primarily concerned with the public interest. Some have economic interests that conflict with public health and safety. Others have political agendas that may not benefit from a public that possesses a full, balanced understanding of a risk, allowing its members to reach their own conclusions. They may even want the public to fail, in order to justify transferring authority to technical specialists.

Such uses could undermine the public acceptability and reputation of a method. The public itself provides one line of defense against such abuses. Most citizens have developed some proficiency at sensing messages shaped by self-interest. We would like to believe that providing better ways to disseminate information will help the public to act on its own inherent skepticism and evaluate the messages aimed at it. The hope of a democracy has to be that good information will drive out bad.

Of course, not all poor risk communication is intentionally misleading. Some is just done too casually. Media messages are often constrained by the norms of journalism, which sometimes conflict with covering the complexity and uncertainty of risk stories. For example, the desire to keep a story simple can encourage nonquantitative presentations and the omission of critical information. Unless readers receive basic quantitative information on exposure and dose-response relationships, they must make it up, reading between the lines of the story they receive. If recipients guess wrong, then a well-meaning simple story may produce biased perceptions. A news story about a small, uncertain risk may trigger undue alarm if it creates public awareness without providing quantitative perspective, even though it follows the canons of journalistic rigor (Sandman et al., 1987; Nelkin, 1987). Alternatively, a story about a large, well-defined risk may fall on deaf ears unless it provides recipients with a context for thinking about the issues. A "balanced" story, lining up equal numbers of experts on opposing sides of a risk debate, may convey uncertainty when the scientific community actually has great consensus. In such cases, journalists become unwitting accomplices of political and economic actors whose public relations aides strive for such confusion.

Risk professionals can counteract these tendencies by speaking out about specific risks and informing media professionals about the problems that their stories can create and the methods available for addressing them. In addition to public comment, they can write friendly private letters to reporters, pointing out problems with the exposition and likely reader responses – and complimenting good work.

One sign of change is the development of guidance by professional journalists on how to cover risk stories (e.g., Cohn, 1989; Ward, 1997).

Another sign is that we have frequently been approached by reporters wondering how to cover a story. When we have already developed a communication on the topic, and time allows, we send it to them to read before we talk.

9.3   Mental Models Methods in Context

Properly used, the methods described in this book can help individuals and organizations to develop clear and understandable messages about risks. The availability of such messages is an important element in the process of risk communication and management. But while such messages are important, they are only one part of what is needed for the effective and democratic management of risks. Mechanisms must be found that allow interested parties, decision makers, and the general public to hear one another's concerns and work through socially acceptable institutions and processes to reach socially legitimate decisions. Effective two-way communication is one part of these mechanisms, which must also allow meaningful participation, leaving stakeholders with appropriate opportunities to influence risk management.

As we noted in Chapter 1, a clearer understanding of the facts may allow a more focused debate, but it will often not resolve underlying philosophical disagreements. Thus, while good risk communication is an important tool in effective risk management, it is only one part of a much larger and more complex process. Not only is this our view, but it seems to be the emerging view of groups such as the Canadian Standards Association (1997), the National Research Council (1989, 1996), the Presidential/Congressional Commission on Risk Assessment and Risk Management (1997), and the Royal Commission on Environmental Pollution (1999).

9.4   The Bottom Line

If this book has one message, it is that in the absence of evidence, no one can predict confidently how to communicate about a risk. Effective and reliable risk communication requires empirical study.

Risk messages must be understood by recipients, and their effectiveness must be understood by communicators. To this end, it is no longer appropriate to rely on hunches and intuition. Professional standards demand a research-based approach, one segment of which is presented here. Before disseminating a risk message, communicators must characterize expert knowledge about the risk, study current beliefs, examine the risk decisions that people face, develop a communication focused on critical content, and evaluate the message through empirical testing.

Developing good and effective risk communications can be time-consuming and expensive. However, as the bumper sticker says, "If you think education is expensive, try ignorance."

References

Canadian Standards Association. (1997). *Risk Management Guidelines* (CSA-850). Canadian Standards Association, Ottawa.

Cohn, V. (1989). *News and Numbers: A Guide to Reporting Statistical Claims and Controversies in Health and Other Fields.* Iowa State University Press, Ames, Iowa.

Fischhoff, B. (1998). "Communicate unto Others . . . ," *Reliability Engineering and System Safety,* 59:63–72.

Morgan, M. G., and Lave, L. (1990). "Ethical Considerations in Risk Communication Practice and Research," *Risk Analysis,* 10:355–358.

Presidential/Congressional Commission on Risk Assessment and Risk Management. (1997). *Volume 1: Framework for Environmental Health Risk Management; Volume 2: Risk Assessment and Risk Management in Regulatory Decision-Making* (529 14th Street, NW, Suite 420, Washington, DC 20045).

National Research Council. (1989). *Improving Risk Communication.* National Academy Press, Washington, D.C.

(1996). *Understanding Risk.* National Academy Press, Washington, D.C.

Nelkin, D. (1987). *Selling Science: How the Press Covers Science and Technology.* W. H. Freeman, San Francisco.

Royal Commission on Environmental Pollution. (1999). *Setting Environmental Standards.* Her Majesty's Stationary Office, London.

Sandman, P. M., Sachsman, D. B., Greenberg, M. R., and Gochfield, M. (1987). *Environmental Risk and the Press: An Exploratory Assessment.* Transition Books, New Brunswick, N.J.

Ward, B. (1997). *Environmental Reporting.* National Safety Council, Washington, D.C.

APPENDIX A

Reproduction of the risk communication brochure *Global Warming and Climate Change.* In its original form, the three details booklets reproduced at the back of this Appendix are housed in pull-out pouches at the back of Parts 1, 2, and 3 of the main brochure. The general structure of the brochure is shown in Figure A.1. Copies of the original version can be purchased at cost through the Department of Engineering and Public Policy, Carnegie Mellon University.

Figure A.1. General structure of the brochure developed on global warming and climate change. Note hierarchical design, with pull-out "details booklets."

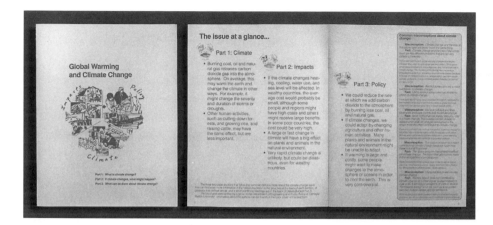

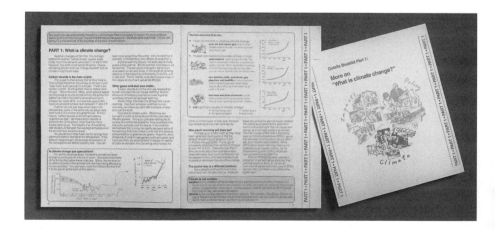

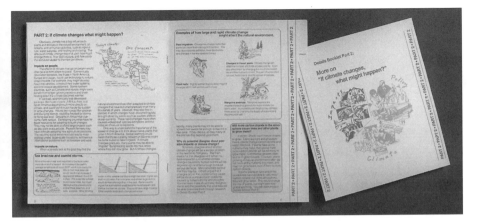

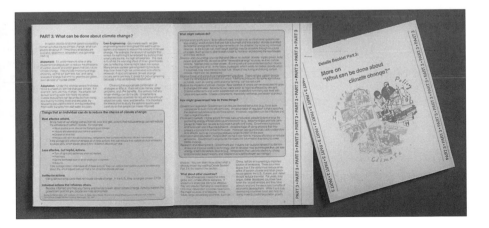

187

Global Warming and Climate Change

Part 1: What is climate change?
Part 2: If climate changes, what might happen?
Part 3: What can be done about climate change?

The issue at a glance...

Part 1: Climate

- Burning coal, oil and natural gas releases carbon dioxide gas into the atmosphere. On average, this may warm the earth and change the climate in other ways. For example, it might change the severity and duration of storms or droughts.
- Other human activities, such as cutting down forests, and growing rice, and raising cattle, may have the same effect, but are less important.

Part 2: Impacts

- If the climate changes heating, cooling, water use, and sea level will be affected. In wealthy countries, the average cost would probably be small, although some people and regions might have high costs and others might receive large benefits. In some poor countries, the cost could be very high.
- A large or fast change in climate will have a big effect on plants and animals in the natural environment.
- Very rapid climate change is unlikely, but could be disastrous, even for wealthy countries.

The three two-page sections that follow this summary tell you more about the climate change issue. You can find even more information in the "details booklets" in the pouches at the back of each section. A glossary, that defines words, and a list of additional readings are in the back of Details Booklet Part 3.

The brochures were written by a group in the Department of Engineering and Public Policy at Carnegie Mellon University. Information about the authors can be found on the back cover of this brochure.

1

190

Part 3: Policy

- We could reduce the rate at which we add carbon dioxide to the atmosphere by burning less coal, oil and natural gas.
- If climate changes, we could adapt by changing agriculture and other human activities. Many plants and animals in the natural environment might be unable to adapt.
- If warming is large and costly, some people might want to make changes to the atmosphere or oceans in order to cool the earth. This is very controversial.

Common misconceptions about climate change:

Misconception: *Climate change and the loss of the ozone layer are pretty much the same thing.*
Fact: *Climate change and the loss of the ozone layer are two different problems that are not very closely connected.*

The largest contributor to global warming is carbon dioxide gas released when coal, oil, and natural gas are burned. CFCs, gases which cause stratospheric ozone depletion, play only a minor role in climate change. The depletion of the stratospheric ozone layer, including the ozone hole, is a serious environmental problem because it causes an increase in ultraviolet radiation which can harm people, animals, and plants. This is a different problem from the problem of climate change.

Misconception: *Aerosol spray cans are a major contributor to climate change.*
Fact: *Using aerosol spray cans has almost no effect on climate change.*

In the past, aerosol spray cans contained CFCs which contributed to the depletion of the ozone layer (not the same as global warming). Under U.S. law, aerosol spray cans no longer contain CFCs.

Misconception: *General pollution and toxic chemicals are major contributors to climate change.*
Fact: *Most forms of pollution play little or no role in climate change. The invisible carbon dioxide released when coal, oil, and gas are burned is the single most important contributor to climate change.*

The burning of fossil fuels, such as coal and oil, to produce energy for electricity, heat and transportation is the primary source of carbon dioxide, which is the most important contributor to global warming. Carbon dioxide does not contribute to general air pollution.

Misconception: *The space program is a major contributor to climate change because it punches holes in the atmosphere.*
Fact: *The space program has almost no effect on climate change. The local changes rockets make in the atmosphere soon disappear.*

Gases released by rocket exhaust have no real impact on global warming. They have only a small, largely short-term, local effect on the different problem of stratospheric ozone depletion.

Misconception: *Using nuclear power causes climate change.*
Fact: *Nuclear power does not contribute to climate change. If nuclear power is used instead of coal or oil, it will reduce emissions of carbon dioxide. "Renewable energy" sources, such as solar power, can also reduce carbon dioxide emissions.*

While nuclear power plants present a variety of other environmental problems, they do not emit gases which contribute to global warming.

2

PART 1: What is climate change?

Weather changes all the time. The average pattern of weather, called climate, usually stays pretty much the same for centuries if it is left to itself. However, the earth is not being left alone. People are taking actions that can change the earth and its climate in significant ways.

Carbon dioxide is the main culprit.

The single human activity that is most likely to have a large impact on the climate is the burning of "fossil fuels" such as coal, oil and gas. These fuels contain carbon. Burning them makes carbon dioxide gas. Since the early 1800s, when people began burning large amounts of coal and oil, the amount of carbon dioxide in the earth's atmosphere has increased by nearly 30%, and average global temperature appears to have risen between 1° and 2°F.

Carbon dioxide gas traps solar heat in the atmosphere, partly in the same way as glass traps solar heat in a sunroom or a greenhouse. For this reason, carbon dioxide is sometimes called a "greenhouse gas." As more carbon dioxide is added to the atmosphere, solar heat has more trouble getting out. The result is that, if everything else stayed unchanged, the average temperature of the atmosphere would increase.

As people burn more fossil fuel for energy they add more carbon dioxide to the atmosphere. If this goes on long enough, the average temperature of the atmosphere will almost certainly rise. You can learn more about how this works, and uncertainties in scientific understanding, from Details Booklet Part 1.

If global warming occurs, not every day or every place will be warmer. But on average most places will be warmer. This will cause changes in the amount and pattern of rain and snow, in the length of growing seasons, in the frequency and severity of storms, and in sea level. Farms, forests, and plants and animals in the natural environment, will all be affected.

Other gases and dust also matter.

Carbon dioxide is not the only gas released by human activities that can cause warming. Human emissions of methane and nitrous oxide together contribute almost half as much warming.

Not all things that enter the atmosphere cause warming. Dust from volcanos, and from human activities, can reflect sunlight (like a window shade) and cool the earth.

Coal and oil contain sulfur. When they are burned the sulfur is transformed into fine particles in the atmosphere. This sulfur pollution contributes to various environmental problems. Most scientists think that sulfur particles cool the planet. In the northern hemisphere, this cooling has partly canceled some of the warming that should have come from the growing concentrations of greenhouse gases. However, since emissions of greenhouse gases continue to grow, and most countries are working hard to reduce emissions of sulfur air pollution, this canceling will probably not

Is climate change just speculation?

No, as the drawings show, the earth's climate has been changing continually for millions of years. Scientists know many of the things that cause these changes. Some, like the amount of carbon dioxide in the atmosphere, are now being affected by human activities. You can learn more from Details Booklet Part 1 in the pouch at the back of this section.

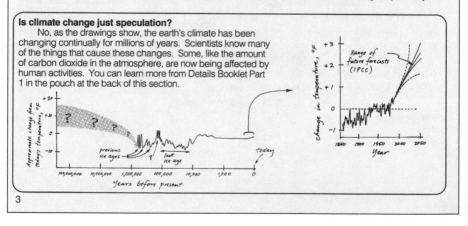

Human activities that are...

- major contributors to possible climate change:

  coal, oil, and natural gas, when burned release carbon dioxide, the most important greenhouse gas.

- modest contributors to possible climate change:

  deforestation: when wood is burned, the carbon contained in the trees is released as carbon dioxide. When wood rots in swamps methane can be produced. Living trees remove carbon dioxide from the atmosphere.

  rice paddies, cattle, coal mines, gas pipelines, and landfills produce methane, another greenhouse gas, which today causes about 30% as much warming as carbon dioxide.

  fertilizers and other chemicals release nitrous oxide, which today causes about 10% as much warming as carbon dioxide.

- *not* significant causes of climate change:
  - aerosol spray cans
  - the space program
  - nuclear power
  - toxic waste

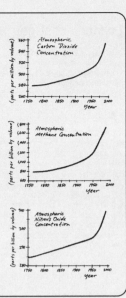

continue in the future. In that case, the average temperature may rise more rapidly.

How much warming will there be?

If things go on pretty much as they have been, scientists' best guess is that the amount of warming will be about 2.5°F (1.4°C) by the year 2050. The range of uncertainty stretches from almost no change to over 4°F (2.3°C). Details Booklet Part 1 tells you more about how scientists reach these estimates, how much confidence can be placed in them, and what actions could increase or decrease the size of the change.

The ozone hole is a different problem.

Many people confuse the hole in the ozone layer with climate change. However, these two problems are not closely related. The ozone layer protects the earth from harmful ultraviolet light that can cause skin cancer and damage plants and animals. The main cause of the hole in the ozone layer is chlorofluorocarbons (CFCs), gases that are used in refrigerators, air conditioners, and industrial applications. While CFCs alone cause warming, their ozone destruction can cause cooling. So far these warming and cooling influences have approximately balanced.

Prior to 1978 CFCs were used as a propellant in aerosol spray cans, but that use has ended in the U.S. Under an international agreement most uses of CFCs are now being phased out to protect the ozone layer.

Climate is not weather.

weather is the condition of the atmosphere at a particular place and time measured in terms of such things as wind, temperature, humidity, atmospheric pressure, cloudiness, and precipitation (rain, snow, etc.). In most places, weather can change from hour-to-hour, day-to-day, and season-to-season.

climate is the average pattern of weather in a place. For example, San Diego, California has a "Mediterranean climate" which means temperatures are generally moderate year round, there is limited rainfall, and humidity is typically low.

4

PART 2: If climate changes what might happen?

Obviously, climate has a big influence on plants and animals in the natural environment, on oceans, and on human activities, such as agriculture, water supplies, and heating and cooling. The effects of climate change depend upon *how much* change there is, *how fast* it occurs, and *how easily the world can adapt* to the new conditions.

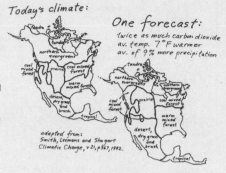

Today's climate:

One forecast:
twice as much carbon dioxide
av. temp. 7°F warmer
av. of 9% more precipitation

adapted from:
Smith, Leemans and Shugart
Climatic Change, v 21, p 367, 1992.

Impacts on people.

The effects of climate change on people would change a lot from place-to-place. Economically developed societies, like those in North America, Europe and Japan, could use technology to reduce direct impacts. For example, they might develop new crop varieties, construct new water systems, and limit coastal development. Some northern countries, such as Canada and Russia, might even benefit from longer growing seasons and lower heating bills if the climate becomes warmer.

In contrast, economically less developed societies, like those in parts of Africa, Asia, and South America depend much more directly on climate, and could be hit much harder by sudden or large changes. Places like coastal Bangladesh and low-lying islands, could be flooded by storms or rising sea level. Droughts in Africa might become more serious. Developing countries have far fewer resources for adapting to such changes. They may not be able to afford large projects such as sea walls or aqueducts. Peasant farmers may have difficulty adopting new agricultural practices. The resulting social tensions could lead to more political unrest, large-scale migrations, and serious international problems such as terrorism and wars.

Impacts on nature.

When scientists look at the past they find the natural environment has often adapted to climate changes that have occurred gradually over many thousands of years. However, they also find instances in which changes have occurred rapidly, brought about by events such as sudden shifts in ocean currents. These rapid changes have often caused widespread species extinctions and the collapse of natural ecosystems.

One way to understand the importance of the speed of change is to think about native plants that grow in North America. Global warming could mean that those currently growing in Georgia might be better suited to New England. If climate changes gradually, many plants may be able to "migrate" by spreading seeds into new areas where they can now grow. But if climate changes

Sea level rise and coastal storms.

Most of the rise in sea level would occur because water expands when it is heated. An increase in the earth's average temperature of about 3.5°F, which is probably too

Even an increase of 3.5°F would not melt most polar ice and glaciers.

little to melt most polar ice, would result in an increase in sea level of between 8 and 30 inches. This is too little to flood most coastal cities, but could damage some coastal plants and animals, beaches, and water supplies. While flooding

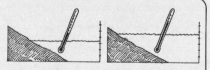

under normal weather conditions might be small, higher sea level would mean that hurricanes and similar large storms could do more damage than in the past. Some experts argue that such storms would become more frequent and intense in a warmer climate. This could have large impacts. Other experts doubt such changes will occur.

5

194

Examples of how large and rapid climate change might affect the natural environment.

Plant migration: Climate may change faster than plants can move from one region to another. This may cause species extinction, lower biodiversity, and changes in the way species interact.

Changes in insect pests: Climate change can affect the number and kinds of pests directly. It can also affect them by changing the mix of plant varieties and their nutrient content. This can influence plant survival, food chains, and the spread of disease.

Coral reefs: Slightly warmer tropical water may kill the algae which reef animals use for food.

Mangrove swamps: Mangrove swamps are important breeding grounds for many animals that live in water. Increased ocean flooding may damage these areas by changing the supply of nutrients and the amount of salt.

rapidly, many plants may not be able to spread their seeds far enough to reach the new area. If they die out, so may many of the animals that depend upon them.

Why do scientist disagree about possible impacts of climate change?

Scientists disagree about whether climate change will be a serious problem in the next 50 to 100 years. The main reason for this disagreement is that nobody knows for sure whether climate changes caused by human actions will be large enough and fast enough to cause serious damage. Many scientists believe that they may be. Others argue that if changes occur, the problems they cause will be minor compared with problems caused by today's storms and droughts. You can learn more about these disagreements and the possibility that scientists will be able to resolve them through research, in Details Booklet Part 2.

Will more carbon dioxide in the atmosphere cause trees and other plants to grow more?

It might. Plants need carbon dioxide to grow. Using sunlight and photosynthesis, plants change carbon dioxide and water into food. If plants have all the nutrients they need, then giving them more carbon dioxide will cause many to grow more. Commercial growers often do this in greenhouses. However, plants growing in natural environments often do not have all the nutrients they need, and may not grow faster, even if there is more carbon dioxide.

If some plants on land and in the oceans are naturally able to take more carbon dioxide out of the atmosphere, they will grow faster. This would change the mix of plants, but might also slow global warming. You can learn more in Details Booklet Part 2.

PART 3: What can be done about climate change?

If carbon dioxide and other gases released by human activities cause climate change, what can people do about it? Three basic strategies are available, abatement, adaptation, and geo-engineering.

Abatement: To *abate* means to slow or stop. Abatement strategies aim to reduce the emissions of carbon dioxide and other gases that can cause climate change. They include improving energy efficiency, so that we burn less fuel, and using sources of energy that emit no greenhouse gases, such as solar or nuclear power.

Adaptation: Under this strategy people find ways to live successfully with the changed climate. For example, land use may change. Aqueducts can be built to bring water into newly dry areas. Coastal populations can be protected from rising sea level by building dikes and sea walls, by relocating populations inland, and by protecting fresh-water supplies from salt-water intrusion.

Geo-Engineering: *Geo* means earth, so geo-engineering means to engineer the earth's atmosphere and oceans to reduce the amount of climate change. For example, the amount of sunlight that strikes the earth might be reduced by putting more small particles into the high atmosphere. The idea is to off-set the warming effect of more greenhouse gas by reflecting more sunlight back into space. Many people oppose geo-engineering because they think there might be unintended side effects. However, if rapid and severe climate change occurs, some are likely to press for geo-engineering because it may be relatively inexpensive.

Choosing the appropriate combination of strategies is difficult. Each will cost money, pose problems, and offer benefits. It is unlikely that any single strategy can do the job. Uncertainty is added because scientists do not yet know enough about the costs, risks, and benefits. It is important for researchers to study the options quickly and carefully so that people can make informed

Things that an individual can do to reduce the chance of climate change:

Most effective actions.

Since most of our energy comes from oil, coal and gas, actions that reduce energy use will reduce the emissions of carbon dioxide. For example:

- When you buy a car, choose one that gets good mileage.
- Insulate and weatherize your home or apartment.
- Carpool or drive less.
- Replace old, worn-out appliances (e.g., refrigerators, heat pumps) with the most efficient new models.

If the average U.S. citizen undertakes all of these actions, they can reduce their carbon dioxide emissions by about 25%, which equals about 5 tons of carbon dioxide per year.

Less effective, but helpful, actions.

- Turn off lights and appliances when not needed.
- Plant trees.
- Set the thermostat lower in winter and higher in summer.
- Recycle.

If the average citizen undertakes all of these actions, they can reduce their carbon dioxide emissions by about 3%, which equals just over half a ton of carbon dioxide per year.

Ineffective actions.

Using aerosol spray cans does not cause climate change. In the U.S., they no longer contain CFCs.

Individual actions that influence others.

Become informed and help your family and friends to learn about climate change. Actively support the government policies you decide are most appropriate.

Source for the numbers: J.M. DeCicco, J.H. Cook, D. Bolze, and J. Beyea, Chapter 6 in *Energy Efficiency and the Environment*, American Council for an Energy Efficient Economy, Washington, DC, 1991.

7

What might nations do?

Improve energy efficiency: More efficient cars, appliances, and industrial systems use less energy, which means that less fuel is burned and less carbon dioxide is emitted. Substantial energy efficiency improvements can be obtained by replacing individual devices. In the longer run, even larger savings may be possible through structural changes, such as being able to work closer to home or redesigning the way houses and cities are built.

Develop and use energy sources that emit little or no carbon dioxide: Hydro power, solar power and windmills, as well as other "renewable energy" sources, emit no carbon dioxide. Neither does nuclear power. Burning natural gas emits less carbon dioxide than burning coal or oil. In the future, hydrogen, which emits no carbon dioxide when it is burned, may become a practical fuel. Ways of capturing and storing carbon dioxide might also be developed.

Improve forest and agricultural management practices: Trees remove carbon dioxide from the atmosphere and store it in wood. Methane produced by some agricultural activities, such as raising cattle and rice farming, can be reduced.

Reduce the impacts of climate change: New varieties of crops can be developed to grow in changed climates. Aqueducts can carry water to regions affected by drought. Coastal settlements and water supplies can be protected from rising sea level with dikes and sea walls. Coastal ecosystems, especially wetlands, are harder to protect.

How might government help do these things?

Government regulation: Government can require desired behaviors (e.g., force auto companies to build more efficient cars). An advantage of regulation is that it specifies the desired outcomes and can force action. However, regulation can be inflexible and discourage innovation.

Prices and markets: Higher prices for fossil fuels encourage people to save energy by promoting energy efficient devices and behavior (e.g., expensive gas prompts companies to make and people to buy more fuel efficient cars). Government subsidies and taxes can also influence behavior. An advantage of using prices is that they present a constant incentive to innovate. However, using prices can have undesirable side effects, such as imposing a relatively larger burden on the poor.

Information and education: People often do not know how to improve efficiency or reduce emissions. Government can provide them with the information they need to make better choices.

Research and development: Government and industry can support research to demonstrate and improve existing technology, and to develop new technologies that use less energy or emit no carbon dioxide (e.g., refrigerators that use less electricity, cheap practical solar water heaters, and inexpensive solar/hydrogen technology).

choices. You can learn more about what is already known by reading Details Booklet Part 3 in the back of this section.

What about other countries?

The atmosphere covers the entire globe and climate affects everyone. If abatement strategies are to be effective they will require international cooperation. Until now, developed countries have been the major sources of emissions. In the future, large developing countries, such as China, will be an increasingly important source of emissions. These countries argue that if the world must reduce emissions of carbon dioxide and other greenhouse gases, the U.S., Europe, and Japan should reduce the most. For years, they argue, these developed countries have been the largest emitters and they have already enjoyed the associated benefits of economic development. While this is true, developing countries could also help by doing more to control population growth.

8

197

Who wrote these brochures?

The primary authors of these brochures were Granger Morgan and Tom Smuts of Carnegie Mellon University. They had help from a number of colleagues including Hadi Dowlatabadi, Baruch Fischhoff, Lester Lave, and Ed Rubin. Before the brochures were published they were reviewed by a number of experts and groups of laypeople who offered extensive advice on how the brochures could be improved. While we followed much of this advice, the final product is the authors' responsibility.

Granger Morgan is Head of the Department of Engineering and Public Policy at Carnegie Mellon University. He holds a Ph.D. in applied physics and has worked for many years in environmental problems and risk analysis. Tom Smuts holds a BA in philosophy and is particularly interested in ethical issues related to the environment. Hadi Dowlatabadi holds a Ph.D. in physics and directs Carnegie Mellon's program of integrated assessment of climate change. Baruch Fischhoff holds a Ph.D. in psychology and is an expert in risk communication. Lester Lave holds a Ph.D. in economics and has worked extensively on risk and environmental economics. Ed Rubin holds a Ph.D. in mechanical engineering and is an expert on energy systems and their environmental impacts.

In preparing these brochures, the authors have worked hard to present a balanced and impartial treatment of this controversial topic. A number of laypeople assisted us with evaluations. In addition, we thank the following for their assistance and reviews: Peter Ashcroft, Cindy Atman, Jesse Ausubel, Matt Ball, Ann Bostrom, Edith Brown-Weiss, Stewart Cohen, Rob Coppock, Cliff Davidson, Michael Fischer, Paul Fischbeck, Ann Fisher, Shane Frederick, Willett Kempton, Millett Morgan, Eleanor Morgan, William Nierenberg, Ted Parson, Anand Patwardhan, George Perkins, Daniel Read, Sue Rowley, Tom Schelling, Stephen Schneider, Jhih-Shyang Shih, Mitchell Small, Richard Sonnenblick, Patti Steranchak, Billy Turner, Randy Urbano, and Robert White. The drawings for the brochures were done by Frederick Carlson. The work was supported by a grant from the Scaife Family Foundation.

Department of Engineering and Public Policy
Carnegie Mellon University
Pittsburgh, PA 15213

Details Booklet Part 1:

More on
"What is climate change?"

This details booklet provides additional information for people who would like to learn more about the subject of "Part 3: What can be done about climate change?" of the brochure "Global Warming and Climate Change." This booklet does not repeat many of the key points made in Part 3, so it would be best if you read Part 3 of the main brochure first.

Table of Contents

200

Why is it important to distinguish between weather and climate?

Many people use the words weather and climate as if they mean the same thing. They do not. It is important to understand the difference in order to understand the idea of climate change.

Everyone knows what *weather* is. It's what is going on in the atmosphere at a particular place and time. Weather is measured in terms of wind speed, temperature, humidity, atmospheric pressure, cloudiness, and precipitation. In most places, weather changes from hour-to-hour, day-to-day, and season-to-season. The word *climate* refers to the *average pattern* of weather in a region.

An example may help. If on a day in July, you are asked, "What's the *weather* been like in New Orleans?" you might answer, "Today it's clear and cool, but yesterday was hot and muggy." On the other hand, if you are asked, "What's the *climate* like during the summer in New Orleans?" it would be correct to answer, "In the summer it's hot and muggy." The fact that on a particular July day New Orleans happens to be clear and cool doesn't mean its climate has changed.

When climate *does* change, it usually changes slowly. For example, the *climate* or average weather of Iowa involves cold snowy winters and hot summers. While the specific weather in Iowa varies from year-to-year, the *average pattern* is pretty much the same today as it was back in our grandparents' days.

Because the specific weather we experience may be a bit different from one year to the next, a couple of very hot summers, or a couple of very rainy winters, may lead people to conclude that the climate is changing. Of course, rapid climate change might cause such shifts, but it is far more likely that these differences are just natural year-to-year variability. However, because everyone notices a really hot summer, and television and newspapers sometimes talk about climate change in the same story as they talk about recent unusual weather, it is easy to get the two confused.

Weather ≠ Climate

1

What is the "greenhouse effect" and how does it keep temperatures on most of the earth moderate?

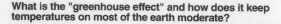

A clear summer night in Kansas stays warm

because the water in the moist air traps the heat through the "greenhouse effect".

The same night in the desert of New Mexico gets cold

because there is little water in the air to trap the heat and the energy radiates out into space.

The greenhouse effect is what keeps the earth a good deal warmer than our neighbor planet, Mars. Unlike Mars, the earth has a thick atmosphere that can trap and redistribute energy from the sun. Perhaps the easiest way to understand how the trapping works is by thinking about what happens when you park your car in the sun with its windows closed. The inside of the car gets warm because light energy can easily pass through the glass of the car windows and enter the car. Some of the light energy bounces off the lighter colored surfaces of the car's interior and is reflected back out through the windows, but much of it is absorbed by the darker seats and other things inside the car. If that was all that was going on, the inside of the car would just keep getting hotter and hotter. However, as the seats and other things in the interior warm up, they give off heat in the form of infrared energy. Unlike light, this infrared heat energy cannot pass easily through the glass of the car's windows, so only a little of it gets back outside. However, as the temperature rises, more energy gets through the window glass. Finally, a balance point is reached at which the amount of sunlight energy that is being absorbed is just balanced by the amount of heat energy that escapes in the form of infrared. At this point, the inside of the car reaches a stable temperature.[†]

The same kind of balancing goes on with the earth. You can think of the earth's atmosphere as playing roughly the same role as the glass in the car window. Sunlight can easily pass through the atmosphere. About a third of the sunlight is immediately reflected back out into space by light colored surfaces such as clouds, sand, snow, and ice. Most of the rest is absorbed by darker surfaces. If this were the whole story, the earth's surface would keep heating up and soon we would all fry. To reach a balance, the energy that is absorbed must somehow get back out into space as infrared heat energy.

Water vapor, ozone, carbon dioxide, and several other natural and man-made gases in the atmosphere, all absorb infrared energy, so infrared energy has trouble getting out to space. Just as with the car (or a glass-covered greenhouse), the earth's system reaches a temperature level at which the amount of light coming in is just balanced by the amount of infrared heat energy that is escaping. This process is what is commonly known as the "greenhouse effect."

[†]While the car example provides a useful analogy, it is not strictly equivalent to the atmosphere. Much of the heating in a car occurs because the closed windows block convection which would otherwise carry heat away from the warm surfaces.

2

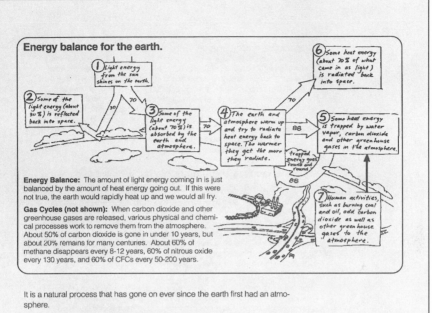

Energy balance for the earth.

① Light energy from the sun shines on the earth.

② Some of the light energy (about 30%) is reflected back into space.

③ Some of the light energy (about 70%) is absorbed by the earth and atmosphere.

④ The earth and atmosphere warm up and try to radiate heat energy back to space. The warmer they get the more they radiate.

⑤ Some heat energy is trapped by water vapor, carbon dioxide and other greenhouse gases in the atmosphere.

⑥ Some heat energy (about 70% of what came in as light) is radiated back into space.

⑦ Human activities, such as burning coal and oil, add carbon dioxide as well as other greenhouse gases to the atmosphere.

trapped energy goes round and round

Energy Balance: The amount of light energy coming in is just balanced by the amount of heat energy going out. If this were not true, the earth would rapidly heat up and we would all fry.

Gas Cycles (not shown): When carbon dioxide and other greenhouse gases are released, various physical and chemical processes work to remove them from the atmosphere. About 50% of carbon dioxide is gone in under 10 years, but about 20% remains for many centuries. About 60% of methane disappears every 8-12 years, 60% of nitrous oxide every 130 years, and 60% of CFCs every 50-200 years.

It is a natural process that has gone on ever since the earth first had an atmosphere.

Because of this natural greenhouse effect, on average, the earth is about 59°F (33°C) warmer than it would be without its atmosphere. About 57°F (32°C) of this extra warmth is due to water vapor, the rest is due to ozone, carbon dioxide, and several other naturally occurring "greenhouse gases."

What is global warming?

The phrase "Global warming" or "Greenhouse warming" refers to the fact that as more carbon dioxide or other greenhouse gases are added to the atmosphere, the temperature of the earth will rise, *assuming nothing else changes.* For the past few hundred years, people have been burning fossil fuels such as coal and oil in ever increasing quantities. While some of the carbon dioxide released is absorbed into the ocean or taken up by plant life, in the short-term about half of it remains in the atmosphere. Industrial activities also have been releasing

3

several other greenhouse gases into the atmosphere. The best estimates today are that these gases should have already increased the average temperature of the earth by about 2.3°F (1°C). Since it appears that the average temperature of the earth has only increased by between 1 and 2°F (.6 to 1°C), it is likely that some other things have also changed. In Part 1 of the main brochure, we discussed one change - small particles that are created from sulfur air pollution and that cool the earth by reflecting sunlight. There are others. Some of these changes may be directly or indirectly caused by the increase in carbon dioxide or other greenhouse gases. These changes are called "feedbacks." It is largely the uncertainties about these feedbacks that makes the science of climate change so uncertain and controversial.

How is heat redistributed by the atmosphere and the oceans?

The largest amount of energy coming in from the sun strikes the equatorial region of the earth. Only a modest amount strikes the area around the poles. While the poles are cooler than the equator, the difference in temperature is much smaller than you would expect on the basis of the amount of sunlight each region receives. This is because the earth's atmosphere and ocean constantly move heat from the equator toward the poles. This giant "heat engine" drives the earth's climate and the weather.

When light from the sun is absorbed at the equator it warms the air and evapo-rates water from the surface. The warm moist air rises. As this air rises, the water condenses to form clouds and rain. This produces the heavy rain that is characteristic of the tropics. As water condenses, it releases heat. Since it is now high up, much of the heat energy that is released can be radiated back into space as infrared energy. That leaves dryer cooler air which is pushed north from the equator and ultimately settles back toward the surface in a region about 30° from the equator.[1] From there it once again makes its way to the equator (in what are known as the trade winds).[11] This circulation pattern, of air rising near

---

[1]These regions where dry air settles back to the surface are known as the "horse latitudes." In the northern hemisphere, they correspond roughly with the deserts of northern Mexico, the Sahara in northern Africa, the Arabian Desert and the great Indian Desert, in the southern hemisphere, with the Atacama Desert of Chile, Peru and Bolivia, the Kalahari Desert of southern Africa, and the deserts of Australia.

[11]The region around the equator where air may be coming together from both the north and the south is commonly called the "doldrums" because at some times of the year the winds in this region can be very light and variable.

4

Planetary circulation and the "Coriolis effect."

When Hadley originally suggested the idea of large scale circulation patterns in the earth's atmosphere in 1735, his idea was that warm air would rise at the equator and then travel all the way to the poles, settling as it went. While this was a plausible first theory, several things prevent it from happening on the real earth. One important complication results from the fact that the earth is rotating. Due to rotation, the surface of the earth moves more rapidly at the equator than it does at the pole. When a parcel of air moves towards the pole it tends to get ahead of the surface below it. Similarly, when a parcel starts to move towards the equator, it tends to lag behind the surface below it. The result is that flows of air that start in a north-south direction curve around in what is known as the "Coriolis effect." One result is that the very large-scale circulation, that Hadley proposed, breaks up into several smaller-scale patterns. You can see one practical consequence of the Coriolis effect in the direction of the trade winds. Rather than flowing straight down the lines of longitude toward the equator, these winds, which are created by the air motion of the tropical Hadley cells, curve toward the west.

Illustration of the Coriolis effect by a child throwing a ball on a merry-go-round.

the equator and settling about 30° toward the pole, is referred to as the "Hadley cell" after the meteorologist who first suggested it in 1735.

The circulation of the Hadley cell moves energy from the equator up to the mid-latitudes. The atmosphere carries energy further north through a different set of mechanisms which include the large circulating high and low pressure weather systems that characterize weather in middle latitudes such as in the United States.[†] The drawing on this page shows a simplified sketch of the general circulation of

---

[†]These weather systems, which are typically many hundred miles across, are referred to by meteorologists as cyclones (around low pressure centers) and anticyclones (around high pressure centers). The flow of air curves around the high or low pressure centers because of the Coriolis effect. For example, as air rushes in to fill a low pressure area its direction gets bent...to the right in the northern hemisphere or to the left in the southern hemisphere, thus setting up a counterclockwise flow in the northern hemisphere, or a clockwise flow in the southern hemisphere. These cyclones should not be confused with tornados, the much smaller intense rotating storms that are sometimes popularly called "cyclones."

the earth's atmosphere. It is best to think of this picture as showing the *average* flow over time. At any given moment, the details may be quite different.[†]

About half the energy carried from the equator toward the poles is carried by the atmosphere. The remainder is carried by currents flowing in the ocean. Some of these currents are directly created by the wind. Others are driven by the different concentrations of salt in different parts of the ocean. Water naturally flows from regions of more salt to regions of less salt in order to try to balance these differences. The drawing on the bottom of the next page shows one very large circulation pattern, often called the "ocean conveyer belt." One important consequence of this ocean circulation is that it carries warm tropical surface water north through the Atlantic ocean so that Europe ends up being much warmer than it would otherwise be. If this "ocean conveyer belt" were suddenly to shut down (as paleontological and other data suggest it has on occasion in the past), very rapid climate change could occur in northern Europe and perhaps in several other regions.

What are "feedbacks?"
How might they effect the way the climate changes?

As more carbon dioxide or other greenhouse gases are added to the atmosphere, the temperature of the earth will rise, *assuming nothing else changes.* As we noted earlier, perhaps the most important set of changes that can occur are called "feedbacks."

Feedbacks come in two kinds: negative feedbacks that work to slow down or offset the warming and positive feedbacks that work to speed up or amplify the warming.

There are many feedbacks in the climate system. For example, carbon dioxide acts as a fertilizer that makes some plants grow faster. As the concentration of carbon dioxide in the atmosphere increases, these plants may grow faster and as a consequence take more carbon dioxide out of the atmosphere. This would result in a *negative feedback, slowing* the rate at which carbon dioxide increases, and hence slowing the rate of warming.

As the earth warms, some ice and snow are likely to melt. Ice and snow are good reflectors of sunlight. The dark ground that is exposed when the snow and ice melts is not as good a reflector. When the ice and snow melt less light energy from the sun will be reflected and more will be absorbed by the earth. This would result in a *positive feedback* that would tend to speed up the rate at which the earth warms.

General circulation of the atmosphere

In middle latitudes "cyclonic eddies" in the jet stream form around high and low pressure areas and move energy poleward.

WINTER

north pole

the jet stream

equator

Hadley cell circulation moves energy poleward.

SUMMER

In summer Hadley cell circulation moves south and reverses direction.

[†]For example, much of the time only one of the Hadley cells is operating.

6

Climate scientists have identified a number of positive and negative feedbacks in the climate system. Some of them are well understood. Others are still only partly understood. For example, water vapor is not typically considered part of the climate change problem. However, the greatest uncertainty in predictions of future climate are related to different views on how water vapor and clouds will respond to changed greenhouse gas concentrations.

Aren't there large computer models of the climate? How good are they?

Yes, there are a number of large computer models called General Circulation Models, or GCMs, that have been built to study and predict climate. These models use the basic laws of science (conservation of mass, conservation of momentum, etc.) to represent the large-scale circulations and interactions of the atmosphere. Recently scientists have begun to connect some of these models to similar models of the oceans and the biosphere.

These models all predict roughly the same amount of warming when the amount of carbon dioxide in the earth's atmosphere is doubled. Some people see these similar predictions as a source of confidence that we can make reliable predictions. However, there are several awkward details. To get them to produce these results the models first must be carefully "tuned up" to get them to reproduce the existing climate. This is largely because many of the important

The "Ocean Conveyor Belt."

Dense, cold, salt-laden water sinks in the North Atlantic. This drives the "Ocean Conveyor Belt" that carries it under the Atlantic and Indian oceans to re-surface in the northern Pacific. The North Atlantic remains more

salty because, the general circulation of the atmosphere carries fresh water (as vapor) from the North Atlantic to fall as rain in the North Pacific. Geological records suggest that on several occasions in the past this large circulation has suddenly shut down, bringing regional climate changes, such as much colder temperatures, to northern Europe.

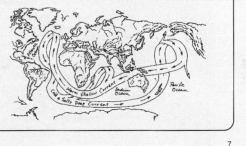

To learn more see: W. S. Broecker, "The Great Ocean Conveyor," *Oceanography*, Vol. 4, No. 2, pp. 79-89, 1991.

processes of the atmosphere and the oceans take place over dimensions of space and time that are too small to be included in the models, so they have to be estimated. The best way to do this is by comparing with past and present climates. Perhaps more troubling, while the GCMs all give roughly the same overall answer, if you look at what is going on in the detailed physical process of each model, things are very different from one model to the next. The same answers come out of the models, but for somewhat different reasons. Finally, while the models all produce about the same result for global averages, the predictions for specific locations are quite variable.

In order to understand and predict the climate system better, we will need a more complete understanding of the basic science of climate process. Many ongoing research programs, both in the United States, and elsewhere around the world, are dedicated to producing this better basic knowledge.

How much will the climate change? How fast will it change?

The answer depends in part on how people behave over the next several decades. If we carry on pretty much with "business as usual," expanding the amount of energy each person uses, the developed world will continue to add large amounts of carbon dioxide to the atmosphere. As developing countries like China and India continue to add population, and become more economically developed, they will begin to add even larger amounts of carbon dioxide.

Recently, a group of leading scientists from around the world were gathered in a special study group called the "Intergovernmental Panel on Climate Change" or IPCC. The estimates made by this group are widely viewed as the best consensus judgment about the science of climate change now available. They are summarized in the drawings on the next page.

The uncertainty and controversy about climate change arise because we are trying to make predictions about how a complex dynamic system will respond when we do things to it which are not quite like anything that has ever been done to it in the past. Most scientists believe that small changes in the "inputs" to the climate system will result in small changes to the resulting climate. But the atmosphere and the ocean, and the interactions they have with living things make up a very complicated system that has many interconnections and feedbacks. Because of these feedbacks, the response of the climate to changes such as more greenhouse gases could be very "nonlinear." While many scientists think it is unlikely, there is some chance that a small change in an input might produce a big change in the resulting climate.

8

208

The IPCC.

In 1988 The World Meteorological Organization and the United Nations Environment Program jointly established the *Intergovernmental Panel on Climate Change* or IPCC. The IPCC consists of a set of committees of leading scientists from all around the world whose task it is to periodically review and report on the state of understanding of the climate problem. The panel operates under the general leadership of Prof. Bert Bolin of Sweden. In 1990, IPCC Working Group 1 on climate change science issued its first "consensus report." This was followed in 1992 with an update. The drawings show three scenarios which IPCC developed of how the earth's temperature might change over the next century.

IPCC projects that "the land surfaces warm more rapidly than the ocean, and high latitudes warm more than the global mean in winter." Night time low temperatures are found to be increasing more than day time high temperatures. They estimate a "global mean sea level rise of about 6 cm [2.4 inches] per decade over the next century (with an uncertainty range of 3-10 cm [1.2-3.9 inches] per decade), mainly due to thermal expansion of the oceans..."

For references to the IPCC reports, see the box labeled "For further reading" on the back cover of Details Booklet Part 3.

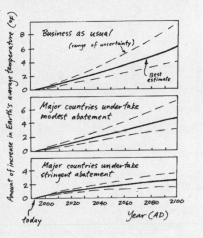

Will more research about climate get us all the answers?

Probably not. More research will certainly improve our understanding and help us to make better predictions. However, the climate system is extraordinarily complex and we may never be able to predict fully how it will respond. Indeed, within limits it may even be a "chaotic system," which would mean that precise predictions would never be possible.

Thus, while our knowledge and our ability to make predictions should get better in the next few decades, we will probably always be stuck with a great deal of uncertainty when we face policy choices about the climate.

9

Details Booklet Part 2:

More on
"If climate changes,
what might happen?"

This details booklet provides additional information for people who would like to learn more about the subject of "Part 2: If climate changes, what might happen?" of the brochure "Global Warming and Climate Change." This booklet does not repeat some of the key points made in Part 2, so it would be best if you read Part 2 of the main brochure first.

Table of Contents

What can we say about the likely economic impacts of climate change in wealthy countries?

Most scientists believe that if significant climate change occurs it will take place gradually over a period of many decades. If change is gradual, the overall economic impact on wealthy countries such as the United States will probably be modest although some regions or groups may experience large costs and others may experience large benefits. After all, American society already exists very successfully in Alaska, Arizona, and Florida and these states span a range of climates much wider than any predicted changes. Farmers would have to adjust their crops, and in some cases, farming regions and other land use patterns would shift. Some water supply systems would have to be modified. Low coastal areas would have to make adjustments. But, our society regularly makes changes to adapt to natural and man-made fluctuations. It could probably handle these additional changes without much trouble, although nationally the total costs could add up to many billions of dollars.

While many of the impacts of climate change would be negative, some might be positive. Heating costs in northern areas might decline, agricultural productivity in places such as Canada, Scandinavia and northern Japan might be improved, and the amount of sunlight available for grain crops might increase as the regions where they grow shifts further north. Of course, not all northern regions would benefit. Some northern soils are not suitable for agriculture, some areas of permanently frozen ground (permafrost) might become large impassable bogs, and various insect pests and diseases might move north.

Several economists have tried to estimate the overall economic cost of climate change for the United States. For the sorts of gradual changes being predicted over the next century, they estimate costs in the vicinity of a quarter of one percent per year of GDP (gross domestic product). Such calculations are, of course, very uncertain.

There is some chance that climate change will be abrupt, perhaps brought on by a sudden shift in the general pattern of ocean circulation. If that happens, the economic costs to wealthy countries like the United States could be very large. Much new investment might be needed in a very short period of time. Agricultural and water systems might not easily be modified in just a few years, especially if uncertainty makes planning difficult. Most scientists believe that such catastrophic change is unlikely, but not impossible.

1

Agricultural impacts.

Of all human economic activities, agriculture is potentially most vulnerable to the effects of climate change. Here are brief descriptions of two recent studies:

Global Impacts: An international group of agricultural researchers used climate projections from three climate models (GCMs) to project regional climate changes at 112 locations in 18 countries under the assumption that the amount of carbon dioxide in the atmosphere had doubled. Average global temperature increased about 8°F (4.5°C). Regional agricultural experts projected the yields of wheat, corn, soybeans, and rice at each location. An economic model was then used to estimate patterns of world food prices and trade. Assuming that farmers employ simple adaptation practices, such as changing planting times and seed varieties to match the changed local climates, they estimate global food output to be unaffected for the case of one climate model, and to drop by 2% and 6% respectively for the other two climate models studied. The developing world is hit harder than the developed world. Including the effects of comparative costs in world trade, developed country output is predicted to rise between 4 and 14% and developing country output to fall by 9 to 12%. World food prices go up. The number of people at risk of hunger (due to higher prices) probably also goes up, perhaps by 50%. This analysis assumed that no major changes, such as construction of new irrigation projects, are undertaken. If such changes are included, the agricultural impact on all but the poorest developing countries probably becomes very small.

Source: C. Rosenzweig and M. L. Parry, "Potential Impact of Climate Change on World Food Supply," *Nature*, Vol. 367, pp. 133-138, 1994 January 13.

Impacts on the U.S. Great Plains: In a study of Missouri, Iowa, Nebraska and Kansas, called the MINK study, researchers studied both best-case and worst-case scenarios of the effect of a 2°F (1.2°C) rise in temperature, similar to the temperature change during the dust bowl era of the 1930s. In the best-case scenario, they assumed that higher carbon dioxide levels would speed plant growth while reducing water consumption. They also assumed that farmers would adapt with such strategies as earlier planting, using plant varieties with a longer growing season, and changing tillage and irrigation practices.

In the worst-case scenario, they assumed that crop growth would not be aided by increased concentrations of carbon dioxide and that farmers would not adapt successfully to the warmer climate. Here are the results:

The Worst-Case Scenario	The Best-Case Scenario
• Crop productivity declines 17.1% or $2.7 billion/year.	• Crop productivity declines 3.3% or $500 million/year.
• Crops need 23% more water, but reduced rainfall means less water is available.	• Crops need about 15% more water, but supply remains limited.
• Farmers use 3 to 4% more energy.	• Farmers adopt to more efficient irrigation systems.
• Regional industries related to farming suffer $1.4 billion in losses/year.	• Regional industries related to farming suffer $410 million in losses/year.
Summary: 2°F warming causes a $4.1 billion/year loss, a *1.3% reduction* of the total regional agricultural output of $309 billion/year.	**Summary:** 2°F warming causes $910 million loss, a *0.3% reduction of* regional agricultural output of $309 billion/year.

Source: N.J. Rosenberg and P.R. Crosson, *The MINK Project: An overview*, Washington, DC: U.S. Department of Energy, 1991.

2

What can we say about economic impacts in poor countries?

Whether it is fast or slow, climate change is likely to have greater economic impacts on poor countries than on rich countries. Two factors lead to this conclusion. First, poor countries are forced to live "closer to the edge" and have less capacity to adapt to changes. Compare the flooding by the Mississippi river in 1993 with various major floods you have heard about in developing countries such as Bangladesh. While the Mississippi floods were serious, the U.S. was able to adjust to them remarkably smoothly. Very few people died, aid was supplied by other parts of the country, food prices were hardly affected, and people got on with their lives. A similar flood in many poor countries would kill tens of thousands of people and cause massive disruptions in food supply, widespread disease, and economic dislocation for many years.

The second reason that some poor countries are likely to be affected more severely is that the people in many poor countries live traditional lives in cultures that depend much more directly on a specific climate. Their agricultural practices, their housing, and many other aspects of their way of life, are adapted to local climate conditions. These traditional ways have been passed down for countless generations. Because of low education levels and strong cultural traditions, changing these ways in response to climate change may be very difficult.

On the positive side, some countries, such as India and China, may become more wealthy during the next century, and find it easier to cope with climate change. Other countries, that remain very poor, may have so little capital investment to loose that changing to new circumstances may be less costly for them than for partly developed countries.

How could climate change affect natural ecosystems?

We know that climate affects plants and animals in the natural environment. Many of us have seen the effects of such short-term climatic variations as droughts. On a longer time scale, scientists have reconstructed the history of past climates, such as ice ages, and shown that the ecology of entire continents has undergone profound shifts.

Of course, many factors other than climate can affect natural ecosystems. Among these, changes in human land use are probably the most important. For example, consider the enormous ecological impacts that were associated with the European settlement of the North American continent over the past 300 years.

3

While the ecological disruptions caused by climate change may not be as large as those caused by major changes in human land use, they still could be severe. How severe depends critically on how rapidly climate changes. Individual birds and animals can move. Plants and trees can only move from one generation to the next. If climate warms slowly, trees and plants will gradually migrate north. For example, most forests could probably cope with warming of 1-3°F over the next century. In contrast, while it is unlikely, warming of 5 to 10°F over the next century would undoubtedly cause great problems.

Not all species are likely to move at the same rate. Thus, even if change occurs relatively slowly, the various mixes of species that occur in the ecosystems of a warmer world might be somewhat different from the mixes of species that make up current ecosystems. Differences in things such as soils and soil microbes may also affect the ease with which different kinds of plants can move. Even if

The effects of climate change on tree growth.

Different species of trees grow best in different climates. Sugar maple trees do not grow in Florida, palm trees do not grow in New Hampshire. If climate changes, the regions in which different tree species occur may shift. The drawing shows estimates based on the results of two different climate models of how the locations where sugar maples can grow might shift in North America.

Region in which sugar maples would grow if carbon dioxide doubles; based on the GFDL climate model.

Region in which sugar maples would grow if carbon dioxide doubles; based on the GISS climate model.

Region in which sugar maples now grow.

Results based on research by Margaret Davis and Catherine Zabinski of the University of Minnesota.

If they have the climate they need, and if they have plenty of water and nutrients, most trees are able to grow better in air that contains more carbon dioxide. The carbon dioxide acts as a fertilizer. However, it is not clear whether, as the amount of carbon dioxide in the atmosphere increases, natural forests will grow more vigorously. This is because natural forests often do not have enough water and nutrients to take advantage of the increased carbon dioxide.

As carbon dioxide levels increase, trees and many other plants may take up more carbon and offset much of the increase. Alternatively, as climate changes, many trees and other plants may die, and as they decay, the carbon they contain may be released to the atmosphere, accelerating the rate of carbon dioxide buildup. Scientists do not know which of these processes will be more important.

Since different plants respond differently both to different climates, and to different levels of carbon dioxide, the mixture of trees and other plant species that occur together may change over time. At a given location, some trees and other plants will find it easier to grow, some will find it harder. Balances may shift in complicated ways. This is particularly true when we add such complicating factors as pests and fire.

4

216

Learning from past climate change.

The earth's climate has changed continually through the past. If we can better understand some of these past changes, we may be better able to anticipate the impacts of possible future changes. The last ice age ended about 13,000 years ago. Studies of pollen in sediments suggest that stands of trees moved slowly north at a speed of between six and thirty miles per decade. The fastest rate recorded is about 125 miles per decade, for spruce moving back into northern Canada about 9000 years ago.

After a period of rapid warming, about 11,000 years ago there was a sudden and quite dramatic cooling which climatologists call the "Younger Dryas" cooling. This may have happened because of sudden changes in ocean circulation, perhaps triggered by fresh water runoff from melting glaciers. Temperatures may have dropped by up to several degrees in just a few years. Pollen in sediments, and other evidence, suggest that large-scale ecological disruptions may have occurred in Europe and North America.

More recently, there has been a smaller and more gradual period of cooling that began in about 1450 and ended in the late 1800s. Historical records suggest that the coolest periods were in the mid and late 1600s, and early and late 1800s. Known as the "little ice age," the beginning of this period of cooler weather and locally expanding glaciers was probably responsible for putting an end to Norse settlements in Greenland.

Dust from volcanos can produce brief periods of cooling. Dust from the 1991 Mt. Pinatubo eruption in the Philippines caused slight cooling for several years. A much more dramatic example is provided by the eruption of Tambora in Indonesia in April of 1815. This was followed by unusually cold temperatures for the next two years, 2 to 4.5°F (1-2.5°C) cooler than normal, and serious crop losses. In New England, 1816 was known as "the year without a summer."

Despite some disruptions such as the Younger Dryas cooling, the little ice age, and the year without a summer, overall the climate during the "interglacial" period since the last ice age has been pretty stable. The previous "interglacial" period may have been less stable. Evidence from ice cores collected in Greenland suggest that the climate may have hopped around between three different states: one similar to today's climate, one several degrees warmer than today's climate, and one several degrees colder than today's climate. Some of these changes occurred in periods of just a few decades. It is unclear if these were global- or hemispheric-scale changes, or just local changes in the vicinity of Greenland. If they were global, future studies may help us understand how rapid changes can occur and how ecosystems respond.

Scientists use a variety of methods to reconstruct past climates. On time-scales of thousands of years, they use both human records as well as tree rings and other direct biological evidence. On time-scales of tens of thousands of years, they use data collected from deep ice cores in arctic and antarctic glaciers. Tiny bubbles of gas trapped in the ice give some information about temperature as do grains of pollen and dust. They can also use data from sediments from stable locations such as the deep ocean. On time-scales of millions of years or more, scientists have to rely on evidence such as fossil remains in rocks.

5

change is slow, some species may become trapped by natural barriers such as mountain ranges or large cities, and be unable to move. Unless humans intervene with preservation efforts, these species could be lost.

People value natural ecosystems partly in terms of what they have gotten used to. For example, many of today's New Englanders place a high value on the maples, birch, and white pines that make up their forests. The assurance that in the future such a forest may be preserved in Quebec or Ontario, while New England acquires a red pine and oak forest like that in the Carolinas, may offer small solace to these people! On the other hand, most of their great great grandchildren may not be aware that any change has occurred, just as today's New Englanders do not recall the deforested landscape of the 1860s.

Can you be more specific about some of the possible effects of climate change?

Because of the many uncertainties, it is not easy to be more specific. However, the paragraphs below provide some details about the topics of disease and health, insects, coral reefs, and mangrove swamps.

Disease and health are always issues of concern. Some scientists have suggested that diseases borne by insects, such as mosquitoes, might become more common in a warmer world, or shift their ranges into populations that do not have as many natural defenses. In a recent review of the available evidence, a scientific workshop conducted by the U.S. Environmental Protection Agency concluded that "...it is not well understood how changes in climates, particularly gradual changes, will affect disease patterns...Without knowing exactly what changes in climate will occur...it is impossible to predict what the impacts will be." Compared to current threats to human health such as viral epidemics and environmental pollution, risks from gradual climate change are likely to be modest.

At extremes of heat or cold, temperature itself can cause health effects such as heat stroke or frostbite. Studies of the patterns of deaths in U.S. cities suggest that the residents of very warm or cold climates take measures to adapt and protect themselves. Thus, it seems unlikely that temperature changes from global warming would have direct health consequences in the U.S.

Insect populations that feed on farms, forests, and natural ecosystems might be affected by climate change. In natural ecosystems, since different plant species would likely migrate at different speeds, and with different levels of success, the mix of pests with which they would have to cope might change significantly.

6

218

Under certain circumstances plants grow more rapidly in the presence of carbon dioxide. How this might interact with pest populations is unclear. On the one hand, more plant mass might mean more food for pests. On the other hand, if the ratio of carbohydrates to other nutrients in plant tissue were to change as a result of growth in a carbon dioxide rich atmosphere, pests might have to eat more in order to get the nutrient material they need to survive. How all these changes might interact and affect overall pest populations, or the levels of destruction they cause, is something that we will not be able to estimate until biological scientists have conducted many more studies.

Coral Reefs, which sustain two-thirds of all marine fish species and support human communities by providing fisheries and storm protection, may be affected in at least three ways. First, corals may "bleach." Corals thrive in a fairly narrow range of water temperatures. If the temperature becomes too high, corals expel the algae which give them their color and supply their food. With their food source gone, the corals stop growing and, if the algae do not become re-established, may die within a few months. In recent years, scientists have observed a number of instances of bleaching, but the causes are uncertain. Whether modest global warming would damage corals through bleaching is unclear. Second, if storms increase in a warmer world, corals may be physically broken up and be unable to re-establish themselves. Wave action is particularly damaging to branching corals. Third, sea level rise may affect corals, but it can be either beneficial or destructive, depending on how much and how rapidly it occurs. Some scientists believe that the rates of sea level rise currently predicted will be "moderately beneficial" to reefs, allowing some to expand their current boundaries while not adversely affecting the others.

Mangrove swamps are found in coastal tide-lands in Florida, India, Australia, Africa, and other subtropical and tropical zones. Mangrove trees grow above the water but have branching roots that are often flooded. They provide protective habitat for a wide variety of species and act as sediment traps, maintaining water quality, and both building up and protecting coastlines from erosion. Many coastal tropical fish are highly dependent on mangrove swamps for nursery, feeding, and spawning grounds.

Already under severe pressure from human activities such as coastal development and water pollution, mangrove ecosystems are further threatened by the sea level rise associated with global warming. The IPCC predicts that global warming would cause sea level to rise just under 2 inches (4.5 cm) per decade. Most mangrove ecosystems can at most tolerate a rise of only about 0.5 inches (1.3 cm) per decade. Furthermore, it would be difficult if not impossible to protect mangrove ecosystems from the rising seas because traditional methods

7

of coastal protection such as sea walls cut off the circulation of nutrients and sea-water necessary for mangrove survival. In a recent survey, the World Wildlife Federation concluded that, because of the impact of human activities, the rate of sea level rise and the very limited options for protection, "the world's mangroves are likely to face severe disruption in the next few decades."

How much might the sea level rise?

Tides and winds move the level of the oceans up and down all the time. "Sea level" refers to the ocean's average level over a long time. In many parts of the world, sea level changes gradually as the coast or the ocean floor rises or falls due to natural geological changes or human actions such as pumping large amounts of oil out of the ground. In addition to these often large local changes, over the past century the average sea level has been rising at a rate of between 0.4 to 0.8 inches (.5 to 1 cm) per decade. Scientists are uncertain why this is occurring. There is no persuasive evidence that the rate of rise has increased in recent years.

If the climate becomes warmer, the oceans will warm. As water warms, it expands slightly. Thus, in addition to the local variations that now occur in sea level, global warming might cause a general increase in sea level all around the world. As Part 2 of the main brochure explains, scientists estimate that a warming of 3.5°F (2°C), which will probably not occur before about 2075, will cause sea level to rise between 8 and 30 inches (30-76 cm).

If warming were to continue long enough, and become large enough, mountain glaciers and polar ice caps might melt. This could release large amounts of additional water into the oceans and result in significantly greater sea level rise. This is unlikely to occur any sooner than 150 years from now. Nor is it clear that if warming continues, glaciers will melt. A somewhat warmer climate causes more precipitation. In polar regions, this means more snow. Modest warming could actually work to build glaciers and slow or even reverse sea level rise.

What might happen if sea level rises?

If global warming were to cause sea level to rise a couple of feet over the next century, two types of problems would result: permanent flooding of very low lying areas, and increased storm damage. Permanent flooding could pose problems for certain coastal ecosystems, for highly vulnerable cities such as Venice, and for some coastal drinking water supplies. However, the larger problems are likely to come with storms. When storm winds blow onto shore they cause water to "pile up." If the sea level rises, the amount of this "storm surge" may increase, with the

8

220

result that coastal ecosystems may be flooded more often, some beaches may be eroded more rapidly, and building and other structures along the coast may suffer greater and more frequent damage. The box below presents a case study of this problem for Ocean City, Maryland.

Developed countries like the U.S., and even low lying developed countries like the Netherlands, can use a combination of land use laws, and technologies such as dikes and storm surge barriers to minimize damage. In contrast, heavily populated coastal areas in developing countries such as Bangladesh might suffer enormous losses of life and property.

In the long run, if sea level continued to rise, even developed countries might begin to experience serious costs. Many of the world's biggest cities are in low lying coastal locations. If, as seems likely, these cities respond to sea level rise by building dikes, rather than by gradually relocating, the result over hundreds of years could be that a growing proportion of the world's population would live in locations below sea level that are vulnerable to sudden catastrophic floods.

A case study of the impacts of rising sea level.

Ocean City, Maryland is a beach resort located on Fenwick Island, a long thin barrier island half a mile off the Maryland coast. In the center of town, on the ocean-side of the island, there is a boardwalk that runs north-south along the wide sandy beach with hotels, restaurants and gift shops. Along the bay-side of the island there are sheltered marinas and private residences. There are also private beach-front residences both to the north and south of the central strip. As of today, the annual economic benefit from recreational activity in Ocean City is estimated to be $28 million per year.

Even without climate change the beach gets washed away by storms. On several occasions, the U.S. Army Corps of Engineers has had to dredge sand from offshore to rebuild the beach. Occasionally, large storms also cause property damage through wave action and flooding. Without any sea level rise, over the next fifty years, it is expected that the property losses from these storms will average about $7 million per year. We say "average" because in some years there will be no losses, and in other years, large losses.

Over the next 100 years scientists estimate that sea level at Ocean City may rise between 4 and 35 inches (10-90 cm). If this happens, and if storm patterns remain unchanged, computer studies conducted by Anand Patwardhan at Carnegie Mellon University, suggest that the *additional* property losses due to storms will range between $0.5 and $2 million per year. In addition, he estimates that the economic losses due to impacts on recreational use will average between $2 and $5 million per year. If, as some scientists predict, climate change produces more frequent or more intense storms, these costs would probably rise.

Ocean City might reduce these costs by moving or abandoning structures, or by building bulkheads. However, Dr. Patwardhan's studies find that for reasonable planning assumptions (discount rates of less than 10%), the best strategy is to continue the practice of rebuilding the beach with sand from offshore.

9

Details Booklet Part 3:

More on
"What can be done about
climate change?"

This details booklet provides additional information for people who would like to learn more about the subject of "Part 3: What can be done about climate change?" of the brochure "Global Warming and Climate Change." This booklet does not repeat many of the key points made in Part 3, so it would be best if you read Part 3 of the main brochure first.

Table of Contents

Who is the "decision maker" on the issue of climate change?

There is no single decision maker who is responsible for either the choices that are likely to lead to climate change, or for the actions that people might take to respond to change. At the international level many countries add greenhouse gases to the atmosphere. Today's top emitters of carbon dioxide are:

Country	% of current human carbon dioxide emissions.	% of world's population.	Annual metric tons of carbon dioxide per person.
United States	22.0	5.0	20.0
Former Soviet Union	18.0	6.0	13.5
People's Republic of China	10.0	22.0	2.3
Germany	4.6	1.5	14.0
Japan	4.5	2.5	8.5
India	2.7	17.0	.8
United Kingdom	2.5	1.0	10.0

Data are for 1988 and are drawn from "Trends '90: a compendium of data on global change," Carbon Dioxide Information Analysis Center, Oak Ridge National Laboratory, 1990.

In the future, emissions from a number of developing countries such as China and India are likely to rise dramatically as these countries follow the example set by the developed countries and burn large amounts of coal and oil in order to raise their people's standards of living. The effect will be further amplified if the population in these countries continues to grow.

Any serious effort to control the future emissions of carbon dioxide and other greenhouse gases will require international cooperation.

In order to protect the ozone layer, an agreement to phase out most uses of CFCs was reached in 1987. In many ways, this agreement was much easier than the kinds of agreements that will be needed to control carbon dioxide emissions to slow climate change. CFCs play a key role in only a few parts of the economy. It has been relatively easy to develop affordable substitutes. The "world environment summit" held in Rio de Janeiro, Brazil in 1992 reached a much looser agreement on carbon dioxide and other greenhouse gases. Nations pledged to work to reduce their emissions. While the wording is vague, and there are no legally binding obligations, there is now an international framework for monitoring and reviewing progress towards reducing emissions.

1

The burning of coal and oil, which is the principle source of carbon dioxide, underlies almost all economic activities. So far, abundant low cost alternative sources of energy have not been identified. Developed countries could probably afford to reduce their energy consumption, and invest in more energy efficient technologies. Without help in such forms as economic assistance and technology transfer, developing countries may find the cost of such changes unacceptable. After all, in the name of some very general long term "common good" they are being asked to give up on some of the very real short-term economic benefits that their citizens will experience through development.

For this reason, many developing countries argue that the developed countries should take the lead and contribute the most to reducing emissions of green-house gases.

The same situation of "many decision makers" applies on the response side of the climate problem. Residents and regional managers in areas such as the low lying coastal resort of Hilton Head, South Carolina are likely to have very different views about climate change from the residents and regional managers of a city such as Fairbanks, Alaska. Wealthy Sierra Club members in Boulder, Colorado are likely to have very different views from the impoverished members of a rural economic development cooperative in central China as they struggle to build a stronger economy.

In short, the problem of climate change is not a single problem. It is a multitude of problems that will be faced by many different groups with different needs and different concerns. At the end of this details booklet we will elaborate on these issues. First, however, we need to explore some of the specific things that might be done.

2

What impact might specific policy options have? How much might they cost?

As we explained in Part 3 of the main brochure, there are three broad policy options for dealing with the climate problem. These are: abatement, adaptation, and geo-engineering. The next five pages explore these options in somewhat more detail and consider how effective they may be and how much they may cost. Of course, a number of other considerations will play an important role in determining the options a country, state or business chooses, including whether the policies are acceptable to the public, whether they are fair, and whether they are more important than other goals society might have. These considerations can be very important, but they are basically a matter of a choice among different values. There is no single right answer to such choices. Economists and engineers are still somewhat uncertain about how effective some policies might be and what they would cost, but rough estimates are possible. In the discussion that follows, we will focus only on how much each option can reduce U.S. carbon dioxide emissions and how much it will cost. We leave it to you to consider the other value choices each option involves.

Abatement options are strategies that reduce emissions. We will consider three kinds, improved energy efficiency, use of cleaner energy sources, and changes in agriculture and forestry.

Improving energy efficiency will reduce emissions of carbon dioxide, the most significant greenhouse gas. If it is pursued wisely, it should also improve economic performance. Here are examples of three strategies that the U.S. might pursue to improve its energy efficiency:

> *Reduce energy use in buildings.* About 1/3 of all the energy used in the U.S., and 2/3 of all the electricity, goes into buildings. Most goes to heating, cooling and lighting. Researchers estimate that with improved insulation, glazing, weather-stripping, furnaces and air conditioners, and lighting in residential and commercial buildings, U.S. carbon dioxide emissions could be reduced by about 360 million tons per year, about 5% of total U.S. emissions. They also estimate that such changes would lead to reduced energy use, and actually save money, between $25 and $75 per ton of carbon dioxide saved.

> *Improve fuel efficiency of new cars.* Currently the average mileage obtained by new cars in the U.S. is 27.5 mpg. If this were raised to 32.5 mpg, and held there, over time, U.S. emissions would decline by about 250 million tons per year, about 4% of U.S. emissions. Estimates of the costs of such a program range from a savings of $76 per ton of carbon dioxide removed to a cost of $16 per ton of carbon dioxide. The savings result if the reduced fuel cost outweighs other cost increases.

> *Make appliances more efficient.* Currently available technology allows refrigerators, dishwashers, water heaters and other home appliances to be substantially more efficient than they are. If this

3

coal

0.9 lbs of carbon dioxide

1 kilowatt hour of energy

What is energy efficiency?

When we drive a car chemical energy stored in gasoline is converted into mechanical energy and used to create motion. When we use an electric stove, a power plant first converts chemical energy stored in coal to electrical energy which is carried through the electrical system. Then the stove converts it to heat energy. The proportion of the original energy which ends up being used for the final purpose (motion, cooking) measures the *energy efficiency*. Nature sets some basic limits on how efficiently energy can be used, but in most cases our products and manufacturing processes are still a long way from operating at this theoretical limit.

Why does energy efficiency matter?

If we can make things like cars and appliances do their job just as well while using less energy, then we do not need to burn as much coal and oil. Burning fossil fuels like coal and oil produces carbon dioxide. Increasing the energy efficiency in transportation, homes, offices, and factories is the best way we have to reduce carbon dioxide emissions without lowering our standard of living.

technology were used in place of older, less efficient technology, the U.S. could reduce carbon dioxide emissions by about 75 million tons per year (1.3% of U.S. emissions) while at the same time saving $35 to $44 per ton.

Replacing coal, oil and gasoline with cleaner energy sources and technologies would reduce carbon dioxide emissions and improve efficiency. The main issue for this strategy is whether there are enough abundant, low cost alternatives to coal, oil, and gasoline.

Instead of gasoline, use ethanol, hydrogen or electricity in cars and trucks. Technology currently exists to allow cars to run on these and other alternative fuels. Ethanol is a kind of alcohol made from corn. If ethanol were made from sustainable agriculture, or if hydrogen or electricity were generated by renewable means, converting all vehicles would eventually reduce carbon dioxide emissions by over 1000 million tons per year (17% of U.S. emissions). However, the technology for some alternative fuel options (i.e., electric and hydrogen powered cars) is presently too expensive to be widely adopted by consumers, and researchers do not know whether farmers can produce enough corn for ethanol to replace gasoline. Such changes would cost between $50 and $177 per ton of carbon dioxide saved.

Switch 10% of building electricity use from electric resistance heat to natural gas heating. Natural gas, whether it is used to warm rooms or heat water, is more efficient than electric heat. As a result, it

4

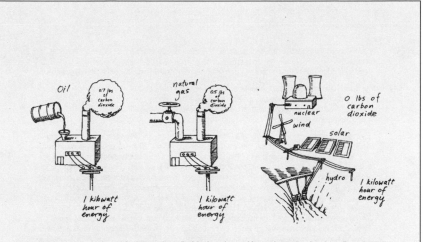

is also cheaper and releases far less carbon dioxide than the coal burned to make electricity. By switching only 10% of commercial and residential electricity use to natural gas heating systems, U.S. carbon dioxide emissions could be reduced by about 75 million tons per year (1.3% of U.S. emissions) at an estimated savings of $90 per ton.

Replace all existing coal and oil fired electric power plants with new high efficiency plants that use natural gas. The combustion of natural gas emits less carbon dioxide than the combustion of coal. If all existing coal and oil power plants were replaced by modern high efficiency natural gas systems, the U.S. would reduce its greenhouse gas emissions about 1000 million tons per year (17% of U.S. emissions). Some scientists doubt that there is enough natural gas to make this possible. The cost of such a plan, though uncertain, is estimated between $0 and $177 per ton of carbon dioxide.

Replace half of the existing oil and coal fired power plants with solar power plants. The amount of solar energy reaching the earth's surface each year is enormous, thousands of times greater than worldwide annual fossil fuel use. While costs are still high, technology currently exists to use this solar energy to provide electricity, light, heat, and steam for buildings and industry. If it were used wherever possible, it could reduce greenhouse gas emissions by about 1000 million tons per year (17% of U.S. emissions). However, substantial progress is necessary before solar technology is affordable as a basic source of electricity. The cost of reducing emissions through this program is estimated to be between $76 to $177 per ton of carbon dioxide.

Where possible, replace all fossil fuel plants with nuclear power plants. Nuclear power currently provides about 7% of electricity in the U.S., but concerns over the safety, cost, and environmental impacts of nuclear energy have halted development. Improvements in nuclear power might allow it to be considered as an

5

option for reducing carbon dioxide emissions. If nuclear power were widely adopted in the U.S., the reduction in carbon dioxide emissions could reach as high as 1500 million tons per year (25% of U.S. emissions). Estimates of the cost of this policy range from $0 to $51 per ton of carbon dioxide saved.

Agriculture, deforestation and other human activities are also responsible for significant quantities of greenhouse gas emissions. Reductions can be achieved through improved waste management, altered use and formulation of fertilizers, and changes in land use.

Establish an international "forestry fund" to prevent deforestation. Deforestation in the developing world accounts for over 20% of the man-made greenhouse effect. The U.S. can play a role in policies to limit deforestation. Because deforestation is due largely to population and economic pressures, tropical rain forests will be preserved only if they have more value standing than cut down. One idea is an international "forestry fund," an endowment, funded by the developed world, which places $80 per acre ($200 per hectare) of protected forest into an investment account. The interest from the account is given to people living near or in the protected forests, to help them develop sustainable forestry practices, and to support them during the transition away from "slash and burn" agriculture. Residents would receive the interest as long as they practiced sustainable forestry. Fully implemented, the program could reduce global carbon dioxide emissions by 7000 million tons annually, at a cost of about $0.40 per ton of carbon dioxide saved.

Reduce methane emissions by improving waste management practices and changing agricultural techniques. Though it accounts for only a small share of the man-made greenhouse effect, methane is a powerful greenhouse gas. Emissions come from rice paddies, cows and other "ruminant" animals, and from decomposing waste. Emissions can be reduced by cultivating fast-growing rice or high-density paddies, by placing ruminant animals on diets that reduce the amount of methane they emit as a byproduct of digestion, and by handling plant and animal wastes in a manner that reduces the amount of methane produced as they decompose. Such actions could reduce greenhouse gas emissions by over 200 million tons of carbon dioxide equivalent per year, at a cost of $0 to $5 per ton.

Adaptation options are actions taken to minimize the global environment's impact on humans.

Relocation of people, agriculture and industry is one way to adapt to the changes in temperature, sea level and water distribution that might result from climate change. For example, state and federal governments often subsidize the rebuilding of homes and replenishment of beaches in areas that have experienced severe storms or floods. If sea level rise makes devastating storms and floods more common in certain regions, government could use these subsidies to help people relocate to less vulnerable areas, instead of rebuilding in the same spot. Banks and insurance companies may begin to influence building choices if they believe climate change may affect the properties they finance or insure. In the U.S. people migrate all the time for a variety of reasons. For this reason, it is difficult to say which portion of the costs of relocation should be assigned to climate change.

Improving irrigation and developing new crop strains would allow agriculture to adapt to moderate climate change. The efficiency of irrigation systems improved 35% between 1950 and 1980, and some researchers believe efficiency can be improved substantially more by making some relatively cheap changes to existing technology. As for crops, state, federal, and private labs today cultivate and test thousands of strains of agricultural plants. There are, for example, about 450 different strains of corn in commercial use. The costs of adapting to modest climate change would probably be a few percent or less of the overall costs of agriculture. Maintaining funding for research on crop varieties is a good way to prepare for the possible impacts of global warming on agriculture.

Migration corridors for plants and animals in the natural environment might help the re-establishment of ecosystems in new locations as a response to climate change. As discussed in Details Booklet Part 2, gradual change would allow many natural ecosystems to migrate with the climate. However, natural migration of ecosystems can be blocked by human development, such as cities, highways, and farms. One way to help these ecosystems adapt to global warming might be to provide them with "corridors" of undeveloped land through which ecosystems can migrate as necessary. The costs are uncertain partly because such corridors might have other "open space" benefits and partly because it is unclear how many would be needed to be effective.

Geo-engineering options are potentially powerful, but as yet untested, ways either to stop the accumulation of carbon dioxide in the atmosphere, or to counteract its effects on our climate.

Global reforestation programs could be designed to plant large numbers of trees to extract carbon dioxide and store it. A global reforestation program could remove 250 million tons of carbon dioxide per year (4% of U.S. emissions) at a cost of $3 to $10 per ton.

Almost everyone thinks planting trees is a good idea. However, because there may be unintended side effects, many people are strongly opposed to other forms of geo-engineering. At the same time, because they may be cheap, and can be done "once we're in trouble," there will probably be some strong supporters of other geo-engineering strategies if serious warming occurs.

Adding iron to fertilize the ocean may cause phytoplankton in the top layers of the ocean to absorb more carbon dioxide. While not all scientists agree that this strategy is safe, and recent tests in the ocean suggest it might not work, the absorption potential is very large, from 600 million to as high as 3000 million tons of carbon dioxide per year (10% to 50% of U.S. emissions). If it turns out to be a safe, viable option, it would probably cost somewhere between 10¢ and $15 dollars per ton of carbon dioxide removed.

Screen out sunlight to counteract the effects of increased concentrations of greenhouse gases. Either large thin screens in low orbit or small particles of dust placed very high in the atmosphere could be used to reduce the amount of sunlight striking the earth. Thus, as the earth's atmosphere trapped more heat, less heat energy would be put into the earth's system by the sun, maintaining basically the same temperature. While untested, this strategy has the potential to counteract the warming effect of large amounts of carbon dioxide, at a cost of between 3¢ and $2.5 dollars per ton of carbon dioxide.

7

How can people decide for themselves what should be done about climate change?

The climate problem affects everyone, and everyone has a stake in deciding what should be done. It is for you to decide what actions you should take as an individual (in your home, your car, and so forth). Equally important, as a citizen you must decide which policies to support or oppose. It may be tempting to decide that the climate problem is just too complicated to deal with. Without telling you *what* to choose, we can offer some advice on how to organize the choices and make decisions.

We will simplify the problem by reducing it to a choice between three broad policy alternatives:

POLICY 1: *no abatement*;

POLICY 2: *moderate abatement*;

POLICY 3: *stringent abatement*.

First, we will discuss the goal of each of these policies. Then we will suggest some of the factors that might be important to you in making a choice. Finally, we will give examples of the sorts of people who might choose each one.

As its name suggests, the *no abatement* policy takes no immediate action on climate change or greenhouse gas emissions. Proponents of this policy may view the science of global warming as too uncertain to justify action, may believe that the impacts of global warming will be very small, or may think that abatement actions are too expensive.

The goal of *moderate abatement* is to slow greenhouse gas emissions and give society more time to solve the problem. One version of this policy would commit every economically developed nation to reduce greenhouse gas emissions to 20% below 1988 levels per dollar of gross domestic product (GDP) by the year 2000. Because this emissions limit is stated in terms of GDP, total emissions could still grow as the population or economy expands. Moderate abatement would not prevent climate change. But, if all the world did it, it would reduce the impacts of climate change by about 25% by the middle of the next century.

Stringent abatement is the most ambitious climate change policy. By reducing total greenhouse gas emissions worldwide to 60% below 1988 levels and holding them there permanently, it aims to prevent climate change altogether. Unlike moderate abatement, which allows emissions to rise as the economy grows, moderate abatement does not allow any emissions growth beyond 60% below 1988 levels. Thus, in order for the world economy to grow and for living standards to rise in the developing world, ever more innovative ways to prevent

8

emissions from growing would have to be found. If all the world did it, stringent abatement would prevent global climate change.

Suppose you or a friend wants to decide which of these three policies to support. Your decision should depend on at least two considerations:

1. *What do you think the impacts of climate change are likely to be?* That is, how much do you think climate will change, and what impact do you believe that change will have on the things you care about? Again to make things simple, assume that there are only three possible beliefs about the impacts of climate change: it can be *not bad, moderately bad,* or *very bad.* Of course your judgment not only depends on what you believe about climate change, but also on what you value. For example, two people might agree that climate change will destroy many of the world's most sensitive ecosystems, but disagree about how much they value those ecosystems. These people would rate the impact of climate change differently. The person who values them highly will probably rate the impacts of climate change as *moderately bad* or *very bad.* The other person, who is perhaps mainly concerned with the economic impacts of climate change and doesn't think sensitive ecosystems are of great importance, might rate the impact of climate change as *not bad.* In short, how you rate the impacts of climate change depends on what you value.

2. *How much do you think abatement will cost?* Again, for the sake of simplicity assume that there are only three possible beliefs about the cost of abatement: *low, medium,* or *high.* Unlike the case above, where we were dealing with values which are very difficult, if not impossible, to measure in dollars, here we are dealing with costs that can be quantified. By *low cost* we mean that moderate abatement can be achieved in the U.S. at a net *savings* of $50 billion per year (because the energy conservation involved would save money), while stringent abatement would cost about $250 billion per year (or about $1000 per person per year). By *medium cost* we mean that moderate abatement will cost nothing in the long-term, while stringent abatement will cost about $500 billion per year. By *high cost* we mean that moderate abatement will cost about $60 billion per year, while stringent abatement would cost as much as $3 trillion per year (about 60% of GDP).

By combining your beliefs about these two considerations, you or a friend can come to a general conclusion about which abatement strategy to support.

To show how this might work, consider three friends named Ann, Sue, and Pat. Like you, each of these imaginary citizens must consider the two questions outlined above: (1) "What do you think the impacts of climate change are likely to be?" and (2) "How much do you think abatement measures will cost?" The two pages that follow give a summary of their positions.

9

233

ANN

SUE

Beliefs: She thinks climate change is a possibility, but isn't convinced it will occur. If climate change does occur, she believes it may damage the environment to some extent, but have only minor effects on the economy.

Values: She cares about the environment, but cares more about the economy and impacts on people's incomes and jobs.

How Ann reasons: Using the terms discussed above, Ann concludes that the impacts of climate change will be *not bad*. She acknowledges that there may be some environmental impact, but is concerned only if the environmental impact is really serious. It's the economy she cares about, and she thinks that won't suffer much. That's why she rates the impacts of climate change *not bad*.

As a result, the policy she chooses will depend on how she assesses their costs. If she expects abatement costs to be *low* or *medium*, she will support moderate abatement because this will either result in a net savings or have no cost.

On the other hand, if she expects abatement costs to be *high*, she will support the "no abatement" policy at least until environmental harm is shown to be important. This is because she cares more about the economy than the environment and does not want to spend a lot of money to reduce what she judges to be small and perhaps unlikely environmental damage.

Beliefs: She thinks climate change is very likely and believes the environmental consequences would be disastrous.

Values: She cares a great deal about the environment, and much less about the economy.

How Sue reasons: Sue thinks that the accumulation of greenhouse gases in the atmosphere will cause a great deal of environmental damage. She also thinks global warming is very likely to come about unless we dramatically reduce greenhouse gas emissions. Because she cares so much about protecting the environment, she rates the impacts of global warming as *very bad*. She would do this even if she believed the economic impacts would be *high*. Therefore, her top priority is preventing climate change altogether, not just slowing climate change with the policy of moderate abatement. If abatement costs are *low* or *medium*, she'll favor the "stringent abatement" policy. She is optimistic about the costs of energy efficiency and new energy technologies and doesn't believe that abatement costs will be *high*, but if she did, she would probably still favor stringent abatement.

10

PAT

Beliefs: She is uncertain about the possibility of climate change and worried about the unlikely but catastrophic consequences.

Values: She wants to avoid huge impacts on both the environment and the economy.

How Pat reasons: Pat rates the impacts of climate change as *moderate*. Neither the environment nor the economy is more important to her, and she wants to protect both against large losses.

If she thinks abatement costs will be *low*, she supports "stringent abatement." She reasons that $250 billion is a reasonable price for the U.S. to pay to completely prevent global warming.

If she expects abatement costs to be *moderate*, she supports moderate abatement. At *moderate* cost, stringent abatement costs $500 billion, which she thinks is too expensive given the uncertainties associated with the issue. Moderate abatement, which under this scenario costs nothing in the long-term, seems reasonable to her because it provides protection against the most catastrophic consequences of global warming.

If she believes abatement costs are *high*, she supports the "no abatement" policy. Under the *high* cost scenario, stringent abatement costs $3 trillion, enough to cripple the economy. "Moderate abatement" under this high cost scenario is a lot cheaper, only $60 billion, but it also provides a lot less protection. In Pat's opinion, too little protection for the money.

While these examples are for the U.S., they assume that the rest of the world does the same thing. Readers who would like to see the more detailed technical analysis on which these examples are based, are referred to: L.B. Lave and H. Dowlatabadi, "Climate Change: The effects of personal beliefs and scientific uncertainty," *Environmental Science & Technology*, Vol. 27, No. 10, pp. 1962-1972, 1993.

11

235

Glossary

aerosols: Extremely small particles of liquid or dust in the atmosphere. Burning coal releases sulfur dioxide which in the atmosphere is transformed into sulfate aerosols. One geo-engineering strategy would put more aerosols into the atmosphere to reflect sunlight back to space.

afforestation: Establishing new forests on unforested land. *Afforresting* large areas of land so that trees will absorb and store carbon from the atmosphere could slow carbon dioxide buildup.

albedo: The fraction of sunlight that is reflected by earth, ice, and clouds back into space. The value for today's earth is about one-third (i.e., two-thirds of the sunlight is absorbed).

biodiversity: The number of different kinds of plant and animal species that live in a region. On land, tropical rain forests have the highest biodiversity.

biomass: The amount of living matter in a particular region, usually expressed as weight (mass) per unit area (e.g., tons per acre).

carbon cycle: The processes by which carbon is cycled through the environment. Carbon, in the form of carbon dioxide, is absorbed from the atmosphere and used by plants in the process of photosynthesis to store energy. Plants and animals then return carbon dioxide to the atmosphere through respiration when they consume this energy. On a *much* longer time-scale, carbon is also cycled into and out of rocks.

carbon dioxide: A gas made up of two atoms of carbon and one atom of oxygen which is produced whenever carbon-based fuels are burned (or oxidized more slowly in plants and animals). Carbon dioxide is the most important "greenhouse gas" which may cause climate change. Human sources of carbon dioxide include burning fossil fuels for electricity, transportation, heating, cooling, and manufacturing. Burning trees in the process of deforestation also produces carbon dioxide. Abbreviated CO_2.

chlorofluorocarbons: A family of greenhouse gases used in air conditioning, as industrial solvents and in other commercial applications. Abbreviated CFCs. CFCs destroy ozone in the stratosphere (see ozone). CFCs were once widely used in spray cans but in the U.S. this use has now been banned. Other uses are also being eliminated under an international agreement negotiated in Montreal in 1987.

climate: The average pattern of weather in a place. While weather may change substantially from day-to-day, when changes in climate occur, they usually happen gradually over many years.

deforestation: Cutting most or all of the trees in a forested area. Deforestation contributes to warming by releasing carbon dioxide, changing the albedo (amount of sunlight reflected from the surface) and reducing the amount of carbon dioxide taken out of the atmosphere by trees. Today, deforestation may contribute about 20% of possible warming.

discount rate: A measure of how cost and benefits that will happen in the future compare to cost and benefits today.

energy intensity: The amount of energy used by an appliance or an industry to produce a product or service. For example, a fluorescent light requires only 20 watts to produce the same amount of light as a regular 100 watt light bulb, so its energy intensity is 5 times lower. Reducing energy intensity is one way to increase energy efficiency and emit less carbon dioxide.

feedback: The mechanism by which changes in one part of the earth-atmosphere system affect future changes in other parts of that system. Feedbacks come in two kinds. In climate change, negative feedbacks work to slow down or offset warming while positive feedbacks work to speed up or amplify warming.

fossil fuel: Coal, oil (from which gasoline is make), and natural gas are called *fossil* fuels

12

because the chemical energy they contained is left over from plants and animals that lived long ago.

greenhouse effect: The process by which energy from the sun is trapped under the atmosphere to cause warming. Light energy can easily pass in through the atmosphere. Once some of this light is absorbed by dark surfaces, the resulting heat energy has greater difficulty getting back out. Through the naturally occurring greenhouse effect, water vapor, ozone and carbon dioxide have kept temperatures on the earth moderate for several billions years. Today, people are adding more gases which might increase the temperature.

greenhouse gas: Any gas in the atmosphere that contributes to the greenhouse effect. These include carbon dioxide, methane, ozone, nitrous oxide, CFCs, and water vapor. Most occur naturally as well as being created by people.

methane: A greenhouse gas consisting of one molecule of carbon and four molecules of hydrogen. Pound-for-pound it produces between 5 to 10 times more warming than carbon dioxide. Methane is produced naturally from rotting organic matter. Human sources of methane include agricultural activities such as growing rice and raising live stock, land-fills, coal mines, and natural gas systems. Abbreviated CH_4.

Montreal protocol: An international treaty signed in 1987 that limits production of chlorofluorocarbons.

natural gas: Gas obtained from wells used as a fuel. While it contains many chemicals the principle component of natural gas is methane.

nitrous oxide: A greenhouse gas consisting of two molecules of nitrogen and one molecule of oxygen. Pound-for-pound it produces about 300 times more warming than carbon dioxide. Nitrous oxide is created when fuels are burned and is also released during the use of nitrogen-based crop fertilizers. Abbreviated N_2O.

ozone: An unstable gas in which three molecules of oxygen occur together. Ozone is a greenhouse gas.

In the atmosphere ozone occurs at two different altitudes. Low altitude *tropospheric ozone* is a form of air pollution (part of smog) produced by the emissions from cars and trucks. High in the atmosphere a thin layer of *stratospheric ozone* is naturally created by sunlight. This ozone layer shields the earth from dangerous (cancer-causing) ultraviolet radiation from the sun. Chlorine gas from chlorofluorocarbons speeds the breakdown of ozone in the ozone layer. While important, this is largely a different problem from the problem of global warming. Abbreviated O_3.

sea level rise: An increase in the average level of the ocean caused by expansion when water is warmed and by addition of more water when ice caps melt.

sequester: To remove or segregate. Scientists sometimes say that activities, such as planting trees, which remove carbon dioxide from the atmosphere, *sequester* carbon dioxide.

sink: A place where material is removed or stored. For example, the oceans absorb about 50% of the carbon dioxide released into the atmosphere. Scientists refer to the oceans as a carbon dioxide *sink*.

stratosphere: The upper part of the earth's atmosphere, above about seven miles.

sustainable development: Economic activities which can meet the needs of the present without compromising the ability of future generations to meet their own needs.

troposphere: The lower portion of the atmosphere in which we live.

weather: The condition of the atmosphere at a particular place and time measured in terms in wind, temperature, humidity, atmospheric pressure, and precipitation (rain, snow, etc.). In most places, weather can change from hour-to-hour, day-to-day, and season-to-season.

How to learn more.

For a comprehensive summary of the issues discussed in these brochures, see:

• U.S. Congress, Office of Technology Assessment, *Changing by Degrees: Steps to Reduce Greenhouse Gases*, OTA-O-482 (Washington, DC: U.S. Government Printing Office, 1991).

• *Policy Implications of Greenhouse Warming – Mitigation, Adaptation and the Science Base*, National Academy of Sciences, National Academy Press, Washington, DC, 1992.

For a summary of the basic science of global climate change written by an international committee of leading scientists, see:

• *Climate Change: The IPCC Scientific Assessment*, J.T. Houghton, G.J. Jenkins, J.J. Ephraums, eds., Cambridge University Press, 1990.

• *Climate Change 1992: The IPCC Supplementary Report*, J.T. Houghton, B.A. Callander and S.K. Varney, eds., Cambridge University Press, 1992.

For a semi-technical discussion of warming, alternative energy, and environmental policy-making, see:

• "Managing Planet Earth," A special issue of *Scientific American*, September 1989.

For a guide on what you can do to save energy, and thus produce less carbon dioxide, see:

• A. Wilson and J. Morrill, *Consumer Guide to Home Energy Savings*, American Council for an Energy-Efficient Economy, 2140 Shattuck Ave, No. 202, Berkeley, CA 94704.

238

APPENDIX B

Reproduction of the risk communication brochure *Fields from Electric Power*. In its original form, the three details booklets reproduced at the back of this appendix are housed in pull-out pouches at the back of Parts 1, 2, and 3 of the main brochure. The general structure of the brochure is shown in Figure B.1. Copies of the original version may be purchased at cost through the Department of Engineering and Public Policy, Carnegie Mellon University.

Figure B.1. Brochure on fields from electric power.

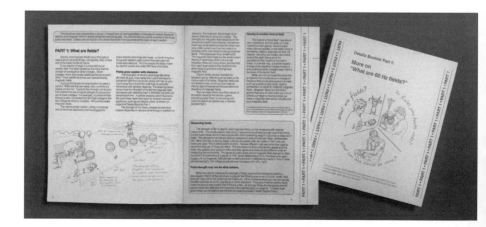

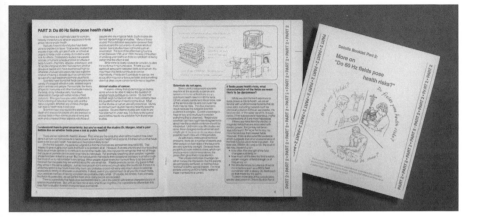

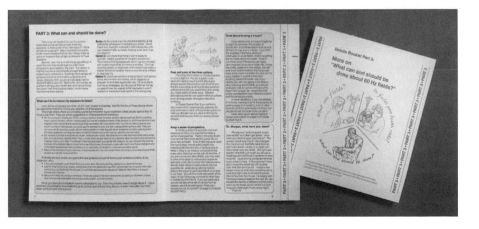

Fields from Electric Power

What are they?
What do we know about possible health risks?
What can be done?

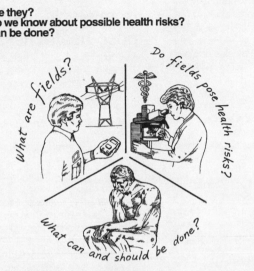

While the evidence is ambiguous, there is some reason to suspect that exposure to the electric and magnetic fields associated with electric power may pose risks to public health. This set of brochures is designed to give you the basic facts you need to understand this issue. The first two pages give a quick overview. Then, the key points are discussed in three sections:

    PART 1: What are fields?
    PART 2: Do 60 Hz fields pose health risks?
    PART 3: What can and should be done?

Additional important details can be found in the "Details Booklets" in the pouches at the end of each section. A glossary is available at the back of Details Booklet Part 3. Information about the author can be found on the back cover of this brochure.

Department of Engineering and Public Policy
Carnegie Mellon University
Pittsburgh, PA 15213

243

The issue at a glance...

Part 1: What are power-frequency fields?

- Like gravity, electric and magnetic fields involve one of the basic forces of nature. They are found almost everywhere. A particular kind of electric and magnetic field, called a power-frequency, or 60 Hertz (Hz) field, is produced by electric power systems, wiring in buildings, and appliances.
- Electric fields are produced by electric charges. More charge means higher voltage and a stronger electric field. Magnetic fields are produced by moving charges called currents. More current means a stronger magnetic field.
- Just like the heat from a camp fire, or the light from a candle, the strength of most electric and magnetic fields decreases rapidly as you move away from their source. For example, while a power line may make a strong field on the ground directly beneath the wire, a few hundred feet away the field is usually very weak.

Part 2: Do fields from electric power pose health risks?

- There have been a number of experiments with cells, animals and people which indicate that power-frequency fields can produce biological changes. It is not clear whether these changes can cause health risks.
- A number of studies of the patterns of cancer in people who live near unusual field sources show a statistical association between field exposure and a small increase in the amount of cancer. These studies raise concern, but do not prove that fields cause cancer.
- In summary, *nobody knows whether exposure to fields causes health risks but there is some basis for concern.* It could be several more years before scientific research will give clearer answers.

> These brochures are about fields from electric power. They do not address radio-frequency fields such as those produced by radio stations, mobile telephones, and some electronic equipment. While some of the issues are similar, in several fundamental ways, radio-frequency fields are different from power-frequency fields.

1

244

Part 3: What can and should be done?

- There is no scientific answer to the question, "What should we do?" The answer depends on your values, and your beliefs about how you and society should spend limited resources, time and attention.
- Basically individuals and society face a choice among three options:
  1. Some people argue that until we know more we should do nothing. They say that there are plenty of risks we *do* know about and we should spend our scarce money and attention on reducing *those* risks.
  2. Some people say that, even if we cannot be sure there is a risk, prudence suggests we should start getting people out of fields when we can do this with little cost or inconvenience.
  3. Some people say we should start major programs to reduce exposures to power-frequency fields now. These programs could be very expensive and might not end up reducing risk.

Common misunderstandings about fields:

- **Misunderstanding:** *Any power line you can see exposes you to fields.*
  Fact: *Fields are fairly closely confined to the vicinity of most lines.*
  The strength of fields decreases rapidly as you move away from lines. Once you are at a distance of several hundred feet, the fields from even very large lines have dropped to very low levels.

- **Misunderstanding:** *If there is a public health problem with fields, stronger fields will certainly be more dangerous.*
  Fact: *If there is a risk, the strength of the field may be what is most important, but it is also possible that other features of the field, such as its time pattern or how rapidly it changes, may be what matter.*
  Because of experience with chemical pollution, we are used to thinking that "if it's bad, more is worse." However, there is significant evidence from laboratory studies with cells and animals that suggests that other aspects of the field may be important.

- **Misunderstanding:** *If there is a public health problem with fields, high voltage transmission lines will pose the greatest risk.*
  Fact: *If there is a public health problem with fields, power lines in the streets, building wiring, and appliances may pose the greatest risk.*
  While high voltage transmission lines make strong steady 60 Hz fields, few people are close enough to them to be exposed. On the other hand, building wiring and appliances can produce strong, often fluctuating, fields to which many people are exposed.

- **Misunderstanding:** *A statistical association between field exposure and cancer is pretty clear evidence that fields contribute to cancer.*
  Fact: *A statistical association may mean there is a cause and effect relationship, but this is not always true.*
  The best explanation is an example. The number of storks in Europe has been decreasing. The number of children born in Europe has also been decreasing. Thus, there is a statistical association between the number of storks and the birth rate (they are going down together). However, contrary to the old folk-tale, this does not prove that children are brought by storks. The correlation observed in the statistical studies of fields and cancer might be caused by a similar coincidence.

- **Misunderstanding:** *If scientists would just stop fooling around and expose some animals to see if they get cancer, we could quickly resolve the uncertainty.*
  Fact: *Animal cancer studies are complicated and expensive. Doing them properly takes a long time, and often requires multiple studies.*
  If there is a risk, it probably involves very small increases. Designing and running studies that can detect these increases, especially when we do not know what aspect of the fields may be important, is a difficult job. Remember it took many years to clearly demonstrate that smoking causes cancer, and that is a risk that is ten to thirty times greater than the kinds of risk levels that some studies suggest may be caused by fields.

SUMMARY • SUMMARY • SUMMARY • SUMMARY • SUMMARY • SUMMARY • SUMMARY

2

PART 1: What are fields?

Electric and magnetic fields occur throughout nature and in all living things. Like gravity, they involve one of the basic forces of nature.

Every electric charge is surrounded by an *electric field*. This field represents the force that the charge will produce on other charges. When charges *move* they create *additional* forces on each other. These additional forces are represented by *magnetic fields*.

A group of charges moving together is called a current. Materials that can easily carry currents are called *conductors*. Currents flow through conductors from places that are at higher voltages to places that are at lower voltages. For example, a current will flow through a wire connected from the high voltage to the low voltage terminal on a battery. All currents create magnetic fields.

The electric power system, wiring in buildings, and all electrical appliances that are plugged in,

make electric and magnetic fields. In North America the power system uses current that alternates 60 times each second. For this reason the fields made by electric power are called 60 Hertz (Hz) fields.

Fields grow weaker with distance.

The strengths of electric and magnetic fields diminish as you move away from electrical objects — just as the light from a candle grows dimmer as you move away from it and the heat from a campfire decreases with greater distance. The drawing below shows how the strength of the 60 Hz magnetic field decreases with distance from a 345,000 volt (345 kV) transmission line. A similar drawing which illustrates the even more rapid decrease for a small compact appliance, such as an electric clock, is shown on page 6 of Details Booklet Part 1.

The strength of the fields created by electrical objects depends on several other things in addition to

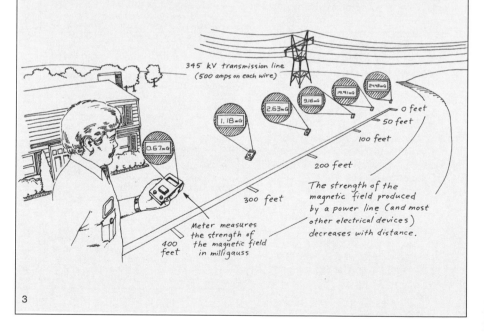

345 kV transmission line
(500 amps on each wire)

2.48mG

19.91mG

9.16mG

2.63mG

1.18mG

0.67mG

0 feet
50 feet
100 feet
200 feet
300 feet
400 feet

The strength of the magnetic field produced by a power line (and most other electrical devices) decreases with distance.

Meter measures the strength of the magnetic field in milligauss

3

distance. For example, the strength of an electric field depends on the voltage. The strength of a magnetic field depends on the amount of current that is flowing. Sometimes even very small electrical devices which use only a little current, such as the motor in a bedside clock, can produce strong magnetic fields. This is because they contain coils. The magnetic field made by the small current flowing in each loop of the coil is small. However, there are many loops, and the field from each loop adds to the fields from the other loops to produce a strong local magnetic field.

Electric fields can be shielded (or blocked out) by objects such as trees or the roof or walls of a house. Magnetic fields are not shielded very much by most objects. Hence, typical houses do not provide much shielding of magnetic fields.

You can learn more about the nature of the fields made by the electric system, including power lines, house wiring and common electrical appliances, in Details Booklet Part 1.

Gravity is another kind of field.

The idea of a "force field" may sound very mysterious, but it is really no more mysterious than gravity. Around every mass (like our bodies, or the earth) there is something called a gravitational field. All objects, including our bodies, are pulled toward the earth because of the gravitational field made by the earth's mass. In a similar way, a positive electric charge pulls negative charges toward it, and pushes positive charges away from it, because of its electric field.

While we can compare the force that an electric field produces on a charge to the force that gravity produces on a mass such as a stone or your body, such a comparison is harder to make for magnetic fields. Magnetic fields are sort of like gravity that turns on only when you move! Unless a charge is moving it does not make a magnetic field and is not affected by a magnetic field.[†]

[†]A changing magnetic field can produce an electric field. In some circumstances this electric field may be large enough to have a significant effect on charges that are not moving.

Measuring fields.

The strength of 60 Hz electric and magnetic fields can be measured with special instruments. The words used in describing measurements of field strength sound technical, but the basic ideas are no more complicated than measuring weight in pounds or distance in miles. The strength of an electric field is measured in units of volts per meter, abbreviated V/m. When the field is strong, larger units of a thousand volts per meter or "kilo" volts per meter are used. This is abbreviated as kV/m. Several different units are commonly used to report the strength of magnetic fields. The two most common units are the gauss and the tesla. Like gallons and quarts or miles and feet, gauss and tesla are just different units for measuring the same thing. The gauss is a fairly large unit so magnetic field strength is often reported in thousandths of a gauss or "milli" gauss (abbreviated mG). The tesla is an even bigger unit, so magnetic field strength is often reported in millionths of a tesla or "micro" tesla (abbreviated μT). Ten milligauss equals one microtesla (10 mG = 1μT).

Field strength may not be what matters.

While it is easy to measure the strength of fields, some of the biological evidence, discussed in Part 2 of this brochure, suggests that if fields pose a risk to public health, field strength may not be the most important attribute. Other characteristics such as how rapidly the field switches on or off, may be as or more important. Thus, you must be careful not to make the simple assumption that if there is a risk, all stronger fields are dangerous and all weaker fields are safe (second "common misunderstanding" on page 2). To learn more about these complications see the box on page 6 and also Details Booklet Part 2.

4

247

PART 2: Do 60 Hz fields pose health risks?

While there is a legitimate basis for concern, nobody knows for sure whether exposure to fields poses risks to public health.

Basically three kinds of studies have been done to explore this issue: 1) laboratory studies that expose single cells, groups of cells, or individual organs to fields under a variety of conditions and look for effects; 2) laboratory studies that expose animals or humans to fields and look for effects in body function, chemistry, disease, or behavior; and 3) "epidemiological studies" that examine whether groups of people who have experienced high (or otherwise unusual) field exposures have a greater chance of having a disease (such as cancer) than groups who have experienced more usual fields.

Scientists have found that fields can produce a variety of biological effects in cells, isolated organs and in animals and people. For example, the levels of specific hormones and other chemicals made by the body, or by individual cells, have been observed to change with certain kinds of field exposure. Changes have also been observed in the functioning of individual nerve cells and the nervous system. Whether any of these changes can lead to health risks is less clear.

Scientists have also studied the statistics on death and disease for people who are exposed to unusual fields in their normal course of living and work and compared these statistics with those of people who are in typical fields. Such studies are termed "epidemiological studies." Many of these studies find a statistical association between field exposure and the occurrence of certain kinds of cancer. Some studies have not found such an association. The size of the effect being found is small (between 1/5th and 1/20th the size of the effect of smoking and health) so there is a problem of being certain that the effect is real.

While there is clearly a basis for concern, to date the evidence is not conclusive. If there is a real statistical association between fields and cancer, this may mean that fields contribute to cancer. Alternatively, if fields don't contribute to cancer, the association may occur because fields and something else that does cause cancer tend to occur together.

Animal studies of cancer.

It seems unlikely that epidemiological studies alone will ever be able to resolve the question of whether fields contribute to cancer. Studies that expose large numbers of rats or mice probably have the greatest chance of resolving this issue. Most animal studies of cancer are very expensive. Money to conduct such studies has only recently become available. Several lifetime studies with rodents are now planned or under way. It is likely to be several years before results are available from these large studies.

I understand there's great uncertainty, but you've read all the studies Dr. Morgan, what's your bottom line on whether fields pose a risk to public health?

There are two questions I need to answer. First, what are the odds that when all the research has been done it will turn out that exposure to fields poses a risk to public health? And second, if it does turn out that fields pose a risk to public health, how serious is the problem likely to be?

On the first question, my personal judgment is that the chances are somewhere around 50:50. That means I'd give roughly even odds that there is no problem at all. However, if we are unlucky and it turns out that fields do promote cancer (or contribute to some other health risk), it is important to remember that not all things that cause or promote cancer pose large risks to *individuals*. For example, breathing other peoples' cigarette smoke has been linked to cancer. But, the *individual* risk that results from occasional exposure is small enough that most of us do not consider it very serious. When people object to smoke it is more likely to be because of the smell than because they are worried about the very small risk. If fields promote cancer, my guess is that they will be in this same category. Just as most people don't worry very much about the health risk if once in a while they spend a few hours in a smoky room, you probably should not worry very much about occasional exposures to strong or otherwise unusual fields. Indeed, even if you spend much or all your life in such fields, your personal chances of having a problem are probably pretty small. Of course, like smoke, if we ultimately find fields do pose risks, we will control them since *many* people are exposed.

There is a possibility that fields pose substantial risks to just a few people with special characteristics or in special circumstances. But, until we have some idea what those might be, it is impossible to differentiate this case from a situation in which everyone faces a small risk.

5

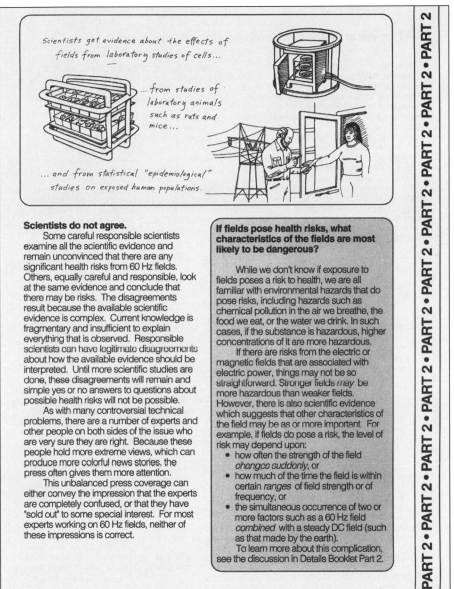

Scientists get evidence about the effects of fields from laboratory studies of cells...

... from studies of laboratory animals such as rats and mice ...

... and from statistical "epidemiological" studies on exposed human populations.

Scientists do not agree.

Some careful responsible scientists examine all the scientific evidence and remain unconvinced that there are any significant health risks from 60 Hz fields. Others, equally careful and responsible, look at the same evidence and conclude that there may be risks. The disagreements result because the available scientific evidence is complex. Current knowledge is fragmentary and insufficient to explain everything that is observed. Responsible scientists can have legitimate disagreements about how the available evidence should be interpreted. Until more scientific studies are done, these disagreements will remain and simple yes or no answers to questions about possible health risks will not be possible.

As with many controversial technical problems, there are a number of experts and other people on both sides of the issue who are very sure they are right. Because these people hold more extreme views, which can produce more colorful news stories, the press often gives them more attention.

This unbalanced press coverage can either convey the impression that the experts are completely confused, or that they have "sold out" to some special interest. For most experts working on 60 Hz fields, neither of these impressions is correct.

If fields pose health risks, what characteristics of the fields are most likely to be dangerous?

While we don't know if exposure to fields poses a risk to health, we are all familiar with environmental hazards that do pose risks, including hazards such as chemical pollution in the air we breathe, the food we eat, or the water we drink. In such cases, if the substance is hazardous, higher concentrations of it are more hazardous.

If there are risks from the electric or magnetic fields that are associated with electric power, things may not be so straightforward. Stronger fields *may* be more hazardous than weaker fields. However, there is also scientific evidence which suggests that other characteristics of the field may be as or more important. For example, if fields do pose a risk, the level of risk may depend upon:

- how often the strength of the field *changes suddenly*, or
- how much of the time the field is within certain *ranges* of field strength or of frequency, or
- the simultaneous occurrence of two or more factors such as a 60 Hz field *combined* with a steady DC field (such as that made by the earth).

To learn more about this complication, see the discussion in Details Booklet Part 2.

6

PART 3: What can and should be done?

First, research needs to be continued and expanded so that we can answer three key questions: Is there a risk? If so, how big is it? What can be done about it? Many scientists and public health experts believe that too little money is being spent on research that will get us answers to these questions.

Second...well, this is where things get difficult. It would be nice if we could spell out a few clear conclusions about actions. We can't. The reason is that the science is not complete enough today to support such conclusions. Anything more we say will go beyond science and involve judgments and values. Basically both you as an individual making decisions about your own exposures, and society as a whole making public health decisions about things like power lines and building codes, must choose from among three options:

Option 1. Conclude that the present evidence is not sufficiently persuasive to warrant any action. Don't make any changes in people's field exposures until new research tells us clearly there is a risk and, if so, how big it is.

Option 2. Conclude that there is some basis for concern. Adopt a position of "prudent avoidance." This means limiting exposures which can be avoided with small investments of money and effort. Don't do anything drastic or expensive until research provides a clearer picture of whether there is any risk and, if there is, how big it is.

Option 3. Conclude we have a real problem and spend some serious time and money on an aggressive program to limit field exposures now. Do analysis to find robust strategies, but recognize that the money we spend may be wasted either because it wasn't needed or because it was spent in the wrong way.

What can I do to reduce my exposure to fields?

Look at how you spend your time, all of it, both awake and asleep. Identify the two or three places where you spend the most time. Focus your attention on those places.

The single place where you probably spend the most time is your bedroom. Most people spend 6 to 10 hours a day there. Here are some suggestions on limiting bedroom exposure:

- Do not use electric bedding (or, if that is too big a sacrifice, switch to newer low field electric bedding). Electric bedding means electric blankets, electric mattress pads, and electric waterbed heaters. Older designs for all of these devices make magnetic fields that are at least as strong as those associated with large power lines. If you do not want to give up your electric blanket or mattress pad, you could use it to preheat the bed, and then unplug it before going to bed. There are some people (for example, people with circulatory problems in their legs) for whom an electric blanket is very important. For these people the cost of going without an electric blanket may be too high to make this a prudent step.
- Do not sleep right next to small electric motors. Small electric motors, like those found in older bedside clocks and in small fans, produce strong magnetic fields. Thus, a motor driven electric clock on your bedside table may produce a fairly strong magnetic field by your head. The strength of the field decreases very rapidly with distance. So, you can push the clock to the back of the bedside table or move it to the top of the bureau. If you want a clock right next to your head, change to one of the digital varieties that make low fields or (if you are really concerned) to a mechanical windup variety.
- Measure the fields around your bedroom. If there are places in the room where there are strong or otherwise unusual fields, position your bed so as to avoid them.

Probably the spot where you spend the next greatest amount of time is your workplace (office, shop, classroom, etc.).

- If you use a computer, push it back from you on the desk. Get some reading glasses if you need them to see.
- Look for small motors (e.g., clocks, cooling fans) and other electrical things that might be right next to you for extended periods (e.g., local lighting). The strength of most fields decreases *very rapidly* with distance. See if there is a way to increase your distance.
- Measure the fields around your workplace. If there are places in the room where there are strong or otherwise unusual fields, and you have the option to move your work location, consider doing it.

Once you have done whatever seems reasonable to you, then it is probably wise to forget about it. Life is short and you probably have better things to do than spend it worrying about uncertain risks after you have taken some prudent precautions!

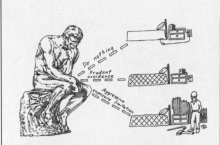

Pros and cons of the three options.

Deciding which option to choose requires a value judgment. You (and public health decision makers) need to think about your attitude toward risk and then ask whether you find the incomplete and fragmentary evidence sufficiently troubling to spend time and money you might spend in other ways. Different attitudes toward risk can lead to different actions even among people who agree about the evidence.

In Details Booklet Part 3 you will find a discussion which systematically explores the pros and cons of each of these three options to help you decide how you want to choose for yourself and how you think our society should choose.

Keep a sense of perspective.

In thinking about the possible risks from exposure to fields, it is important to keep a sense of perspective. There is still a significant chance that fields from electric power do not pose risks to health. Even if field exposure does turn out to pose risks to public health, the individual risk that any one of us faces due to fields is likely to be modest compared to the many other risks that we live with all the time. If you are concerned about fields, you may want to take some steps to reduce your exposure (see box to left), but it would not make sense to devote major efforts or resources to this one possible risk, while doing nothing more to reduce the many known risks that all of us face in our lives. You will find more discussion of the issue of how fields may compare to other risks in Details Booklet Part 3. If you are particularly concerned about the risk of cancer from all causes, see the boxed section "How can I reduce my risk of cancer?" on page 5 of Details Booklet Part 3.

What about buying a house?

If you are buying a house it might be prudent to consider the location of distribution and transmission lines as one of many things you consider. If you think the property may have strong or otherwise unusual fields, check by getting some measurements made. Keep in mind that even if fields are ultimately demonstrated to pose a health risk, things like traffic patterns in the streets, fire risk, and even radon levels in the house are likely to be more important for your own or your children's overall safety than anything related to fields. But, if you decide you are not going to be able to stop worrying about fields, you should probably look for some other property. Apart from actual risk, remember that public perceptions may influence current and future house prices.

In most situations, if you are already in a home, moving only for the purpose of getting away from existing lines or other sources of fields goes beyond what most people would consider to be prudent.

More discussion about buying a house is provided on page 7 of Details Booklet Part 3.

Dr. Morgan, what have *you* done?

People say "actions speak louder than words" so I often get asked, "what have you done in your own home?" The answer is not very much. We changed the clock on our bedside table from an old motor driven variety to a digital one that makes very low fields. We don't use electric blankets (although we still use a heating pad if we have a sprained or sore muscle). I pushed my computer terminal back a few inches. In the summer I have also moved the small fan off my desk over onto the window sill. I made a few measurements and discovered my son's bed was right next to where the power line comes into the house. He sleeps with his head pressed against the wall. So, we moved the bed to a different corner of the room so his head would not be in a high magnetic field eight hours every night. That's it!

Who wrote these brochures?

The primary author for these brochures was Dr. Granger Morgan of Carnegie Mellon University. He had help from a number of colleagues including Dr. Indira Nair, Dr. Keith Florig, and Dr. Jack Adams. Before the brochures were published they were reviewed by a large number of experts and laypeople who offered extensive advice on how the brochures could be improved. While we followed much of this advice the final product is Dr. Morgan's responsibility. The judgments expressed in these brochures are his and may be quite different from those of some of the reviewers and some of the agencies that supported this work.

We thank the following for their assistance and reviews of these brochures: Caron Chess, Bill Hallman, Miles Kahn, Edwin Mantiply, Hank May, Robert McGaughy, Kjell Hansson Mild, Raymond Neutra, Charles Petko, Jack Sahl, David Savitz, Maria Stuchly, Dan Wartenberg, and Richard Wilson. We also thank the reviewers of previously developed material, some of which has been reused here. These reviewers included: Carl Blackman, T. Dan Bracken, David Carpenter, Connie Cortés, Anita Curran, Wendy Davis, Fred Dietrich, Dan Driscoll, John Dunlap, Baruch Fischhoff, Reba Goodman, Julia Greenlee, Gordon Hester, Jim Hoburg, Lester Lave, Kai Lee, Alvin Leonard, Don MacGregor, Joseph Norton, Gilbert Omenn, Hamilton Oven, Ron Owen, Richard Phillips, Richard Rankin, Greg Rauch, Emilie Roth, Asher Sheppard, Miichael Silva, June Small, Amy Stiffey, Paul Slovic, Stan Sussman, Ola Svenson, Richard Tell, Nancy Wertheimer, Chris Whipple, Susan White, Susan Wiltshire, and Luciano Zaffanella. Finally, we thank several anonymous groups of laypeople who served in focus groups and performed read-aloud protocols to help improve the material. Their assistance was particularly valuable.

Granger Morgan is Head of the Department of Engineering and Public Policy at Carnegie Mellon University where he is also a professor in the Department of Electrical and Computer Engineering. He was educated in science and engineering at Harvard, Cornell and the University of California. He has worked for many years on environmental problems and in risk analysis. Most of his work on these topics has been funded by the US National Science Foundation. He has served as a member of a number of scientific advisory panels for the US Environmental Protection Agency. He is a Fellow of the Institute of Electrical and Electronics Engineers.

Dr. Morgan and his colleagues at Carnegie Mellon have worked hard to remain impartial on this very controversial topic. They have never testified on behalf of any electric utility company. They have never been a participant in any power line siting controversy. They make no profit from selling these brochures. Power-frequency fields is just one of several areas in which Dr. Morgan does research.

Preparation of these brochures was supported by US Environmental Protection Agency, National Institute of Environmental Health Science, and the Conference on Radiation Control Program Directors, Inc. Earlier work done at Carnegie Mellon on this topic has been supported by a number of different organizations including the US National Science Foundation, the Electric Power Research Institute, the US Department of Energy, and Southern California Edison Company. All views expressed are the author's alone.

Department of Engineering and Public Policy
Carnegie Mellon University
Pittsburgh, PA 15213

Details Booklet Part 1:

More on
"What are 60 Hz fields?"

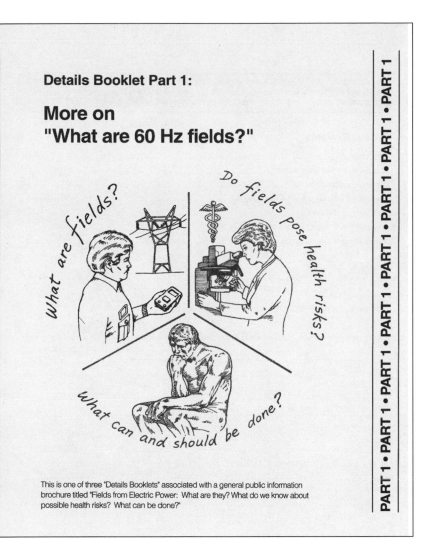

This is one of three "Details Booklets" associated with a general public information brochure titled "Fields from Electric Power: What are they? What do we know about possible health risks? What can be done?"

This details booklet provides additional information for people who would like to learn more about the subject of "Part 1: What are fields" of the brochure "Fields from Electric Power." This booklet does not repeat very much of the material that is in Part 1, so it would be best if you read the main brochure first.

Table of Contents

254

Where do electric and magnetic fields occur?

As the main brochure explains, electric and magnetic fields occur throughout nature and in all living things. The molecules in our bodies, and in all other living and nonliving things, are held together by electric fields. The messages that flow in our nervous systems involve electric and magnetic fields. When you get a shock from static electricity by touching someone on a rug on a dry winter day, the spark is caused by strong electric fields from the many charges you have picked up from the rug. When you use a magnetic compass to locate north it is responding to the natural magnetic field which is created by charges flowing deep inside the molten core of the earth. Almost all electrical wiring and appliances produce electric and magnetic fields.

Both electric and magnetic fields are made by charges. All the objects in our world contain positive electric charges (protons) and negative electric charges (electrons). A positive and a negative charge attract each other. Two positive charges repel or push each other apart. Similarly, two negative charges repel each other. Charges are tiny — many may be contained in a single atom.

What are electric fields?

Electric fields represent the forces that electric charges exert on other charges at a distance *because they are charged*. It is because of its electric field that a positive electric charge pulls negative charges toward it, or pushes other positive charges away from it. The forces that electric fields produce on charges are unaffected by whether the charges are moving.

The total (or "net") charge on an object determines its voltage. In general, the higher the voltage of an object, the more charges it carries. Each of the charges makes its own electric field. These separate fields all add together and act like a single field. Because objects at higher voltages carry more "net", or excess, charge, they make stronger electric fields.

The electric power system, and appliances we connect to it, produce electric fields because charges are "pumped" into wires by the electric generators at power stations.

1

What are magnetic fields?

When charges *move* they create *additional* forces on each other. A magnetic field represents these forces that a moving charge exerts on other moving charges *because they are moving*. Magnetic fields are not created by charges unless they are moving.

A group of charges moving in the same direction is called a current. The more charges that are moving in a current, the stronger the current is. The size of a current is measured in amperes (abbreviated A, sometimes Amp). All currents produce magnetic fields. Larger currents make stronger magnetic fields. Magnetic fields exert forces *only* on moving charges or currents. Magnetic fields do not exert forces on charges that are standing still. A changing magnetic field can produce an electric field. In some circumstances this electric field may be large enough to have a significant effect on charges that are not moving.

Materials that can easily carry currents are called *conductors*. Materials that cannot easily carry currents are called *insulators*. Currents flow through conductors from places that are at higher voltages to places that are at lower voltages (for example, a current will flow through a wire connected from the high voltage to the low voltage terminal on a battery). A steady or DC current flowing in a wire from the high voltage to the low voltage terminal of a battery will turn a compass needle because it makes a steady magnetic field that exerts a force on many charges all moving in the same direction inside the iron atoms of the needle.

Several different units are used to measure magnetic fields. The most common is the milligauss (abbreviated mG). Another unit, which many scientists prefer, is the microtesla (abbreviated µT). Ten mG are equal to one µT.

Magnetic field lines form continuous loops around current

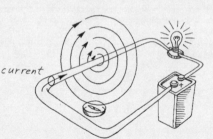

current

While a compass needle will be influenced by a DC current, it will not be influenced by AC currents which change direction too fast for the needle to follow. Thus you can not use a compass to check if there are currents flowing in house wiring.

2

256

What are field lines or "lines of force"?

The forces that electric fields can produce on a charge are often drawn as electric field lines or "lines of force." *Electric fields begin and end on electric charges.* The sketch below shows the electric field lines between a positive and a negative charge. In such drawings, fields are strongest where the lines are closest together. There is no such thing as a magnetic charge on which magnetic field lines can start or stop. *Magnetic field lines form continuous closed loops around currents.* They have no beginning or end. The sketch on the bottom of page 2 shows the magnetic field lines around a wire carrying a steady current. As you can see from the sketches, electric and magnetic fields involve *direction* as well as strength.

If a charge is placed in the field it experiences a force. The direction of the force is parallel to the field line, as shown by the direction of the arrows. The magnitude of the force is proportional to the spacing between the field lines, as shown by the length of the arrows.

Electric field lines begin and end on charges

What are 60 hertz electric and magnetic fields?

The electric power that we use in our homes, offices and factories uses AC, or alternating current. This is in contrast to DC, or direct current, that is produced by batteries. An alternating current does not flow steadily in one direction. It alternates back and forth. The power we use in North America alternates back and forth 60 times each second. Scientists call this 60 Hertz (abbreviated Hz) power. In Europe and some other parts of the world, the frequency of electric power is 50 Hz rather than 60 Hz.

Because a 60 Hz current changes directions back and forth 60 times each second, the magnetic field that it produces also changes directions back and forth 60 times each second. Such a field is called a 60 Hz magnetic field. *A 60 Hz current flowing in a wire will not turn a compass needle because it changes directions back and forth faster than the needle can respond.*

The charges on a wire carrying a 60 Hz alternating current are not constant. At one instant, the wire will have positive charges on it. A moment later it will have negative charges on it. This means that the electric field produced by 60 Hz power changes directions back and forth 60 times each second. Such a field is called a 60 Hz electric field.

3

257

The electric power system.

Electric power is produced by generating plants and then transferred to homes, businesses, and factories by a transmission and distribution system. Transmission lines use very high voltages and go long distances. Distribution lines consist of "primary" lines which operate at intermediate voltages and serve a region and "secondary" lines which bring power to individual homes. Transmission lines, and many distribution lines, use three "phase" or "hot" wires. While the voltages on all three wires oscillate at 60 Hz, the oscillations are not "in phase" with one another. As the voltage on one wire is peaking, the voltage on one of the others is one-third of a cycle ahead and the voltage on the remaining wire is one-third of a cycle behind.

For this reason, the three wires are referred to as the three phases of a power network. Although commercial and industrial facilities use three-phase power to run large motors and other heavy loads, the 120 V power in homes is generally supplied by just a single phase. Utility companies try to connect equal numbers of houses to each phase of a residential distribution network in order to balance the load across the phases. Throughout the system there are circuit breakers (most are not shown in the drawings) which will automatically disconnect if a short circuit or other safety problem occurs.

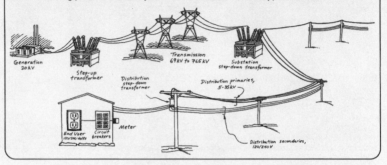

Everything that carries or uses 60 Hz electric power produces 60 Hz electric and magnetic fields. This includes high voltage power transmission lines (large lines usually on big steel towers), intermediate and lower voltage distribution lines (on wooden poles in the street), wiring in homes and offices, and electrical appliances such as electric blankets, electric clocks, electric typewriters, or hair dryers. The drawing on the next page gives an approximate indication of the strength of fields associated with a number of common electrical objects.

4

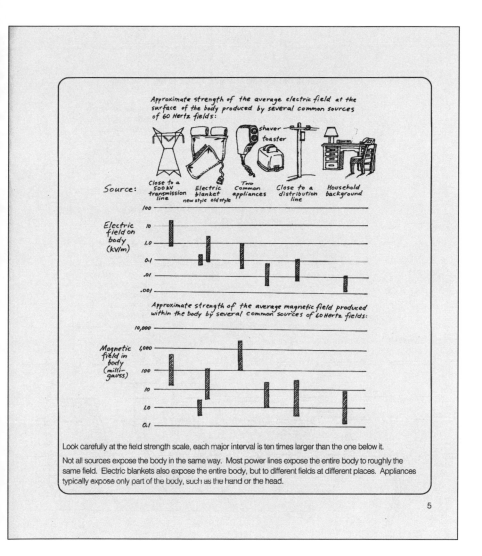

Approximate strength of the average electric field at the surface of the body produced by several common sources of 60 Hertz fields:

Source:

| Close to a 500 kV transmission line | Electric blanket new style old style | Two Common appliances | Close to a distribution line | Household background |

Electric field on body (kV/m)

100
10
1.0
0.1
.01
.001

Approximate strength of the average magnetic field produced within the body by several common sources of 60 Hertz fields:

Magnetic field in body (milli-gauss)

10,000
1,000
100
10
1.0
0.1

Look carefully at the field strength scale, each major interval is ten times larger than the one below it.

Not all sources expose the body in the same way. Most power lines expose the entire body to roughly the same field. Electric blankets also expose the entire body, but to different fields at different places. Appliances typically expose only part of the body, such as the hand or the head.

5

259

Do fields get weaker as you move away from electrical objects?

Yes, the strengths of electric and magnetic fields decrease, often quite rapidly, as you move away from electrical objects. This is shown for a high voltage power line in the drawing on page 3 of the main brochure. The drawing across the bottom of these pages shows the same thing for a motor driven electric clock. Fields made by objects that are large or long, such as power lines, fall off more slowly with distance than fields made by small compact objects, such as toasters or electric clocks.

What else besides distance affects the strength of fields?

The strength of an electric field depends on the voltage of the object creating it. For example, a high voltage power line produces a stronger electric field than a low voltage power line (at the same distance from the two lines).

Because charges make electric fields, current does not have to be flowing for an electric field to exist. Thus, a toaster or an electric blanket that is plugged in, but not operating, may still produce an electric field. This is particularly true of older appliances. You may have noticed that modern appliances usually come with either a three prong plug, or a two prong plug that has one prong that is larger than the other. In these appliances, the switch is wired so that the 120 volt side of the line is disconnected when the switch is "off." In appliances that do not have such "polar- ized plugs," the on/off switch may interrupt only the low voltage side of the line, leaving the wiring inside the appliance at 120 volts. In this case, electric fields will be present even though the appliance is turned off.

Field strength decreases with distance

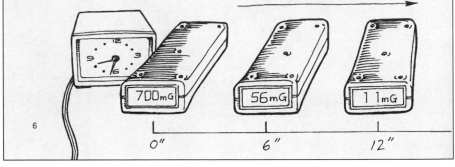

700mG   56mG   11mG

0"   6"   12"

6

The strength of a magnetic field depends on the strength of the current that produces it. For example, a power line will produce a stronger magnetic field when it carries a large current than it does when it carries a small current. The amount of current a power line carries is determined by how much electrical load has been connected to it. A typical line in a residential neighborhood might carry a large current in the early evening when all the lights are on, or on a hot day when all the air conditioners are running. It might carry a much smaller current on a pleasant afternoon when neither lights nor air conditioning are running.

While power line *currents*, and the magnetic fields they make, change with changing load, the power system is operated so that its *voltages* are kept nearly constant. Electric field strength is determined by voltage. This means that the strength of the electric field associated with a power line, or with other operating wiring or appliances, is likely to remain nearly constant even as loads change.

Because fields have direction, when fields from two sources are combined, they may either add or subtract. Fields with the same direction will add, those with opposite directions will subtract. The strength of the electric or magnetic fields associated with objects like power lines, wiring and appliances depends upon things such as the location of the object, the location of other nearby objects, the configuration of wiring, and the conditions of use.

The *power* of an electrical device depends both on the voltage at which it operates and the amount of current it uses (the actual equation is power equals voltage multiplied by current). You can get the same amount of power by using lots of current at a low voltage (like the headlight on an automobile) or very little current at a high voltage (like high voltage street lights). The same power, carried over a high voltage transmission line, will require a smaller current and produce a weaker magnetic field than when it is carried over a lower voltage line. When the voltage is

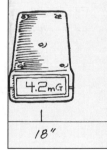

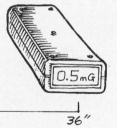

4.2mG   1.8mG   0.5mG

18"   24"   36"

7

increased, the associated electric fields increase. When the current is increased, the associated magnetic fields increase.

Not all devices which use lots of power expose nearby people to strong fields. For example, for reasons of efficiency, some high-power devices, such as transformers or motors, are designed to keep most of their fields contained inside. Similarly, not all devices that use very little power make very weak fields. For example, a small motor driven clock draws very little power, but fairly strong magnetic fields leak out from the many windings in its simple electric motor.

Can fields be shielded?

Magnetic field from a single wire...

Magnetic fields from two wires with identical currents add...

Magnetic fields from two wires with opposite currents subtract...

Electric fields can be shielded (or blocked out) by conducting objects. This is because electric field lines start and stop on charges. If you put an object like a row of trees, or the wall or roof of a house in the path of an electric field, most of the field lines will stop on charges on that object. The amount of shielding that a house will provide varies somewhat with construction material and relative humidity. A typical house shields about 90% of electric fields from outside. For example, if such a house is next to a power line that makes an electric field of 1000 volts per meter (1 kV/m) near the house, the electric field inside the house will be only about 10% as large, or 100 volts per meter. The fraction of the electric field that a house blocks can be increased with the proper use of shielding materials such as grounded aluminium roofing and siding.

Magnetic fields cannot be shielded very much by most ordinary objects. Hence, typical houses do not provide much shielding of magnetic fields. This is because magnetic field lines do not stop on anything, they form continuous loops around conductors carrying currents. Although they are out of sight, wires inside walls or buried under ground can still produce fields. Unless special low-field designs are used, power lines buried under streets can expose people to stronger magnetic fields than overhead lines.

While magnetic field lines can travel through most materials (wood, air, people, etc.), they travel most easily through a few materials such as iron or steel. Hence, while magnetic fields are not easily shielded, in certain structures such as commercial buildings which have large steel beams, many of the field lines may be deflected to funnel through the beams instead of traveling through the spaces where people are. However, such beams can also be a *source* of magnetic fields if, as is often the case, they carry currents flowing to the ground. Without a measurement, it is typically impossible to predict how a steel beam will affect nearby magnetic fields.

Special kinds of materials are being developed that can shield magnetic fields, but they are not yet in general use.

8

Fields change dramatically as we move from place-to-place.

The drawings below show the recordings of the magnetic field that three different people experienced during the course of their day. The figures were recorded by little meters which the people wore on their belt in order to keep track of the fields they were in. The people kept notes to record where they were, and what they were doing. Look carefully at the field strength scale, each major interval is ten times bigger than the one below it. Notice that in these examples, the fields to which these people are exposed vary enormously throughout the day. In most cases the largest fields are encountered when people are traveling, using an old-style electric blanket, and using various appliances. The Washington measurements were made by staff working at the US Environmental Protection Agency.

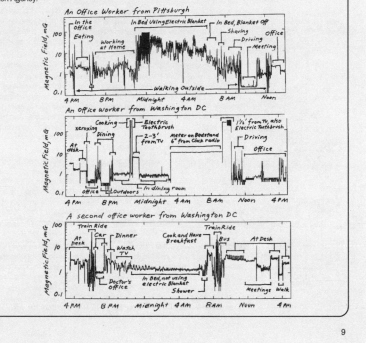

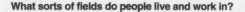

What sorts of fields do people live and work in?

The fields around us change all the time. The fields in the middle of your living room are likely to be higher in the early evening when you and all your neighbors are using a lot of power to run your lights and prepare dinner than they are in the middle of the morning when lights and electric stoves are mostly turned off. Similarly, as you move around from place-to-place, you enter and leave places with a variety of different fields. Most of the fields from electric power have a frequency of 60 Hz. However, some of the fields produced can be at higher frequencies.

Small field measuring instruments have been designed that people can wear. These specialized research instruments measure the fields every few moments and store the results in a little computer memory. At the end of the day the data can be taken out of the memory and turned into a graph which shows the fields the person encountered over the course of the day. The drawings on page 9 show examples of fields encountered by three office workers.

If fields pose health risks, it is unclear what aspects of the field exposure matters. Some of the fine details in the time pattern of exposure may be important. A common way of describing fields that leaves out such details is the average field strength. Suppose that you go around and measure the field in the middle of the living room of 12 houses. An example of the results you might get is shown in the margin of this page. The simplest way to summarize these results is to compute the average field. To do this for our example we add the twelve measurements together (the result is 18) and then divide by the number of measurements (in this case 12) to get the average, which in this case is 1.5 mG.

We can look at an actual example of someone who has done something very similar to this. During the summer of 1991, Dr. David Brodeur measured fields just outside the front doors of 974 homes and workplaces around Peabody, Massachusetts. He reported his findings to the EPA in public testimony. Peabody is an old eastern city. Except for the downtown region, all the power lines are above ground and run along the streets. Dr. Brodeur computed the average of his 974 measurements to be 4.39 mG. This value is higher than the average for many communities in the United States, especially in neighborhoods with relatively new houses.

A slightly more complicated way to summarize a set of measurements is with a diagram called a "histogram." In this case, we plot the number of measurements that we obtained in each of a number of ranges of field strength in order to show the "distribution" of the measurements. If we do this for the 12 example measurements we discussed above, we get the result shown in the sketch to the left. We measured three living rooms with a field between 1 and 2 mG (1.1, 1.4, 1.6). Three measurements amount to 25% of our total of 12 measurements. So, since the

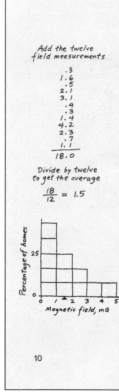

Add the twelve field measurements

```
  .3
 1.6
  .5
 2.1
 3.1
  .4
  .3
 1.4
 4.2
 2.3
  .7
 1.1
─────
18.0
```

Divide by twelve to get the average

$$\frac{18}{12} = 1.5$$

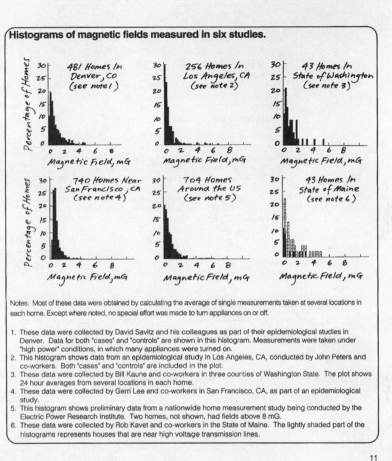

Histograms of magnetic fields measured in six studies.

(Top-left graph) 481 Homes In Denver, CO (see note 1)

(Top-middle graph) 256 Homes In Los Angeles, CA (see note 2)

(Top-right graph) 43 Homes In State of Washington (see note 3)

(Bottom-left graph) 740 Homes Near San Francisco, CA (see note 4)

(Bottom-middle graph) 704 Homes Around the US (see note 5)

(Bottom-right graph) 43 Homes In State of Maine (see note 6)

(All graphs: y-axis "Percentage of Homes" with marks at 0, 5, 10, 15, 20, 25, 30; x-axis "Magnetic Field, mG" with marks at 0, 2, 4, 6, 8)

Notes: Most of these data were obtained by calculating the average of single measurements taken at several locations in each home. Except where noted, no special effort was made to turn appliances on or off.

1. These data were collected by David Savitz and his colleagues as part of their epidemiological studies in Denver. Data for both "cases" and "controls" are shown in this histogram. Measurements were taken under "high power" conditions, in which many appliances were turned on.
2. This histogram shows data from an epidemiological study in Los Angeles, CA, conducted by John Peters and co-workers. Both "cases" and "controls" are included in the plot.
3. These data were collected by Bill Kaune and co-workers in three counties of Washington State. The plot shows 24 hour averages from several locations in each home.
4. These data were collected by Gerri Lee and co-workers in San Francisco, CA, as part of an epidemiological study.
5. This histogram shows preliminary data from a nationwide home measurement study being conducted by the Electric Power Research Institute. Two homes, not shown, had fields above 8 mG.
6. These data were collected by Rob Kavet and co-workers in the State of Maine. The lightly shaded part of the histograms represents houses that are near high voltage transmission lines.

11

265

measurements in three of the rooms lie between 1 and 2 mG, our distribution has a height of 25% in this interval. In the drawing, we have also used a dark triangle to indicate the location of the average field measured, which was 1.5 mG.

The drawings on page 11 show the histograms of measured fields in a number of different parts of the United States. Notice that most homes have fields that are below 1 or 2 mG, some have fields between 2 and 4 mG, and a few have fields higher than that.

What are ground currents?

Power distribution systems in the United States are usually wired as shown in the sketch below. The "hot" sides of the line are insulated from the ground. Both for reasons of safety and economics the "neutral return" path for the current is commonly grounded at the customer's home and at every few poles along the line. While some of the current flows back to the utility through the "neutral return" wire, in many cases much of it also flows through the ground itself or through metal pipes used for water, sewer or gas, or along other conductors such as the outer sheath of cable television cables. While the voltages involved are very low, these ground return currents can be quite large. They may produce magnetic fields of several milligauss or more.

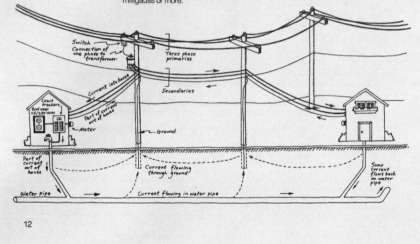

266

Additional common misunderstandings about fields:

The box on page 2 of the main brochure lists the most common misunderstandings about fields. Here are a few more:

- **Misunderstanding:** *You can see, hear or feel 60 Hz fields under normal circumstances.*

  Fact: *You cannot see, hear or feel 60 Hz fields under normal circumstances.*

  Sometimes you can hear buzzing or humming noises around electrical equipment. You are not hearing the fields themselves. Usually such noise comes from mechanical vibrations in things like the metal in transformers. In high voltage systems, noise can also come from an electrical discharge to air, called corona. In *very* strong electric fields (over 5-10 kV/m), people can feel a slight tingling sensation from things like the vibration of hairs on their skin. Usually the only place where you can be in a field that strong is right under the highest voltage power transmission lines. People cannot feel even very strong magnetic fields.

- **Misunderstanding:** *60 Hz fields can contaminate food or other things.*

  Fact: *Fields do not build up or accumulate over time.*

  Fields are present only as long as the charges and currents that make them are present. When the charges or currents are removed the fields disappear. No trace of them is left. The only exceptions to this involve very special materials, such as magnetic recording tape.

- **Misunderstanding:** *60 Hz fields are like X-rays or microwave radiation.*

  Fact: *60 Hz fields are very different from X-rays or microwave radiation. The mechanisms by which X-rays and microwave radiation produce biological effects do not work for 60 Hz fields.*

  X-rays, and other forms of ionizing radiation, cause health risks by breaking up biological molecules. 60 Hz fields don't carry enough energy to do that.

  Microwaves do not carry enough energy to break molecules but they can cause biological damage by heating tissue. 60 Hz fields don't carry enough energy to do that, either.

- **Misunderstanding:** *Lead is particularly good for shielding 60 Hz fields.*

  Fact: *Lead is not unusual in its ability to shield 60 Hz fields.*

  Lead is a conductor so it can shield electric fields, but it does this no better than any other conductor, such as aluminum or copper. Lead is not effective in shielding 60 Hz magnetic fields. Lead is very good at shielding ionizing radiation such as X-rays, but that has nothing to do with 60 Hz fields.

- **Misunderstanding:** *There is a special relationship between water and fields.*

  Fact:*The interactions that 60 Hz fields have with water are just like those they have with any other conducting material.*

  There *is* a hazard associated with using electrical appliances close to water: a greater chance of shock and electrocution. This is because if you are in water, you are probably well grounded. If you touch a hot wire, or drop an appliance in the bath tub while you are sitting in it, your chances of electrocution are high. But, none of this means there are *special* interactions between water and fields.

13

267

PART 1 • PART 1 • PART 1 • PART 1 • PART 1 • PART 1 • PART 1 • PART 1 • PART 1

A Summary of Basic Electrical Facts

Here's a summary of the basic electrical facts that are presented in this brochure:

- There are things called *charges*.
- Charges may be positive or negative. Charges with the same signs repel each other; charges with opposite signs attract each other.
- These forces of attraction or repulsion are carried from one charge to another charge through space by the *electric field*.
- If other things are held constant, the total quantity of charge on an object determines its *voltage*.
- Because objects at higher voltages generally have more charges on them, they make stronger electric fields.
- When a group of charges all move together in the same general direction they are called a *current*.
- Materials that can easily carry currents are called *conductors*. Materials that cannot easily carry currents are called *insulators*.
- Currents flow through conductors from places that are at higher voltages to places that are at lower voltages (for example, a current will flow through a wire connected from the high voltage to the low voltage terminal on a battery).
- Currents (that is moving charges) make *magnetic fields*.
- Stronger currents make stronger magnetic fields.
- Magnetic fields exert forces on moving charges or currents. Magnetic fields do not directly exert forces on charges that are standing still.
- The strengths of electric and magnetic fields decrease as you move away from the charges and currents that make them.
- Fields made by objects that are large or long, such as power lines, decrease in strength more slowly with distance than fields made by small compact objects, such as toasters or electric clocks.
- The *power* of an electrical device depends both on the voltage at which it operates and the amount of current it uses. You can get the same amount of power by using lots of current at a low voltage (like the headlight on an automobile) or very little current at a high voltage (like high voltage street lights). When the voltage is increased the associated electric fields increase. When the current is increased, the associated magnetic fields increase.
- Not all devices which use lots of power make strong fields. Not all devices that use very little power make very weak fields.
- The current carried by a power line goes up and down as the electrical load increases and decreases. The operating voltage of a power line is held quite steady. This means that the strength of magnetic fields produced by power lines may vary a lot over time, while the strength of electric fields will not.
- Electric fields can be shielded (or blocked out) by conducting objects. Magnetic fields cannot be shielded very much by most objects.

See page 2 of the main brochure as well as page 13 of this booklet for a list of things which are not true about 60 Hz fields.

Department of Engineering and Public Policy
Carnegie Mellon University
Pittsburgh, PA 15213

268

Details Booklet Part 2:

More on
"Do 60 Hz fields pose
health risks?"

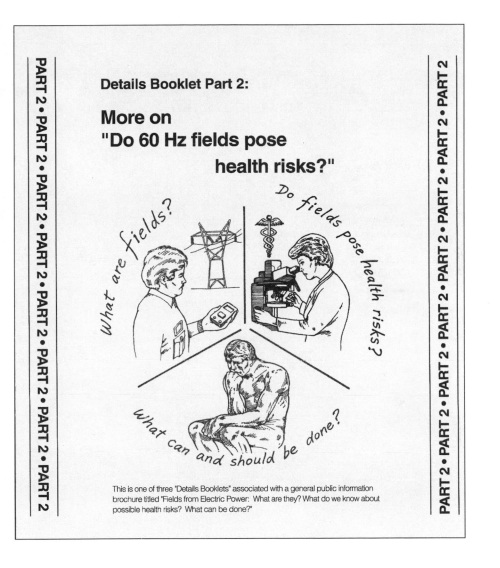

This is one of three "Details Booklets" associated with a general public information brochure titled "Fields from Electric Power: What are they? What do we know about possible health risks? What can be done?"

This details booklet provides additional information for people who would like to learn more about the subject of "Part 2: Do 60 Hz fields pose health risks?" of the brochure "Fields from Electric Power." This booklet does not repeat some of the key points made in Part 2, so it would be best if you read the main brochure first.

Table of Contents

Do fields from the electric power system pose health risks?

Nobody knows for sure. As we noted in the main brochure, scientists have found that fields can produce a variety of biological effects. In addition, a number of epidemiological studies have found a statistical association between fields and the occurrence of certain kinds of cancer.

Some careful responsible scientists examine all the scientific evidence and remain unconvinced that there are any significant health risks from 60 Hz fields. Others, equally careful and responsible, look at the same evidence and conclude that there may be risks. The disagreements result because the available scientific evidence is mixed. Current knowledge is fragmentary and insufficient to explain everything that is observed. Responsible scientists can have legitimate disagreements about how the available evidence should be interpreted. Until more scientific studies are done, these disagreements will remain and simple yes or no answers to questions about possible health risks will not be possible.

As with many controversial technical problems, there are a number of experts and other people on both sides of the issue who are very sure they are right. Because these people hold more extreme views, which can produce more colorful news stories, the press often gives them more attention.

This unbalanced press coverage can either convey the impression that the experts are completely confused, or that they have "sold out" to some special interest. For most experts working on 60 Hz fields, neither of these impressions is correct.

What kinds of "biological effects" do 60 Hz fields produce?

A variety of experiments show that under certain circumstances fields can interact with cells and trigger changes in the way the cell operates. The fields contain too little energy to cause such changes directly. Some structure on or in the cell must act to detect and amplify the weak field into a stronger chemical signal in the cell that can change things like the rate at which the cell makes hormones, enzymes and other proteins. These chemicals play roles in the operation of the cell and in signaling to other cells and tissues.

Modern biology tells us that the surface of the cell is made up of a double layer of "phospholipid" molecules, similar to a double-layered soap bubble. In this "bilayer" float various large complex molecules which act as receptors for communication between the cell and its surroundings and serve as channels that can move selected material into and out of the cell. Although the details remain unclear at

1

present, a variety of experiments have shown that fields, even fairly weak fields, can interact with the cell surface, or with some of the receptor molecules in that surface, and produce changes in how the cell operates.

There may also be mechanisms by which fields can interact with structures inside cells. For example, many cells are connected together by little passages called "gap junctions" which might allow groups of cells to work together in sensing fields. Also, some cells (e.g., in people, pigeons, bees, and single cell animals that live in soil) have been shown to contain trace amounts of magnetic material which could be involved in sensing some magnetic fields.

What kinds of specific findings have been reported from the laboratory studies?

While a number of biological effects have now been observed, they haven't been easy to find. In early studies large numbers of rats, mice and other animals, as well as various individual cells were exposed to see if anything happened. Most of these "screening studies" didn't find any differences between animals or tissues exposed to fields and those not exposed to fields. The few studies that did find interesting changes have been followed up with more detailed experiments.

In studies performed in cells, several effects have been observed including:
- changes in the rate of growth of several different kinds of cells exposed to strong "pulsed" magnetic fields (that is, fields that turn on and off rapidly) such as bone cells involved in bone growth, slime mold, and a type of laboratory cell that was derived from human cells,
- changes in the amounts of calcium found inside and on the surface of some cells exposed to weak magnetic fields,
- changes in the way in which certain "receptor molecules" on the surface of cells respond to chemicals outside the cell, when exposed to pulsed magnetic fields,
- changes in the rate of activity of some enzymes that are involved in cell growth in cells exposed to weak magnetic fields, and
- changes in the rate and amount of RNA copied from DNA and changes in the size of the proteins which cells copy from RNA when they are exposed to pulsed or to weak continuous magnetic fields.

In studies performed in animals, effects that have been observed include:
- changes in the production of various hormones including melatonin which is important in daily biological cycles called circadian rhythms in rodents (and possibly people) exposed to pulsed or strong continuous magnetic fields,
- changes in the reaction time of primates, and people exposed to strong magnetic fields, and

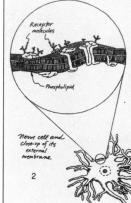

Receptor molecules

Phospholipid

Nerve cell and close-up of its external membrane

2

- changes in the number of defects in chicken eggs exposed to pulsed magnetic fields.

Science places great importance on being able to repeat or "replicate" a study. Only a few of these studies have been replicated and a great deal of attention is now being given to replicating several others.

While all of the reported effects may prove significant for our eventual understanding of how fields affect cells and animals, it is important to recognize that some of the experiments have involved exposure conditions that are quite different from those that people normally encounter when they are exposed to fields.

It is also important to understand that a biological effect is not the same thing as a health risk. The effects that have been observed are intriguing. They will certainly help us to better understand the role of electric and magnetic fields in living systems. Whether they are also an indicator of a chain of biological events that can lead to a health risk, is still not clear. However, in some cases, such as the change in the hormone melatonin, scientists have begun to propose theories about how this could lead to changes in cancer rates.

If you are interested in looking at some detailed reviews of the laboratory studies, you can find an introductory guide to reviews of that literature in the Appendix at the back of Details Booklet Part 3.

Can people and animals sense fields?

People can sense very strong electric fields (more than about 2 kV/m) as a slight tingling sensation which is mainly caused by vibrating hairs. People cannot sense the presence of the magnetic fields they encounter in daily life.

A few animals, including some fish and birds, have highly specialized sense organs which allow them to detect the presence of very weak (mainly DC) fields. Some use this ability to help in navigation. Some bottom feeding fish use weak electric fields to help find prey.

With all this evidence why do some scientists still doubt that weak fields can produce any biological effects?

Some scientists say there actually isn't much evidence. They point out that few of the studies have been precisely repeated, and they raise questions about the way in which some of the studies were designed and conducted.

Some scientists argue that the biological results that show effects from weak 60 Hz fields must all be wrong because there is no physical explanation of how weak fields could produce such effects.

3

273

X-rays (and other forms of "ionizing radiation" such as gamma rays) produce effects in living systems because the energy carried by the X-rays is so large that it can break molecular bonds. It can actually break the chemical bonds in DNA, the molecules that make up the genes. This is how X-ray exposure can start cancer. However, all scientists agree that the energy carried in 60 Hz fields is *much* too small to break molecular or chemical bonds.

Microwaves do not carry enough energy to break chemical or molecular bonds but they are absorbed by the water in tissue. They can also create strong electric currents. This causes heating. This heat is what makes a microwave oven work. If a person, such as a maintenance worker, gets right in front of a very powerful micro-wave antenna, such as some of those used for radar or communication, significant health damage can result from heating body tissue. There are safety standards designed to protect people from such exposure.

While 60 Hz fields can also create electric currents in tissue, these currents are *much* weaker. The amount of heat they generate is trivial compared to the natural heat that comes from the cells of the body. All scientists believe that such minuscule amounts of heat are too small to cause health effects.

In addition to the fields and currents in the body that are created by electric power, there are many other fields and currents in our bodies. For example, there are the fields generated by the cells in our nervous system. In addition, we all live in the earth's magnetic field. Whenever we move rapidly in this field, currents are "induced" to flow in our bodies. These fields and currents are larger than many of those created in our bodies by the fields from electric power.

There is one other fundamental problem. The charged atoms and molecules in our bodies are always moving with random heat energy. As these charges move around they make constantly changing fields and currents. Simple physical calculations suggest that these random fields and currents (thermal noise) are larger than most of the fields and currents created in and around cells of the body by electric power. In such a case, the random noise should swamp out the 60 Hz fields from electric power and prevent cells from sensing them, just as the noise from a raging storm prevents you from hearing a quiet whisper.

Some scientists look at all these arguments and conclude that the biological results must be wrong because they see no way they can happen. Others, more inclined to believe that the biologists are seeing real effects, suggest that we need to look harder for physical explanations.

How might the biological results that have been reported be explained? Perhaps the simple noise calculations are too simple. There may be structures in individual cells, or in connected groups of cells, that will allow them to detect the regular

4

repetitive pattern of a weak continuous 60 Hz field in the midst of all the random noise which has no regular pattern.

Alternatively, it may not be the *strength* of the field that is most important. Suppose that what matters is currents that are induced in cells by rapidly changing magnetic fields. Within some limits a fairly weak field could induce a fairly strong current if it is turned on or off fast enough.

It has been shown that some biological tissues contain magnetic material (essentially microscopic bar magnets). Some animals, such as honey bees and pigeons, have been shown to use these materials as an aid in orientation and navigation. Perhaps such magnetic materials are more common in living systems than scientists have thought. It is possible that at least in some cases such material may be involved in sensing some 60 Hz magnetic fields.

There is only one way in which this scientific argument can be resolved. Biologists must find several experiments which many different scientists can run in their labs and all get the same biological effects from weak fields. If this can be done, then the arguments about whether there are effects will disappear. Until it is done, the arguments will continue. Several groups are now working to identify and perform such experiments.

What about the epidemiological studies of cancer?

There have been two kinds of "epidemiological" studies which have looked for an association between exposure to 60 Hz fields and cancer. The first set of studies has looked at the death rates from different diseases for people who are employed in "electrically related" occupations and compared them with the death rates from the same diseases for all other people. The second has compared the *estimated* magnetic field exposures received by people who have specific cancers, especially leukemia, with the *estimated* exposures received by other similar people who did not have cancer. Most of these latter "case-control" studies have involved exposure at home from power distribution lines (lines on the big poles in the street). One cancer that has received particular attention is childhood leukemia.

Some of these studies of both kinds have found a statistical association between increases in estimated field exposure and increased cancer rates. As we discuss on page 9, the phrase "statistical association" is not a synonym for "causes" or for "contributes to." Depending on the study, and the type of cancer, the incidence of cancer in "exposed" populations has been found to be up to several times higher than that experienced by unexposed or less exposed populations. (In contrast, cigarette smoking can increase the risk of lung cancer by 10 to 30 times.) Most of these cancers are fairly rare, for example childhood leukemia affects about one in

5

every 14,000 children per year or about 1 in 1,100 per lifetime.[†]

Most investigators believe that if fields play some role, they will not "initiate" or start cancer. Rather, fields may be a promoter. That is, they aid, or perhaps even make possible, the growth of cancer that has been initiated by one or more other factors.

All of the epidemiological studies involve some level of statistical uncertainty. Some of the results are summarized in the figures on the next two pages. The results are reported in terms of "relative risk." A relative risk of 1 means that "exposed" people in the study had cancer as often as people who are "not exposed" - no more and no less. A relative risk of 3 means that the rate of cancer was three times higher among "exposed" people than the rate among those "not exposed." A relative risk of 0.5 means that "exposed" people in the study had cancer half as often as those "not exposed." The solid dots in the figures show the best estimates of the relative risk for each study. Because the number of people involved in these studies is fairly small, the relative risk cannot be estimated precisely. The vertical bars in the figures show the range of statistical uncertainty. When both ends of the bar are above a relative risk of 1, the study is said to show a positive indication of an association with cancer, and is called a "positive study." In this case "positive" means "demonstrated" rather than "good." When the bar crosses the level 1, it may not be possible to conclude that the study has found an association with cancer. Such a study is sometimes called a "negative study" because no association with cancer has been clearly demonstrated. Modern methods of analysis often move beyond this simple positive/negative characterization to use more subtle statistical methods that examine the overall pattern of the results.

A clustering of results above a value slightly greater than 1 is apparent in the diagrams on pages 7 and 8. Because the increase is so slight, and the results can be influenced by unknown factors, epidemiologist have not yet agreed on whether they imply a true association between fields and cancer. We will discuss this more below, but first we should describe a few of the studies.

The four most widely discussed positive studies involve childhood leukemia. The first two were conducted in the Denver, Colorado, area, the first by Nancy Wertheimer and Ed Leeper, the second by David Savitz and several colleagues. These two studies involved different groups of children. In 1991, a third study was completed by Stephanie London, John Peters, and several colleagues at the University of Southern California in Los Angeles. Finally, in 1992, Maria Feychting

A random distribution can lead to "hot spots"

If we toss 16 beans onto a map of four towns...

...the pattern in which they land is random, but more beans may land in some towns.

Town average 4 beans

Butler   2 beans
Hampton   4 beans
Lincoln   7 beans
Smithtown 3 beans

Lincoln has almost twice the average number of beans. It is a naturally occuring "hot spot."

[†]A simple twofold increase would raise the incidence to one in 7,000 per year or 1 in 550 per lifetime. However, this calculation is misleading since if fields contribute to childhood leukemia, that contribution would already be reflected in the base rate of 1 in 1,100 per lifetime. For quantitative examples of other risks see the table on page 3 of Details Booklet Part 3.

Comparison of some epidemiological results.

This plot shows results for eight epidemiological studies looking at possible associations between residential exposure to power line magnetic fields and childhood cancer.

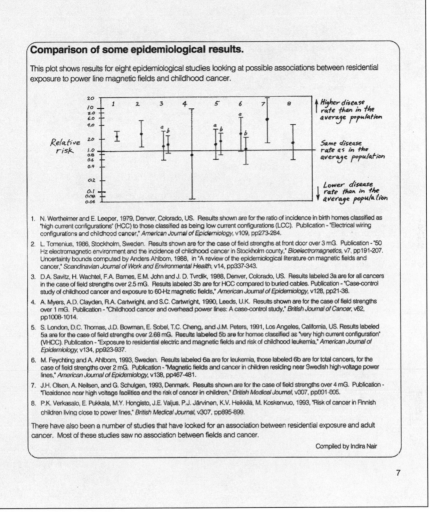

1. N. Wertheimer and E. Leeper, 1979, Denver, Colorado, US. Results shown are for the ratio of incidence in birth homes classified as "high current configurations" (HCC) to those classified as being low current configurations (LCC). Publication - "Electrical wiring configurations and childhood cancer," *American Journal of Epidemiology*, v109, pp273-284.

2. L. Tomenius, 1986, Stockholm, Sweden. Results shown are for the case of field strengths at front door over 3 mG. Publication - "50 Hz electromagnetic environment and the incidence of childhood cancer in Stockholm county," *Bioelectromagnetics*, v7, pp191-207. Uncertainty bounds computed by Anders Ahlbom, 1988, in "A review of the epidemiological literature on magnetic fields and cancer," *Scandinavian Journal of Work and Environmental Health*, v14, pp337-343.

3. D.A. Savitz, H. Wachtel, F.A. Barnes, E.M. John and J. D. Tvrdik, 1988, Denver, Colorado, US. Results labeled 3a are for all cancers in the case of field strengths over 2.5 mG. Results labeled 3b are for HCC compared to buried cables. Publication - "Case-control study of childhood cancer and exposure to 60-Hz magnetic fields," *American Journal of Epidemiology*, v128, pp21-38.

4. A. Myers, A.D. Clayden, R.A. Cartwright, and S.C. Cartwright, 1990, Leeds, U.K. Results shown are for the case of field strengths over 1 mG. Publication - "Childhood cancer and overhead power lines: A case-control study," *British Journal of Cancer*, v62, pp1008-1014.

5. S. London, D.C. Thomas, J.D. Bowman, E. Sobel, T.C. Cheng, and J.M. Peters, 1991, Los Angeles, California, US. Results labeled 5a are for the case of field strengths over 2.68 mG. Results labeled 5b are for homes classified as "very high current configuration" (VHCC). Publication - "Exposure to residential electric and magnetic fields and risk of childhood leukemia," *American Journal of Epidemiology*, v134, pp923-937.

6. M. Feychting and A. Ahlbom, 1993, Sweden. Results labeled 6a are for leukemia, those labeled 6b are for total cancers, for the case of field strengths over 2 mG. Publication - "Magnetic fields and cancer in children residing near Swedish high-voltage power lines," *American Journal of Epidemiology*, v138, pp467-481.

7. J.H. Olsen, A. Neilsen, and G. Schulgen, 1993, Denmark. Results shown are for the case of field strengths over 4 mG. Publication - "Residence near high voltage facilities and the risk of cancer in children," *British Medical Journal*, v307, pp891-895.

8. P.K. Verkasalo, E. Pukkala, M.Y. Hongisto, J.E. Valjus, P.J. Järvinen, K.V. Heikkilä, M. Koskenvuo, 1993, "Risk of cancer in Finnish children living close to power lines," *British Medical Journal*, v307, pp895-899.

There have also been a number of studies that have looked for an association between residential exposure and adult cancer. Most of these studies saw no association between fields and cancer.

Compiled by Indira Nair

7

277

More comparisons of epidemiological results.

This plot shows results for seven epidemiological studies published since 1992 that looked for possible associations between occupational exposure to low frequency magnetic fields and adult cancer.

See the Appendix in Details Booklet Part 3 for reviews of earlier studies.

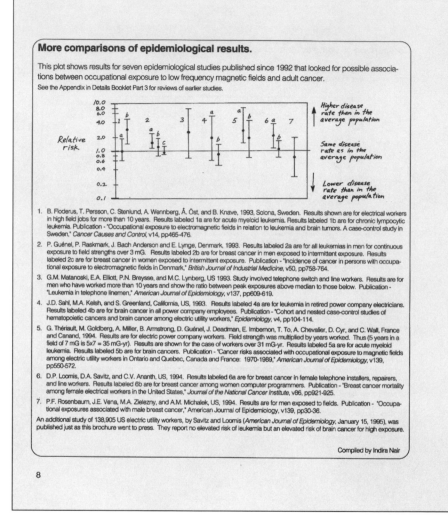

1. B. Floderus, T. Persson, C. Stenlund, A. Wennberg, Å. Öst, and B. Knave, 1993, Solona, Sweden. Results shown are for electrical workers in high field jobs for more than 10 years. Results labeled 1a are for acute myeloid leukemia. Results labeled 1b are for chronic lympocytic leukemia. Publication - "Occupational exposure to electromagnetic fields in relation to leukemia and brain tumors. A case-control study in Sweden," *Cancer Causes and Control*, v14, pp465-476.

2. P. Guénel, P. Raskmark, J. Bach Anderson and E. Lynge, Denmark, 1993. Results labeled 2a are for all leukemias in men for continuous exposure to field strengths over 3 mG. Results labeled 2b are for breast cancer in men exposed to intermittent exposure. Results labeled 2c are for breast cancer in women exposed to intermittent exposure. Publication - "Incidence of cancer in persons with occupational exposure to electromagnetic fields in Denmark," *British Journal of Industrial Medicine*, v50, pp758-764.

3. G.M. Matanoski, E.A. Elliott, P.N. Breysse, and M.C. Lynberg, US 1993. Study involved telephone switch and line workers. Results are for men who have worked more than 10 years and show the ratio between peak exposures above median to those below. Publication - "Leukemia in telephone linemen," *American Journal of Epidemiology*, v137, pp609-619.

4. J.D. Sahl, M.A. Kelsh, and S. Greenland, California, US, 1993. Results labeled 4a are for leukemia in retired power company electricians. Results labeled 4b are for brain cancer in all power company employees. Publication - "Cohort and nested case-control studies of hematopoietic cancers and brain cancer among electric utility workers," *Epidemiology*, v4, pp104-114.

5. G. Thériault, M. Goldberg, A. Miller, B. Armstrong, D. Guénel, J. Deadman, E. Imbernon, T. To, A. Chevalier, D. Cyr, and C. Wall, France and Canand, 1994. Results are for electric power company workers. Field strength was multiplied by years worked. Thus (5 years in a field of 7 mG is 5x7 = 35 mG-yr). Results are shown for the case of workers over 31 mG-yr. Results labeled 5a are for acute myeloid leukemia. Results labeled 5b are for brain cancers. Publication - "Cancer risks associated with occupational exposure to magnetic fields among electric utility workers in Ontario and Quebec, Canada and France: 1970-1989," *American Journal of Epidemiology*, v139, pp550-572.

6. D.P. Loomis, D.A. Savitz, and C.V. Ananth, US, 1994. Results labeled 6a are for breast cancer in female telephone installers, repairers, and line workers. Results labeled 6b are for breast cancer among women computer programmers. Publication - "Breast cancer mortality among female electrical workers in the United States," *Journal of the National Cancer Institute*, v86, pp921-925.

7. P.F. Rosenbaum, J.E. Vena, M.A. Zielezny, and A.M. Michalek, US, 1994. Results are for men exposed to fields. Publication - "Occupational exposures associated with male breast cancer," American Journal of Epidemiology, v139, pp30-36.

An additional study of 138,905 US electric utility workers, by Savitz and Loomis (*American Journal of Epidemiology*, January 15, 1995), was published just as this brochure went to press. They report no elevated risk of leukemia but an elevated risk of brain cancer for high exposure.

Compiled by Indira Nair

8

and Anders Ahlbom, at the Institute of Environmental Medicine, Karolinska Institute in Stockholm completed a study involving all people who lived near high voltage power lines in Sweden. All four studies report an increase in the incidence of childhood leukemia in homes close to power lines that can carry heavy currents.

When we look at these four studies in detail, things get complicated. Several of these studies made short-term measurements of the fields in homes. You might expect the fields to be higher in the homes of children who got cancer. In Savitz' Denver study, children in average fields higher than 2.5 mG have twice the chance of having cancer as those in fields below 1 mG. However, in London and Peter's Los Angeles study, while being close to lines increases the odds of cancer, higher measured fields in homes do not show a statistically significant association with cancer. In this study, leukemia does seem to be associated with being close to various kinds of heavy duty distribution lines as well as with the use of two appliances - black and white television and hair dryers. The Feychting and Ahlbom study in Sweden also finds no correlation with short-term field measurements. However, in this study, detailed power company records allowed the investigators to reconstruct the long-term history of field exposure, and this measure does show a significant correlation with increased cancer.

Male breast cancer is a second form of cancer that has recently received some attention. Three studies - two in the US and one in Norway - have now reported an association between electrical occupations and a higher incidence of this very rare disease. In the US, one study by Genevieve Matanoski and the other by Paul Demers and colleagues found 5-6 times more than the expected number of cases in electrical workers who work in telephone company switching offices and among electricians and telephone linemen. The Norwegian study showed a 2-3 times higher rate for electrical workers. However, because the disease is very rare and only a few cases were observed, one can have only limited confidence in these results. The male breast cancer results are significant because there is some reason to believe that melatonin provides protection against this form of breast cancer, and there is some evidence to suggest that field exposure may affect melatonin levels. Studies on female breast cancer have also begun (see study 6 on page 8).

A positive statistical association of the sort shown in many epidemiological studies may result from the existence of a cause-effect relationship between field exposure and cancer risk. However, it is important to remember that such an association can also exist for other reasons. Taken alone such an association does not prove that fields are involved in causing cancer. In the box on page 2 of the main brochure, we gave an illustration of a statistical association that does not show causation. Consider the fact that both the number of storks and the number of new babies have recently been declining in Europe. A statistical study would show correlation

More comparisons of epidemiological results.

This plot shows results for seven epidemiological studies published since 1992 that looked for possible associations between occupational exposure to low frequency magnetic fields and adult cancer.

See the Appendix in Details Booklet Part 3 for reviews of earlier studies.

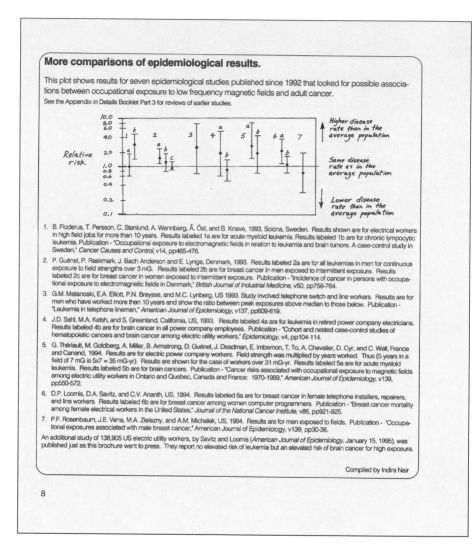

1. B. Floderus, T. Persson, C. Stenlund, A. Wennberg, Å. Öst, and B. Knave, 1993, Solona, Sweden. Results shown are for electrical workers in high field jobs for more than 10 years. Results labeled 1a are for acute myeloid leukemia. Results labeled 1b are for chronic lympocytic leukemia. Publication - "Occupational exposure to electromagnetic fields in relation to leukemia and brain tumors. A case-control study in Sweden," *Cancer Causes and Control*, v14, pp465-476.

2. P. Guénel, P. Raskmark, J. Bach Anderson and E. Lynge, Denmark, 1993. Results labeled 2a are for all leukemias in men for continuous exposure to field strengths over 3 mG. Results labeled 2b are for breast cancer in men exposed to intermittent exposure. Results labeled 2c are for breast cancer in women exposed to intermittent exposure. Publication - "Incidence of cancer in persons with occupational exposure to electromagnetic fields in Denmark," *British Journal of Industrial Medicine*, v50, pp758-764.

3. G.M. Matanoski, E.A. Elliott, P.N. Breysse, and M.C. Lynberg, US 1993. Study involved telephone switch and line workers. Results are for men who have worked more than 10 years and show the ratio between peak exposures above median to those below. Publication - "Leukemia in telephone linemen," *American Journal of Epidemiology*, v137, pp609-619.

4. J.D. Sahl, M.A. Kelsh, and S. Greenland, California, US, 1993. Results labeled 4a are for leukemia in retired power company electricians. Results labeled 4b are for brain cancer in all power company employees. Publication - "Cohort and nested case-control studies of hematopoietic cancers and brain cancer among electric utility workers," *Epidemiology*, v4, pp104-114.

5. G. Thériault, M. Goldberg, A. Miller, B. Armstrong, D. Guénel, J. Deadman, E. Imbernon, T. To, A. Chevalier, D. Cyr, and C. Wall, France and Canand, 1994. Results are for electric power company workers. Field strength was multiplied by years worked. Thus (5 years in a field of 7 mG is 5x7 = 35 mG-yr). Results are shown for the case of workers over 31 mG-yr. Results labeled 5a are for acute myeloid leukemia. Results labeled 5b are for brain cancers. Publication - "Cancer risks associated with occupational exposure to magnetic fields among electric utility workers in Ontario and Quebec, Canada and France: 1970-1989," *American Journal of Epidemiology*, v139, pp550-572.

6. D.P. Loomis, D.A. Savitz, and C.V. Ananth, US, 1994. Results labeled 6a are for breast cancer in female telephone installers, repairers, and line workers. Results labeled 6b are for breast cancer among women computer programmers. Publication - "Breast cancer mortality among female electrical workers in the United States," *Journal of the National Cancer Institute*, v86, pp921-925.

7. P.F. Rosenbaum, J.E. Vena, M.A. Zielezny, and A.M. Michalek, US, 1994. Results are for men exposed to fields. Publication - "Occupational exposures associated with male breast cancer," American Journal of Epidemiology, v139, pp30-36.

An additional study of 138,905 US electric utility workers, by Savitz and Loomis (*American Journal of Epidemiology*, January 15, 1995), was published just as this brochure went to press. They report no elevated risk of leukemia but an elevated risk of brain cancer for high exposure.

Compiled by Indira Nair

8

280

and Anders Ahlbom, at the Institute of Environmental Medicine, Karolinska Institute in Stockholm completed a study involving all people who lived near high voltage power lines in Sweden. All four studies report an increase in the incidence of childhood leukemia in homes close to power lines that can carry heavy currents.

When we look at these four studies in detail, things get complicated. Several of these studies made short-term measurements of the fields in homes. You might expect the fields to be higher in the homes of children who got cancer. In Savitz' Denver study, children in average fields higher than 2.5 mG have twice the chance of having cancer as those in fields below 1 mG. However, in London and Peter's Los Angeles study, while being close to lines increases the odds of cancer, higher measured fields in homes do not show a statistically significant association with cancer. In this study, leukemia does seem to be associated with being close to various kinds of heavy duty distribution lines as well as with the use of two appliances - black and white television and hair dryers. The Feychting and Ahlbom study in Sweden also finds no correlation with short-term field measurements. However, in this study, detailed power company records allowed the investigators to reconstruct the long-term history of field exposure, and this measure does show a significant correlation with increased cancer.

Male breast cancer is a second form of cancer that has recently received some attention. Three studies - two in the US and one in Norway - have now reported an association between electrical occupations and a higher incidence of this very rare disease. In the US, one study by Genevieve Matanoski and the other by Paul Demers and colleagues found 5-6 times more than the expected number of cases in electrical workers who work in telephone company switching offices and among electricians and telephone linemen. The Norwegian study showed a 2-3 times higher rate for electrical workers. However, because the disease is very rare and only a few cases were observed, one can have only limited confidence in these results. The male breast cancer results are significant because there is some reason to believe that melatonin provides protection against this form of breast cancer, and there is some evidence to suggest that field exposure may affect melatonin levels. Studies on female breast cancer have also begun (see study 6 on page 8).

A positive statistical association of the sort shown in many epidemiological studies may result from the existence of a cause-effect relationship between field exposure and cancer risk. However, it is important to remember that such an association can also exist for other reasons. Taken alone such an association does not prove that fields are involved in causing cancer. In the box on page 2 of the main brochure, we gave an illustration of a statistical association that does not show causation. Consider the fact that both the number of storks and the number of new babies have recently been declining in Europe. A statistical study would show correlation

9

Both the number of storks...

... and the number of new babies...

... have recently been decreasing in Europe.

HOWEVER... while the two trends are "statistically correlated" we do not conclude that the one causes the other. Not all correlation means there is causation.

between storks and babies. However, despite this correlation the declining stork population is not the *cause* of the lower numbers of new babies. Similarly, if something else (like air pollution from traffic in streets) is present most of the time that power lines are present, it could be the cause of the association.

There is great controversy about whether the various epidemiological studies reflect a causal relation between field exposure and cancer. Some careful responsible scientists argue that they do. Other responsible scientists point to a variety of very real problems in the design and interpretation of these studies. They argue that the reported findings may be the result of statistical problems or that the cancers may come from various other causes. For example, many of the occupational studies have not "controlled" for other important known carcinogens such as smoking and chemicals in the work place. The number of people exposed to the strongest fields in several of these studies is small. This increases the chance that the results are due to coincidence rather than to a real association between field exposure and cancer. Such uncertainty, and the resulting debate about the meaning of data, are fairly common occurrences in epidemiological studies. Resolution of these issues will require more and better data. Additional epidemiological studies are now in progress. However, in the past when epidemiological studies have succeeded in clearly identifying a hazard (e.g., cigarettes or asbestos) the risks have involved increases of more than tenfold. Even then, it took a long time to establish the association. If fields present a risk of cancer, but the increase in risk is something like two or three, epidemiology alone may never be able to resolve the uncertainty. For this, large expensive studies with animals (typically rats) may be necessary.

You can find references to more detailed introductions to some of the epidemiological literature in the Appendix at the back of Details Booklet Part 3.

Where do things stand with respect to animal studies of cancer?

Most animal studies of cancer are very expensive because they have to expose large numbers of animals for long periods of time. Several lifetime studies with rodents are now planned or under way. It is likely to be several years before they are completed. One Canadian study with mice recently yielded a weakly positive result, but it was not seen when the investigators did the study a second time.

Besides cancer, are there other health effects of possible concern?

Research on cancer has received most of the attention. However work has also been done to explore the possibility of birth defects using mice, rats and small pigs. The

10

282

mouse and rat studies showed no convincing evidence of birth defects from exposure to fields. Results in the pig study are more ambiguous and are complicated by several problems in the way the experiment was designed and conducted.

A study conducted in several laboratories exposed chicken eggs to short pulses of magnetic fields that repeated at 100 times per second (100 Hz). The pulses were turned on rapidly. Some of the laboratories observed a larger fraction of defects in exposed eggs than in eggs that were not exposed to fields. Because the fields were very different from 60 Hz fields and the defects were not found in all the laboratories, the implications of these results for 60 Hz field exposure are not clear. There are many electronic products like video displays, TVs, speed controllers and dimmer switches which produce low frequency pulsed fields which turn on rapidly, so these results cannot be ignored.

Scientists are now conducting a large study of the possible effects of electric blankets on human pregnancies. Earlier studies of this issue have been suggestive but have involved too few women to allow reliable conclusions.

Some animal studies suggest 60 Hz fields may interact with the system that runs the body's biological clock (circadian rhythm) or with the nervous system. There is some reason to think that field exposure might be involved in chronic depression or other systemic neurological disorders. However, there is so little evidence about these effects that, at this point, such arguments are really just speculation.

A recent epidemiological study of workers exposed to fields suggests that there may be an association with the incidence of Alzheimer's disease.

If fields pose health risks, what characteristics of the fields are most likely to be dangerous?

In the box on page 6 of the main brochure, we explained that if fields do pose a risk to public health, their strength may not be what most matters. In other words, "more may not be worse."

Many people find it hard to believe that some characteristic of the field other than its strength may be what is important. An example can help explain how this might be. When a magnetic field changes suddenly it can make fairly strong currents flow in conducting objects such as our bodies. If there were a risk from fields which came from the currents they create in our bodies, strong currents would be created only when the field changes suddenly. If this were the case, it might not be hazardous to spend a long time in a strong steady 60 Hz field, but it could be hazardous to spend time in a somewhat weaker field that switches on and off repeatedly. Suppose this were the case. Then, the steady 60 Hz field created by a nearby high voltage line might not pose a risk, but the switched fields made by an old style electric blanket turning on and off all night could pose a risk.

A yo-yo is an example of a resonant system. It only works if you move your hand up and down at the right times (frequency)...

...and by the right amount (amplitude).

This is just one plausible example. We don't know how things actually work. Let's consider some other plausible examples for other characteristics of the field. For example, there are experiments that show "resonant" effects, that is, effects which appear for fields with some combinations of frequencies and field strengths (amplitudes) but not others. A simple way to understand this is to think of a yo-yo. A yo-yo is a "resonant system." To make it go you must move your hand up and down at the right times (that is at the right frequency) with just the right amount of distance (the right amplitude). If you do use the right frequency and amplitude, the yo-yo works. If you don't, the yo-yo doesn't work. Some of the processes by which fields interact with the surfaces of cells appear to have these same "resonant" characteristics. Thus, for example, there are experiments that show no effect with a strong field but, when the field strength is reduced a little bit, an effect is seen. In at least some of these experiments, it appears that the frequencies and amplitudes at which the resonant responses occur depend upon the strength of the DC (i.e., steady) magnetic field that is present.

There are other laboratory experiments in which biological effects are seen only after being in the field for a very long time. In other cases, effects appear above a certain field strength but then show no additional changes as field strength increases further. Some effects appear only for the first few moments in the field and then disappear. Others are seen only with pulsed fields (that is, fields that turn on and off for brief periods) that have special pulse shapes. It will be some time before scientists can sort out all this complicated evidence and explain it. In the meantime, it seems wise not to assume that weaker fields are necessarily safer than stronger fields, at least across the range of fields people typically encounter.

At the moment the frustrating truth is that no one knows what characteristics of the field, if any, are hazardous. So, no one can tell you if your fields are safe. However, measurements can tell you if your fields are similar to the fields in which other people live. Knowing about the exposures that you and other people experience may help you to better understand the nature of the fields that are all around us, and may also help you to understand whether your situation is common or unique. For information on measurements, see page 6 of Details Booklet Part 3.

Can field exposure produce health benefits?

In certain clinical situations, exposure to fields can be beneficial. Strong pulsed magnetic fields, that turn on and off rapidly, are used in many hospitals to help stimulate bone growth when a broken bone is not growing back together properly.

284

Do 60 Hz fields from power lines pose significant risks to farm crops and animals?

The answer is a simple no. There have been quite a number of studies of field crops grown in strong fields. There have also been quite a number of studies of things like meat and milk production. All of these studies show no significant effects.

If it turns out that fields do pose health risks to people, similar effects may of course be seen in farm animals. But even under the worst assumptions, these effects would be pretty rare. They might be common enough for us to worry about them as a health risk in people, but they will be rare enough that they will have no significant economic implications for farmers. For example, skin cancer from sunlight is something we as people worry about. But farmers don't worry about their pigs getting skin cancer. It's just too rare to matter. That is why we say the answer to this question is a simple no. There is one aspect of electric power that can have very real implications for dairy farmers. This is the so called stray voltage problem. When metal feeders, water troughs, or milking machines are inadequately grounded, cows can be subjected to small but perceptible electrical shocks. This can lead to changes in animal behavior (reluctance to enter a milking stall for instance) and reductions in milk production. The problem can usually be fixed with proper grounding. The problem does not come from the direct effect of exposing the cows to fields. The only other situation that has been identified in which power lines can be important in agriculture is when bee hives are installed directly underneath very high voltage power lines. Again the problem is not from exposing the bees to the field. Rather it comes from voltages that are induced in the hive. Effectively, the bees get shocks as they walk around and, not surprisingly, honey production can drop substantially. If a shield, such as a piece of grounded chicken wire, is installed over the hive, then the problem is eliminated and honey production returns to normal. Still, it is best not to locate bee hives under transmission lines.

Do 60 Hz fields pose significant risks to the environment?

As with agriculture, the answer is again a simple no. Almost all studies of trees and plants have shown no significant effects from 60 Hz or other low frequency electric and magnetic fields. As with agriculture, if there do turn out to be health risks for people, we might expect to see occasional effects in other living things as well. But even under the worst conditions these effects will be so rare that they will only involve individual plants and animals and will not affect the operation of the overall ecosystem.

Some migratory animals like birds and fish appear to use naturally occurring fields as one of their cues in navigation. However, there is no evidence of man-made fields from power lines, radio antennas or other field creating objects causing serious disruptions.

There are experimental studies in which coniferous trees (pines, spruce, firs, etc.) grown right next to very high voltage power lines have experienced needle damage. This is because the fields at the tips of the needles on these trees were so high that they caused the air to break down electrically (like the blue flashes you may see when you stroke a cat in the dark on a dry winter night). Normally trees are trimmed far enough back from transmission lines to preclude this effect.

13

285

Details Booklet Part 3:

More on
"What can and should be
done about 60 Hz fields?"

This is one of three "Details Booklets" associated with a general public information
brochure titled "Fields from Electric Power: What are they? What do we know about
possible health risks? What can be done?"

287

This details booklet provides additional information for people who would like to learn more about the subject of "Part 3: What can and should be done about 60 Hz fields?" of the brochure "Fields from Electric Power." This booklet does not repeat very much of the material that is in Part 3, so it would be best if you read the main brochure first.

Table of Contents

288

What are the alternatives?

Beyond supporting more research, in Part 3 of the main brochure we laid out three broad options for dealing with fields from electric power that might be pursued today. These are:

1. Conclude that the present evidence is not sufficiently persuasive to warrant any action. Don't make any changes in field exposures until new research tells us clearly whether there is a risk and, if so, how big it is.
2. Conclude that there is some basis for concern. Adopt a position of "prudent avoidance," which means limiting exposures which can be avoided with small investments of money and effort. Don't do anything drastic or expensive until research provides a clearer picture of whether there is any risk and, if there is, how big it is.
3. Conclude we have a real problem and spend some serious time and money on an aggressive program to limit field exposures now, while recognizing that we may eventually learn that some or all of this effort and money has been wasted, either because it wasn't needed or because it was spent in the wrong way because we didn't understand the science well enough to allow it to be spent effectively.

What are the pros and cons of the alternatives?

Deciding which option to choose depends on more than the scientific evidence. It requires a value judgment. You need to think about your attitude toward risk and then ask whether you find the incomplete and fragmentary evidence sufficiently troubling to spend time and money on managing fields which you might spend in other ways. Different attitudes toward risk can lead to different actions even among people who agree about the evidence.

Most people who support Option 1 have decided that the current scientific ambiguity about possible health risks from fields is so large, and the possible risks so modest, that no action is justified at this stage. They say that there are plenty of proven risks in life and they think it is better to spend their time dealing with those. In that way, they will know they have made things safer and that they haven't run the risk of wasting their time or money.

Many people who find the evidence sufficiently troubling that they want to take some limited precautionary steps now, support Option 2. They choose to practice "prudent avoidance" — to stay out of strong or unusual fields when that can be done with modest amounts of money and trouble. The key idea here is moderation. These people don't resign from a "high field" job they really like or tear all the wiring

1

out of their house at enormous expense. The box on page 7 of the main brochure lists some of the things these people might consider doing in their home or place of work.

Just as individuals can exercise prudence, government regulators and electric power companies can also exercise prudence. First, however, they have to reach some agreement about what the phrase means. The law uses similar phrases like "beyond a reasonable doubt" or "informed consent" all the time. A number of regulators and power companies have now developed polices for dealing with the problem of managing public and worker exposures to fields based on a strategy of prudent avoidance.

A few people reject the idea of "prudent avoidance" and support Option 3. They call for more drastic action now. They argue that the scientific evidence now shows a clear risk and that the time has come to "solve the problem." While this may sound good, the difficulty is that at the moment we don't know what action to take. Since we don't know what aspect of fields (if any) poses a risk, you as an individual, or society as a whole, could spend a lot of money and possibly end up not making things any safer.

Are there things we should be doing now to prepare for the future?

I believe that the answer is yes.

One important step is to work to improve public understanding of fields and the issues they raise. Another is to develop a careful systematic program of scientific research and provide it with adequate financial support. We are making progress, but despite all the public discussion and controversy I believe this still has not happened to the extent that it should.

Beyond biological and health research, I think we should also expand the amount of work that is being done on developing and testing engineering strategies for reducing or eliminating field exposures from appliances, house wiring, distribution lines and transmission lines. If it turns out that fields do pose health risks, we will certainly not get rid of electric power. The benefits to our health and welfare, and the convenience that electricity brings us, are clearly much larger than any risk that fields may pose.

On the other hand, if fields do pose risks, we will not just put up with them. We will want to redesign the way we distribute and use electric power so as to do what we can to minimize the risks at a reasonable cost. Figuring out how we might do this, poses some engineering challenges that we should start working on now.

2

Can we put bounds on the possible risk?

We do not know enough today to know how to accurately compare the possible risks that fields might pose to the certain risks that we all must live with all the time. Most of the epidemiological studies suggest that *if* there is any cancer risk, the lifetime risk for exposed individuals is probably at or below a level of about 1 in a thousand. The table below provides data on a number of well known risks we all face. Remember that, since we must all die from something, everyone's overall lifetime odds of dying are 1 in 1.

Cause of death.	Approximate number of Americans who die each year from this cause.	Approximate odds that when the average American dies it will be from this cause.
Disease (all kinds)	2,000,000	1 in 1.1
Heart disease	770,000	1 in 2.7
Cancer (all kinds)	480,000	1 in 4.4
Accidents (all kinds)	95,000	1 in 22
Auto accidents	48,000	1 in 44
Diabetes	37,000	1 in 57
Suicide	31,000	1 in 68
Homicide	21,000	1 in 100
Drowning	5,900	1 in 360
Fire	4,800	1 in 440
Asthma	4,000	1 in 530
Firearm accidents	1,500	1 in 1 400
Viral Hepatitis	1,000	1 in 2100
Electrocution	850	1 in 2500
Car-train accidents	570	1 in 3700
Appendicitis	510	1 in 4100
Pregnancy and related	470	1 in 2200
Lightening	78	1 in 27,000
Floods	58	1 in 36,000
Tornado	58	1 in 36,000
Fireworks	8	1 in 260,000
Botulism	2	1 in 1,100,000

There are several reasons why this table uses the words "approximately" and "*average* American." The numbers of death change a bit each year, and some are uncertain for other reasons. Not all people face the same risk. For example, a careful middle-aged driver in a full size car faces a much lower than average risk of being killed in an auto accident. A carefree teenager in a subcompact car faces a much higher than average risk. Numbers based on *Vital Statistics for the United States, 1986*, US Department of Health and Human Services publication PHS88-1122, Washington, DC 1988.

3

You might think of such work as an insurance policy. If we are lucky, we will never need the results. However, developing some options for use in the event that we are not lucky, and fields do pose health risks, could be money well spent. If at some stage it becomes clear that fields do pose a risk to public health, public pressure will rapidly grow to take corrective steps. If, at that time, we haven't done our homework, a lot of dumb, inefficient and wasteful things might happen that could be easily avoided if we do our homework now.

Are there any health or safety standards for fields?

There are several, but they do not really address the central question of possible health risks.

There are standards for transmission lines that are designed to keep fields small enough to prevent dangerous shocks through "induction effects" that can involve large nearby metal objects. The International Radiation Protection Association, whose mission is to review scientific evidence and propose safety standards, has issued draft exposure guidelines for power-frequency electric and magnetic fields. They call for a limit of 5 kV/m for continuous exposures to electric fields and 1 Gauss (1000 mG) for magnetic fields.

In developing these standards, the committee chose not to consider much of the laboratory and epidemiological evidence discussed in Part 2. In some countries, power companies have tried to use these standards to imply that their lines pose no risks. US utilities have not done this.

In the US, regulation of fields from power lines is the responsibility of the states, not the Federal government. Several years ago, when people thought the principle concern was electric fields, a number of states adopted electric field standards for transmission lines that range from 1 to 3 kV/m at the edge of the transmission line right-of-way. These values were chosen on the basis feasibility, not because they assure safety. New York has a magnetic field standard of 200 mG at the edge of the right-of-way. Florida has a standard that ranges between 150 mG and 250 mg for different size lines. There are no Federal standards designed specifically for 60 Hz fields. The state of California has specified that 4% of the cost of new power line projects should be spent on magnetic field reduction. As a matter of prudence, the California Department of Education recommends that new schools be at least 100 feet from 110 kV lines, 150 feet from 235 kV lines, and 250 feet from 345 kV lines.

4

How can I reduce my risk of cancer?

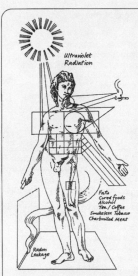

Ultraviolet
Radiation

Fats
Cured foods
Alcohol
Tea / Coffee
Smokeless Tobacco
Charbroiled Meat

Radon
Leakage

On page 7 of the main brochure we discuss a few steps you might take to limit some of your exposure to 60 Hz fields. But fields may not turn out to have anything to do with cancer. If you are concerned about cancer risks, be careful to keep things in perspective. Remember that there are a number of steps you can take which will almost certainly have a greater impact on reducing your cancer risk than anything you might do involving fields. Cigarettes are the leading contributor to cancer today by a very large margin. People who stop smoking, even after many years, greatly lower their cancer risk. Smokers who aren't concerned about their own health but are worried about their children or other family members, should also stop. Associations between smoking and health impacts on nonsmokers in the home have been established. This evidence is significantly stronger than that for fields and cancers. While most lung cancer comes from smoking, perhaps as much as 20% results from exposure to radon, a colorless, odorless, naturally occurring radioactive gas found in all buildings. You can check your home for radon with a simple test kit. If the level measured is more than the EPA action limit of 4 picocuries per liter of air, contact a qualified contractor to discuss ways in which the concentration can be reduced by increasing ventilation and sealing cracks in the basement (radon causes no permanent "contamination" of the home).

Beyond smoking, diet is probably the most important factor in cancer. Current evidence suggests that for most people the basic makeup of their diet is much more important than possible food additives or contamination by toxic materials. The most important things to reduce are fats and red meat. Other things include: charbroiled meat; smoked, cured and pickled foods (things like salami; pepper; celery; mushrooms; alcohol; smokeless tobacco products; and perhaps tea and coffee. On the other hand, things to increase include the amount of fiber; fresh fruits and selected vegetables, especially raw cabbage, broccoli and cauliflower; and foods that are rich in vitamins A, C, and E.

Finally, there is sunlight. While light is essential to well-being, strong direct sunlight, especially at mid-day in the summer, is a leading contributor to skin cancer. If you are concerned about your risk of cancer, you should try to avoid sun burn and exposing your skin to strong sunlight and you should use an effective sun screen when you cannot avoid exposure.

If you would like to learn more about the causes of cancer, we suggest you get the very readable book by Leslie Roberts titled *Cancer Today: Origins, prevention and treatment*, National Academy Press, 1984 (address: 2101 Constitution Avenue, NW, Washington, D.C. 20418). A second very useful book is *Cancer Rates and Risks*, published by the US Department of Health and Human Services, NIH Publication 85-691, 1985. (Available through the US Superintendent of Documents, Washington, D.C. 20402.)

5

Are there safety standards for field exposure outside the United States?

Standards or guidelines for exposures to power-frequency electric fields exist in Britain, Japan, Poland, and Russia. These foreign standards are not significantly different than state standards in the US. For example, guidelines in Russia recommend that fields in publicly-accessible areas be no greater than 10 kV/m and that fields in permanently occupied areas be no greater than 2 kV/m. Although some countries are considering standards, there are presently no national regulations limiting exposures to power-frequency magnetic fields from power lines.

Should I get my fields measured?

As we explain on page 10 of Details Booklet Part 1, many people concerned about fields get their fields measured. While measurements can't tell you if your fields are safe, they may help you to better understand fields, and allow you to compare your fields with the fields in other people's homes and offices.

If you decide to do such a comparison, here's how you might proceed.

First, pick the location where you spend the most time during the day. What was the field measured? Now look at the drawings on page 9 and 11 of Details Booklet Part 1. How does your field compare with the fields these people experienced during their day? If you spent time in other parts of your home or office, how would those fields compare? If you made a measurement at your bed, how does that field compare with the measurements at these people's beds? Do you have any reason to believe that your fields might change more or less over time than the fields these people experienced?

Now look again at the distributions of measurements made in other people's homes that are shown on page 11 of Details Booklet Part 1. These measurements were made in the middle of rooms. How do they compare with the measurements made in the middle of the rooms at your place?

If exposure to fields presents a risk, field strength may not be the most important characteristic of exposure. Can you identify ways in which your exposures might be similar to or different from those received by other people? For example, do you spend a lot of time near particular electrical devices such as "electrical bedding" which cycles on and off?

As explained above, we cannot tell you if any particular field exposure is *safe*. However, measurements may give you some idea about whether the fields to which you are exposed are similar to or different from those that other people experience.

6

294

You may have noticed that in this discussion of measurements we have only talked about magnetic fields. While the initial concern was with electric fields, today, most of the concern about possible risks from fields has shifted to magnetic fields. Electric fields are harder to measure, easily shielded, and probably less important. So, most measurement programs only look at magnetic fields. If you are making your own measurements you will certainly want to measure only magnetic fields.

You can learn how to get measurements made by calling your local electric utility or Department of Public Health. It is also possible to buy a magnetic fields meter.

Dr. Morgan, have you any more advice on buying a house?

If you are thinking about buying a house, and fields are a consideration in your decision, there are two factors you should probably consider: possible risk and future property values. First, if you have some reason to think the property involves strong or otherwise unusual fields, it is probably wise to start by making some measurements. Remember, from Part 1, that the fact that you can see large power lines, or other electrical equipment, does not necessarily mean that their fields will predominate in the house. It is wise to check with some measurements before you put a lot of energy into worrying about what to do.

If the house *does* involve strong or unusual fields, then you need to review the discussion in Part 2 and ask yourself how concerned you are. If fields pose risks, I believe that these risks are likely to be fairly minor, one of many factors which you should consider as you make your decision in choosing between this and other properties. Other factors to consider include:
- how well the property and its location fits your needs
- cost
- other possible risks associated with the property such as fire, flood, neighbor-hood crime, traffic risk to children, radon, asbestos, and so on.

But, you may not share my view that fields should be just one of many factors to consider. If after careful thought you decide that once you have bought the property you are not going to be able to stop worrying about fields, and get on with life, then you should probably look elsewhere.

The second issue to think about is how people's perceptions of fields may affect current and future property values. It is not clear how much effect on property values concern about fields has had. To the extent that it does have an effect, it can cut two ways. It may mean that you can get a really good deal because others are more concerned then you think they should be, and act to push the price down on an otherwise attractive property. On the other hand, if in the future the risks become more likely, or people get more concerned, this could mean that your future resale opportunities and value could be more limited than you would like.

Who is supporting research on possible health risks from 60 Hz fields?

In the United States, support for research on possible health risks from low frequency electric and magnetic fields comes primarily from the Electric Power Research Institute (EPRI), the US Department of Energy (DoE), and the National Institute of Environmental Health Sciences (NIEHS). Several individual states, including New York and California, have programs. A number of power companies support their own research or provide matching funds to augment federally funded research. Total research support in the US amounts to about 30 million dollars per year.

Outside of the United States there are significant research programs under way in a number of other countries including (in approximate descending order of funding levels) Sweden, the United Kingdom, Germany, Canada, Japan, Italy, France, Finland, and Norway. Some research is also being done in Russia, Eastern Europe and China. In 1994, the worldwide research effort, including the US, amounted to about $45 million per year.

Most research has focused on possible health effects. Recently research has also begun on how fields associated with electrical systems might be reduced.

Glossary

AC: The abbreviation for alternating current. An AC current, or an AC field, changes strength and direction in a rhythmically repeating cycle.

amp: The unit used to measure current. Abbreviated A.

charge: The electrical property of matter which is responsible for creating electric fields. There are two kinds of charge labeled positive and negative. Electric fields begin on positive charges and end on negative charges. Like charges repel each other. Unlike charges attract each other.

circadian rhythm: The rhythmic biological cycle (of things like hormone concentrations in the body) that usually recurs at approximately 24 hour intervals.

contact current: The current that flows in the body when a person touches a conducting object (e.g., a metal refrigerator) that has a voltage induced on it because it is in an AC field.

current: An organized flow of electric charge. Current in a power line is analogous to the rate of fluid flow in a pipeline. All currents produce magnetic fields. Current is measured in amps.

DC: The abbreviation for direct current. A DC current, or a DC field, is steady and does not change strength or direction over time.

distribution line: A power line used to distribute power in a local region. Distribution lines typically operate at voltages of between 5 and 35 kV, much lower than the voltages of transmission lines. However, the currents on some distribution lines can be comparable to transmission line currents.

DNA: Deoxyribonucleic acid, the complex, usually helically shaped chemical compounds from which the genetic material of genes and chromosomes is made.

dose: The amount of exposure of a kind that produces effects. In the case of chemical pollutants, dose is usually

8

the amount of chemical that gets into the body. In the case of fields, it is often unclear what aspect of the field, if any, is involved in producing effects. Hence, it is not clear how to measure dose from electromagnetic fields.

electric field: A representation of the forces that fixed electric charges exert on other charges at a distance. The electric field has a strength and direction at all points in space which is often represented diagrammatically by field lines. Electric field lines begin on positive charges and end on negative charges.

electromagnetic field: A field made up of a combination of electric and magnetic fields.

epidemiology: The study of the distribution and factors that cause health related conditions and events in groups of people, often making use of statistical data on the incidence of disease or death.

gauss: A common unit of measure for magnetic fields. Abbreviated G. There are 10,000 gauss in one tesla.

grounding: In order to reduce shock hazard, neutral wires in the electric power system are often grounded by attaching them to a metallic object in contact with the earth. In a home, the neutral is either grounded to a water pipe or to a grounding rod at the main service panel.

hertz: A cycle per second. A unit used to measure frequency. In America, AC power has a frequency of 60 Hz. In most of Europe, AC power has a frequency of 50 Hz. Radio waves have frequencies of many thousands or millions of hertz. Abbreviated Hz.

histogram: A type of plot. All data in intervals of a fixed width is added and then displayed. If the interval is 1 mG, for example, then the reader can see how much of the data is in the interval from 0 to 1 mG, from 1 to 2 mG, and so forth.

hormone: A chemical substance produced by a part of the body and used to send information to some other part of the body. Many people associate the word hormone with sex hormones, substances produced by the sex glands. There are many other kinds of hormones such as insulin which helps the body use sugar and cortisol which helps to control inflammation.

Hz: The abbreviation for hertz. A cycle per second.

impedance: The electrical property of a conductor or circuit which resists the flow of an electric current. Impedance is similar to resistance (see below) but may also involve a change in the current's phase.

initiator: Any agent, such as ionizing radiation and some chemicals, which can start the process of turning normal cells into cancer cells.

kV: The abbreviation for kilovolt. A thousand volts.

kV/m: The abbreviation for kilovolt per meter. A thousand volts per meter. The strength of an electric field is measured in volts per meter.

leukemia: A general word used to refer to a number of different types of cancers of the blood forming tissues.

magnetic field: A representation of the forces that a moving charge exerts on other moving charges (because they are moving). The magnetic field has a strength and direction at all points in space which is often represented diagrammatically by field lines. Magnetic field lines form closed continuous loops around currents. All currents produce magnetic fields.

microwaves: Electromagnetic waves which have a frequency of between roughly 1 billion and 300 billion Hz (a wave length of between roughly 30 centimeters and 1 millimeter). Microwaves have a frequency higher than normal radio waves but lower than heat (infrared) and light. In contrast to x-rays, microwaves are a form of nonionizing radiation (see x-rays below). Strong microwaves can produce biological damage by heating tissue. Sixty Hz fields cannot do this.

phase: The timing with which an alternating current, voltage or field is changing strength and direction. See 'three phase power' below.

pineal melatonin: The endocrine hormone melatonin that is produced by the pineal gland in the brain. Melatonin is involved in the control of circadian rhythm in at least some animals.

promoter: any agent, such as some chemicals, which can aid or accelerate the growth of cancer.

prudent avoidance: The idea of avoiding human exposure to power-frequency electric and magnetic field when it can be done at modest cost and little inconvenience. To be useful, the general idea must be given specific meaning by policy makers and regulators.

radiation: Any of a variety of forms of energy propagated through space. Radiation may involve either particles (for example alpha-rays or beta-rays) or waves (for example, x-rays, light, microwaves or radio waves). Ionizing radiation such as x-rays carries enough energy to break chemical and electrical bonds. Nonionizing radiation like microwaves does not. Most of the energy in the 60 Hz fields associated with power lines, wiring and appliances does not propagate away from them through space. Hence, it is best not to refer to these fields as radiation.

resistance: The electrical property of a conductor that resists the flow of an electric current without changing its phase.

right-of-way: The land on either side of transmission lines in which buildings cannot be built. Right-of-ways exist to reduce potential electric hazard from the lines, and range from nonexistent for some lower voltage lines to several hundred feet across for some high voltage lines. Abbreviated ROW.

RNA: Ribonucleic acid. Complex chemical compounds in cells that are copied from DNA. RNA carries information and material that cells use to make proteins.

stray voltage: A condition that arises when voltages are induced in poorly grounded conductors by strong power-frequency field. It is particularly troublesome on dairy farms in which cows are subjected to small but perceptible electrical shocks which can lead to changes in animal behavior and reductions in milk production. The problem can usually be fixed with proper grounding of equipment. The problem is *not* a direct effect of exposing the cows to fields and can occur without large power lines being involved.

three phase power: Ordinary 60 Hz house current involves only one "hot" wire or phase. Most high voltage transmission lines involve three "hot" wires or phases. The voltage and current in these three wires do not all reach their peak values at the same time. First one, then the next, then the third, reaches maximum, 1/180th of a second apart. The three work together as one line for transmitting electric energy. Three phase power is used because it is a more efficient way to transmit electric power than single phase power.

tesla: A unit of measure for magnetic fields. Abbreviated T. There are 10,000 gauss in one tesla. A microtesla (mT) is one millionth of a tesla or .01 gauss.

transformer: Transformers are used to transform electric power from one voltage to another. Examples of transformers include the "can" type transformers seen on distribution lines, or the much larger transformers used in neighborhood substations.

transmission line: A power line used to carry large quantities of electric power at high voltage, usually over long distances. Transmission lines typically operate at voltages of between 69 and 765 kV. They are usually built on steel towers or very large wooden poles.

voltage: A measure of electric potential, the amount of work that must be done to move a charge from ground to a location in space such as a power line conductor. Voltage in a power line is analogous to pressure in a pipeline. Voltage is measured in volts. Abbreviated V.

V/m: Abbreviation for a volt per meter. The strength of an electric field is measured in volts per meter, or sometimes in thousands of volts per meter (kV/m).

X-rays: A form of electromagnetic waves similar to light but with a much shorter wavelength (higher frequency). X-rays are a form of ionizing radiation. They can damage biological systems by breaking chemical or molecular bonds. Sixty Hz fields cannot do this.

10

298

Appendix: How to learn more.

The scientific literature on 60 Hz fields is large and is growing rapidly. Published every two months by the Bioelectromagnetics Society, *Bioelectromagnetics* is the single most important scientific journal in this field. Many of the most important research results are published there.

There are two commercial newsletters (both fairly expensive but both well done) *EMF Health and Safety Digest* (2701 University Avenue, Southeast, Suite 203, Minneapolis, Minnesota 55414-3233) and *Microwave News* (P.O. Box 1799, Grand Central Station, New York, NY 10163) which carry nontechnical reports on the latest scientific, regulatory and other developments in this field. There are two large scientific meetings each year at which many of the scientific investigators present their latest research findings: the annual meeting of the Bioelectromagnetics Society (usually in June) and the annual DoE/EPRI Research Contractors Meeting (usually in November). Both are open to the public.

The US EPA distributes various information to the public on power-frequency fields. They can be reached at: EPA Public Information Center, Washington, DC 20460 (tel: 202+260-7751). EPA also operates a telephone hotline on fields. The number is 800+363-2383.

A good treatment for the general public can be found in:

*   *Electric Power Lines: Questions and answers on research into health effects*, Bonneville Power Administration, 905 NE 11th Street, Portland, Oregon 97232 (tel: 800+622-4520).

The final pages contain a useful list of papers and reports.

There are a number of published reviews of the scientific literature. They vary considerably in coverage and level of technical detail. Unfortunately, some of the best reviews are in the form of reports, not books. It may take a bit of effort to track down copies of some of them.

At the request of the Office of Technology Assessment of the United States Congress we wrote:

*   US Congress, Office of Technology Assessment, *Biological Effects of Power Frequency Electric and Magnetic Fields - Background Paper*, prepared by I. Nair, M.G. Morgan, H.K. Florig, of the Department of Engineering and Public Policy, Carnegie Mellon University, OTA-BP-E-53 (Washington, DC: US Government Printing Office, May 1989).

11

299

This report, written for a Congressional audience, explains what 60 Hz fields are, discusses human exposure to fields, summarizes many of the biological effects, discusses the epidemiological evidence and discusses alternative policies that might be adopted. While it is a few years old, most of its contents remain useful.

Another review intended for a general audience is:

- *Electrical and Biological Effects of Transmission Lines: A review*, Technical Report prepared by J. Lee, J.H. Brunke, G.E. Lee, G.L. Reiner and F.L. Shon, of the Bonneville Power Administration of the US Department of Energy (Portland, Oregon 97208), 1989.

The Bonneville Power Administration (BPA) is the big Federal power system in the Pacific Northwest. The report focuses heavily on high voltage transmission lines and their associated fields.

A recent technical review of the literature is provided in:

- Thomas S. Tenforde, "Biological Interactions and Potential Health Effects of Extremely-Low-Frequency Magnetic Fields From Power Lines and Other Common Sources" in *Annual Review of Public Health*, v13, 1992, pp173-196.

Two books which provide excellent background for a number of topics are:

- *Biological Effects of Electric and Magnetic Fields*, D.O. Carpenter and S. Ayrapetyan (eds.), v1 - Sources and Mechanisms, v2 - Clinical Applications and Therapeutic Effects, Academic Press, San Diego, California, 1994.

- "Extra Low Frequency Electromagnetic Fields: The question of cancer," edited by B. Wilson, R. Stevens, and L. Anderson, Battelle Press, Columbus, Ohio, 1989.

A paper which describes one model by which exposure to fields might lead to increased health risks is:

- "Neuroendocrine Mediated Effects of Electromagnetic-Field Exposure: Possible role of the pineal gland," B. Wilson, W. Stevens, and L. Anderson in the scientific journal *Life Science*, v45, 1989, pp1319-1332.

One other work about fields and cancer, which provides a fairly thorough review of the literature, is the result of work funded by the Electric Power Research Institute:

12

- "Extremely Low Frequency Electric and Magnetic Fields and Cancer: A literature review" compiled by W. Creasey and R. Goldberg, Report EN-6674, 1989.

An analysis of the number of epidemiological studies can be found in:

- "Residential Proximity to Electricity Transmission and Distribution Equipment and Risk of Childhood Leukemia...," E. Washburn and six other authors in the scientific journal *Cancer Causes and Control*, v5, 1994, pp299-309.

The details of interactions between fields and biological systems at the level of individual cells have emerged as an especially important portion of the literature on low frequency fields. While most of the reviews of this topic are quite technical, the Veterans Administration has produced a 15-minute video tape (made at the Walt Disney studios with illustrations by Frank Armitage who did "The Fantastic Voyage"). The video tape is intended for semi-technical and nontechnical audiences. It is:

- "Cell Membranes and Intercellular Communications," US Veterans Administration, distributed by National Audio Visual Center (8700 Edgeworth Drive, Capital Heights, MD 20743-3701, tel: 301+763-1896).

Some of the ideas presented in this movie are still quite controversial within the research community.

Oak Ridge Associated Universities coordinated the production of a report that concludes that there is "no convincing evidence in the published literature to support the contention that exposure to extremely low frequency electric and magnetic fields generated by sources such as household appliances, video display terminals, and local power lines are demonstrable health hazards." It is:

- *Health Effects of Low Frequency Electric and Magnetic Fields,* Prepared by an Oak Ridge Associated Universities Panel for the Committee on Interagency Radiation Research and Policy Coordination, US Government Printing Office, 029-000-00443-9, 1992.

This report was stimulated by the draft of an earlier EPA report which was never approved for final publication. EPA does not want its draft report to be cited. The last version circulated for public review suggested that evidence on possible risks from fields does warrant concern. EPA is now in the process of producing a new review document.

13

Department of Engineering and Public Policy
Carnegie Mellon University
Pittsburgh, PA 15213

302

Appendix C

Reproduction of the set of risk communication on the risks of HIV/AIDS. The general structure of the communication is shown in Figure C.1. See Chapter 8 for further detail.

Figure C.1. General structure of the seven-part risk communication materials on HIV/AIDS.

how can you tell
if you have HIV?

how can you tell
if you have HIV?

The *only* way to find out if you have HIV (the virus that leads to AIDS) is to be *tested*.

When can you get tested?

When HIV gets into your blood, your body starts to make *antibodies* to fight it. The test looks for those antibodies. But it can take *up to six months* for your body to make enough antibodies to show up on a test. For most people it only takes *three* months for antibodies to show up on a test. Still, the test will miss HIV in a few people after only three months. So if you had unsafe sex less than six months ago, it may be too soon to tell if you have HIV.

If you are worried that you might have HIV, you can get tested right away. To be sure, you can get *another* test six months later.

Where can you get tested?

You can call the *AIDS Hotline* (1-800-342-AIDS) to find out where you can get tested. They will ask you for your zip code and then tell you places to go that are close to you. Many places will do the test for free! If you are under 18 years old, there are places where you don't need your parent's permission to get tested. You can call the place to make sure before you go.

Does it matter where you get tested:

Testing places have different ways of keeping track of the tests. Some places do *anonymous testing*. This means that they never ask for your name. Instead of asking you for your real name, they give you a code name or number, like *007*. Then, *only you* can get the test result.

Other places do *confidential testing*. This is different from anonymous testing because these places *do* ask for your name or social security number. These places won't tell *just anyone* about your test. But they can tell *some* people, like your doctor or your boss. The law decides who can know about your test.

What happens when you get tested?

When you go to get the test, they will take a little bit of your blood. This may hurt a little, but only for a moment. They only use new needles, so you can't get AIDS from the test.

What do they do with your blood?

Your blood will be sent to a lab. Most labs do the *ELISA test*. It looks for HIV antibodies in your blood. If the ELISA test doesn't find any HIV antibodies in your blood, the lab stops testing and tells you that you're OK.

If the ELISA test shows that HIV antibodies *might* be in your blood, the lab does the ELISA test again. If the second test doesn't find any HIV antibodies in your blood, the lab stops testing and tells you that you're OK. But if the second ELISA test also shows that HIV antibodies might be in your blood, the lab does a different test called a *Western Blot test*.

If all three tests show that you have HIV, they may ask you for more blood. They will use this new blood to do a second Western Blot test. They do this to make sure that you really have HIV.

Why do they do all of these tests?
The ELISA test finds any antibodies that look like HIV antibodies. The Western Blot test shows all the different antibodies in your blood. The Western Blot is almost perfect at showing whether HIV antibodies are in your blood or not, but is a harder test for the lab to do. That's why they start with the ELISA test. They only do the Western Blot test if the ELISA test shows that there's reason to worry.

What will they tell you?
The lab tests take about a week. If the lab didn't find any HIV antibodies in your blood, you will be told you are *HIV negative*. This means that you didn't have HIV six months ago. If you haven't done anything in the last six months that could give you HIV, then this means you don't have HIV now. But if you have done something that is a risk for getting HIV, it may be too soon for the test to show that you have HIV. To be sure, you should be tested again in six months.

If the ELISA tests and the Western Blot test found HIV in your blood, you will be told you are *HIV positive*. This means you have HIV. Your doctor can tell you about the different kinds of medicine and help you decide what to do next.

is an HIV test
part of a check-up?

Your doctor will do some tests every time you go in for a check-up, but not an HIV test. The only way to get a test for HIV from your doctor is to ask for one.

what about
home tests?

Another way to get tested is to buy a home HIV test in a drug store, or order one by phone. You will send a little bit of your blood to the lab with a secret code. They will do the same tests as the other labs. You can call in for the result.

what about
other tests?

Some places now do an *oral test* for HIV. It uses spit instead of blood. This test also looks for *antibodies*. There is almost no HIV in spit. But there *are* HIV antibodies in spit. The oral test is just as good as the blood test, but it's still very new and not used in many places.

Scientists are also working on a *urine test*. There is no HIV in urine. But there *are* HIV antibodies in urine. This test will also look for antibodies.

You've heard a lot about AIDS, but some pieces of the puzzle may still be missing. There are some pieces that you might not know, and there are some pieces that scientists are still working on. These pages share what is already known. The more you know the better.

For more answers, call the AIDS hotline for free:

- English: 1-800-342-AIDS (24 hours a day)
- Español: 1-800-344-SIDA (8am-2am)
- TTY/TDD: 1-800-243-7889
  (10am to 10pm Monday-Friday)

Written by Carnegie Mellon AIDS group, SDS
©1997 CMU 2/6/97
To order pamphlets call: (not yet available)
or write: not yet available
        [AIDS puzzle]
        [Pittsburgh, PA 15213]

is AIDS the same as HIV?

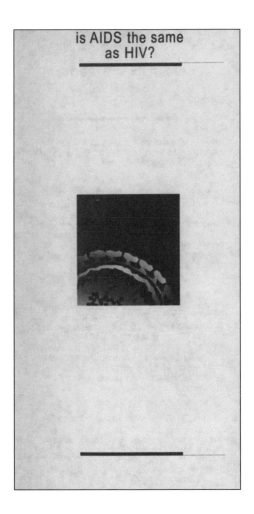

is AIDS the same as HIV?

No, AIDS is not the same as HIV. AIDS is *caused* by the virus called *HIV*. Colds and the flu are also caused by viruses.

How does your body fight HIV?

Your body can fight off many viruses, but not HIV. Your *immune system* fights any living thing that doesn't belong in your body, like bacteria, infections and viruses. *White blood cells* are an important part of the immune system. *T4 cells* are a kind of white blood cell that is very important to HIV.

When a virus gets into your body, the T4 cells do two things. They start making more T4 cells, *and* they send an alarm to the rest of the immune system. This alarm tells the immune system to make *antibodies*. Antibodies are molecules that help the immune system fight viruses. These antibodies stick to the virus. This lets the rest of the immune system know the virus is there, so it can kill the virus.

But HIV isn't like other viruses. Antibodies have trouble finding HIV, so the immune system *doesn't know* it's there. And if the immune system doesn't know HIV is there, then it can't kill HIV.

How does HIV give you AIDS?

HIV kills the T4 cells. First, HIV takes over some T4 cells. Once HIV gets inside the T4 cell, it can't do its job any more. Instead, the T4 cell makes more HIV. Then HIV kills the T4 cell. The new HIV finds other T4 cells to make even more HIV. Then it kills these T4 cells, and so on. If you have more HIV in your body, it is easier for someone to get HIV from having sex with you.

When HIV takes over too many T4 cells, the immune system won't be told to attack anything. It won't even attack weak viruses and common bacteria, things your body can usually fight easily. A test called a *T4 cell count* tells how many T4 cells are still working. When the T4 cell count gets really low, then you have AIDS.

So, what is AIDS?

AIDS is not one disease. AIDS is a *syndrome*, which means that it is a group of diseases that go together. These diseases come from having a very weak immune system. That is where AIDS got its name: *Acquired Immune Deficiency Syndrome.*

What is HIV?

HIV has a similar name: *Human Immunodeficiency Virus*. Its name means that it is the virus that makes the immune system weak, or *deficient*, in humans. There are different kinds of HIV. Some kill T4 cells faster than others, but they all lead to AIDS in the end.

It can take 10 years for the T4 cell count to get very low. So you can have HIV in your blood for 10 years before getting AIDS. With no medicine, most people with AIDS die in less than 5 years.

Is there a cure for HIV?

There is still no cure for HIV or AIDS. For a long time there was nothing a person could do if they had HIV. But now there are medicines that try to slow it down. Each kind of medicine works in a different way.

Some of these medicines, called *RT inhibitors* (such as AZT and 3TC) stop HIV from taking over the T4 cell. If HIV doesn't take over the T4 cell, then it won't make more HIV. But HIV still takes over some T4 cells.

Other medicines, called *protease inhibitors*, stop HIV from making more HIV, even after it has taken over the T4 cell. Together these medicines try to stop HIV.

Each medicine fights HIV in its own way. So doctors give people with HIV more than one kind of medicine at a time. Sometimes, these medicines help people with HIV keep from getting AIDS.

These medicines do not cure AIDS. They only work for some people, and they cost a lot of money. Many people can't get these medicines because they can't pay for them. Also, these medicines don't work as well for people who have had HIV for a long time.

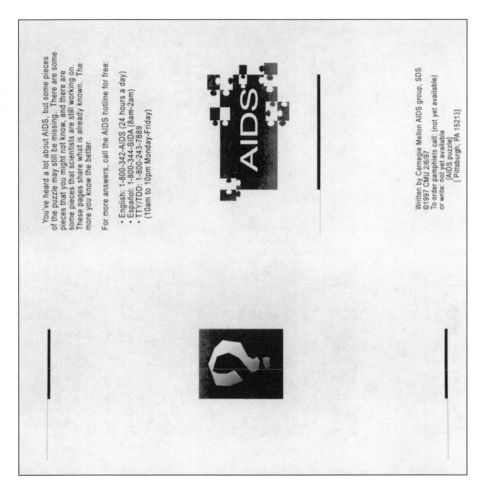

You've heard a lot about AIDS, but some pieces of the puzzle may still be missing. There are some pieces that you might not know, and there are some pieces that scientists are still working on. These pages share what is already known. The more you know the better.

For more answers, call the AIDS hotline for free:

• English: 1-800-342-AIDS (24 hours a day)
• Español: 1-800-344-SIDA (8am-2am)
• TTY/TDD: 1-800-243-7889
  (10am to 10pm Monday-Friday)

Written by Carnegie Mellon AIDS group, SDS
©1997 CMU 2/6/97
To order pamphlets call: (not yet available)
or write: not yet available
          [AIDS puzzle]
          [Pittsburgh, PA 15213]

they say you can get AIDS the first time...

What they really mean is that there's a *chance you will get AIDS* the first time. But there's also a *chance you won't*. This is true for every time. Just because a person didn't get HIV the *first* time, that doesn't mean they won't get it the *next* time. Each time is like a roll of the dice.

Imagine that you are going to roll a pair of dice, and you don't want to roll *snake eyes* (double ones). The first time you roll the dice, you probably won't get snake eyes, but you might. The second time there is another chance, and the third time there is yet another. The more times you roll the dice, the more chances you have of getting snake eyes on at least one of those rolls. If you roll the dice 100 times, you have about a 94% chance of getting snake eyes *at least once*. So if you roll the dice 100 times, there is only a 6% chance that you will *never* get snake eyes.

HIV (the virus that leads to AIDS) works the same way. The first time you have sex, you may or may not get it. But the more times you have sex, the more chances you have of getting HIV. This graph shows the chance of getting HIV from having sex with a person who has HIV. The more times a person has sex, the more chance they have of getting HIV. This is true *with or without* a condom. But the chances go up much more quickly without a condom.

This is also true for having sex with a person who doesn't know if they have HIV. The chances still go up much more quickly *without* a condom. Of course, if you don't have sex at all, then there is *no chance* of getting HIV from sex.

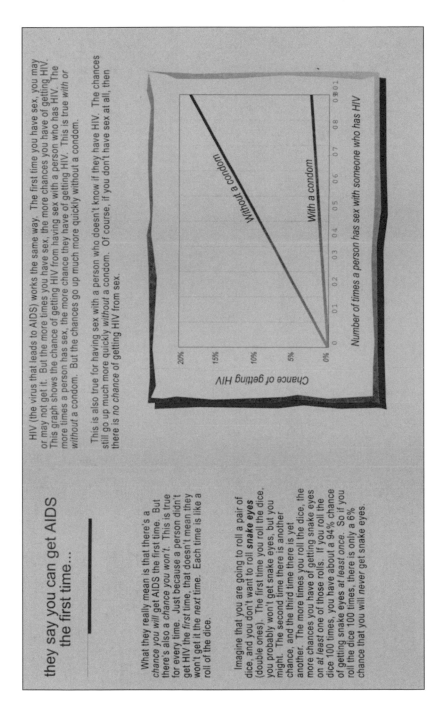

Chance of getting HIV

Without a condom

With a condom

0% 5% 10% 15% 20%

0   0.1 0.2 0.3 0.4 0.5 0.6 0.7 0.8 0.9 1.0

Number of times a person has sex with someone who has HIV

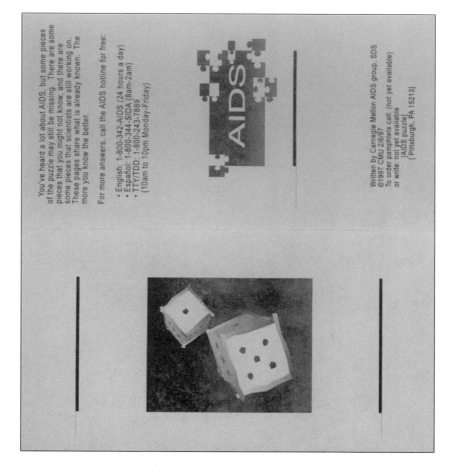

You've heard a lot about AIDS, but some pieces of the puzzle may still be missing. There are some pieces that you might not know, and there are some pieces that scientists are still working on. These pages share what is already known. The more you know the better.

For more answers, call the AIDS hotline for free:

- English: 1-800-342-AIDS (24 hours a day)
- Español: 1-800-344-SIDA (8am-2am)
- TTY/TDD: 1-800-243-7889
  (10am to 10pm Monday-Friday)

Written by Carnegie Mellon AIDS group, SDS
©1997 CMU 2/6/97
To order pamphlets call: (not yet available)
or write: not yet available
[AIDS puzzle]
[Pittsburgh, PA 15213]

do some kinds of sex have more risk for getting HIV?

do some kinds of sex have more risk for getting HIV?

HIV (the virus that leads to AIDS) is in the blood and the fluids the body makes during sex. HIV is spread when these fluids go from one person's body to another's. This can happen during any kind of sex:

- *vaginal sex*: having a man's penis go inside a woman's vagina
- *oral sex*: putting the mouth or tongue on someone's penis or vagina
- *anal sex*: having a man's penis go inside someone's butt

How do you get HIV from having sex?

HIV can get in through small cuts, tears or sores on the skin. These may be too small to see or feel. HIV can also pass through the skin inside the mouth, vagina and butt. This kind of skin is called the *mucous membrane*.

During any kind of sex, cuts or sores on the vagina or penis make it easier for HIV to get in. A person may have sores from *herpes* or another disease that you can get from having sex.

All kinds of sex are more risky for the partner who is getting the penis inside their body. That person gets more of the other partner's fluids inside them. They are also more likely to get cuts and scrapes, which can let HIV in.

What kind of sex is less risky?

Oral sex is the least risky for getting HIV. There isn't very much HIV in spit, but there can be HIV in sex fluids and in blood. You can get sores or tiny cuts in your mouth from brushing your teeth or eating hard food. Then, if you have oral sex, HIV can get in through these sores or cuts.

Vaginal sex is more risky than oral sex because HIV can get in through the mucous membranes. Anal sex is the most risky for both partners. The skin inside the butt is thin, so it can be cut or scraped easily. This makes it easier for HIV to get in.

How can you protect yourself from HIV?

With all kinds of sex, you can lower the chance of getting HIV by using protection. *Latex condoms* with a lubricant can be used on a man's penis for vaginal sex or anal sex. Latex condoms without lubricant can be used for oral sex.

For oral sex on a woman, something needs to cover the vagina. That way, the mouth doesn't touch the sex fluids. A piece of plastic wrap can be used to cover the vagina. Or, roll a condom all the way out, and cut it down the side. Then open it up and use it to cover the vagina. Be sure that the mouth never touches the side with the sex fluids.

cut here

roll
out
flat

What doesn't protect you from HIV?

Natural condoms, such as *lambskin condoms*, do *not* protect against HIV. They have tiny pores that HIV can easily get through.

Birth control pills also don't protect against HIV or any other diseases you can get from having sex. Even if a woman is on the pill, she and her partner still need to use a condom if they want to protect themselves.

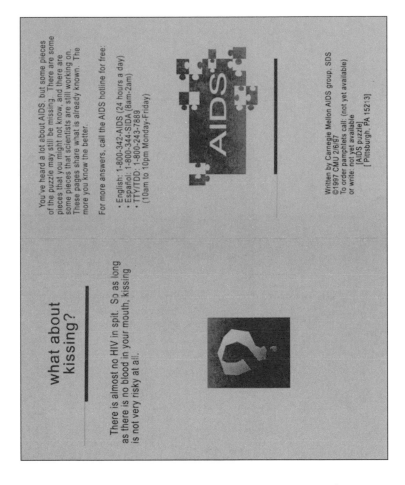

You've heard a lot about AIDS, but some pieces of the puzzle may still be missing. There are some pieces that you might not know, and there are some pieces that scientists are still working on. These pages share what is already known. The more you know the better.

For more answers, call the AIDS hotline for free:

- English: 1-800-342-AIDS (24 hours a day)
- Español: 1-800-344-SIDA (8am-2am)
- TTY/TDD: 1-800-243-7889
  (10am to 10pm Monday-Friday)

Written by Carnegie Mellon AIDS group, SDS
©1997 CMU 2/6/97
To order pamphlets call: (not yet available)
or write not yet available
[AIDS puzzle]
[Pittsburgh, PA 15213]

what about kissing?

There is almost no HIV in spit. So as long as there is no blood in your mouth, kissing is not very risky at all.

does alcohol
make you lose control?

does alcohol
make you lose control?

You may have heard that when people drink they get out of control. But this is not the whole story.

What really happens when people drink?

What *really* happens is that when people drink they don't care as much about things that are important to them when they are not drinking. They may not care if they get in a fight, drive drunk, or have sex. When people drink, they are more likely to do things that might bother them later.

How do people stay in control?

When people drink, they *can* control themselves. But sometimes they just *don't* care enough to do so. They need to decide what they care about *before* they start drinking.

Here are some ways that people say they handle it:

- I like to drink at parties, and sometimes I drink a lot. So I make sure I go with a friend. If we stay together, then we can't do anything stupid.

- I try to just sip at my drinks, so that I don't drink very much. I keep the same drink in my hand, and sip it very slowly.

- If I go to a party and there is alcohol there, I leave, because I'm too young to drink. I don't want to get in trouble with the police.

- Sometimes when I go to a party, I just keep dancing all the time. You know, if you're up dancing you don't have to be sitting around drinking.

- If I go to a party and there is alcohol there, I just drink soda.

These people made their decisions *before* they started drinking. They know that when they are drinking, they don't always remember what is important to them. So, they decide what they want to do before they go out. Then they don't have to make any big decisions when they are drinking. In other words, *they think before they drink.*

What about sex and drinking?

People can also make plans about sex before they start drinking. This can help them avoid bad things, like getting AIDS or some other disease.

Here are some ways that people say they handle it:

- I don't usually have sex when I'm drinking but you never know. So I make sure I have a condom with me.

- When I'm drinking, I may not care if we use a condom. So I never have sex when I'm drinking. We just kiss.

321

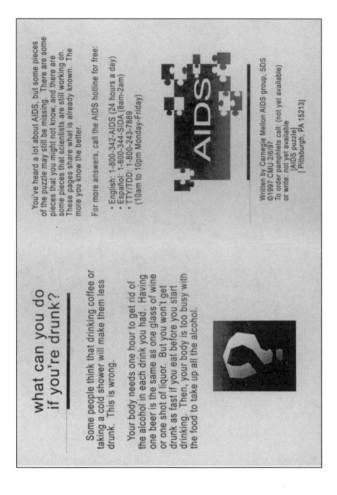

what can you do if you're drunk?

Some people think that drinking coffee or taking a cold shower will make them less drunk. This is wrong.

Your body needs one hour to get rid of the alcohol in each drink you had. Having one beer is the same as one glass of wine or one shot of liquor. But you won't get drunk as fast if you eat before you start drinking. Then, your body is too busy with the food to take up all the alcohol.

You've heard a lot about AIDS, but some pieces of the puzzle may still be missing. There are some pieces that you might not know, and there are some pieces that scientists are still working on. These pages share what is already known. The more you know the better.

For more answers, call the AIDS hotline for free:

- English: 1-800-342-AIDS (24 hours a day)
- Español: 1-800-344-SIDA (8am-2am)
- TTY/TDD: 1-800-243-7889 (10am to 10pm Monday-Friday)

Written by Carnegie Mellon AIDS group, SDS
©1997 CMU 2/6/97
To order pamphlets call: (not yet available)
or write: not yet available
[AIDS puzzle]
[Pittsburgh, PA 15213]

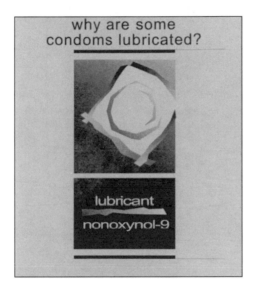

why are some
condoms lubricated?

lubricant

nonoxynol-9

why are some condoms lubricated?

What is a lubricant?

When a woman gets sexually excited, her vagina gets wet. This fluid is a kind of *lubricant*. It makes the vagina slippery, and that makes sex more fun for both partners.

Without a lubricant, the skin is dry and can be cut or torn. This makes having sex hurt. It also makes sex more risky.

Kissing and rubbing parts of the body can make the woman more excited, which helps her body make more lubricant. If the body doesn't make enough fluid, you can also buy a lubricant from a drug store. Even your own spit can be used as a lubricant. You always have spit with you and it's free!

Do you need to use a lubricant with a condom?

A lubricant also makes sex safer if you're using a condom. It makes the condom slide better and keeps it from ripping. This is why most condoms come with a fluid. These are called *lubricated condoms*. Some lubricated condoms have *Nonoxynol-9* in the fluid. Nonoxynol-9 can kill sperm and HIV.

What about lubricant from the store?

A lubricant from the store is safer than spit. Spit dries out. But lubricant from the store stays wet.

If you want to add more lubricant to a condom it should be water-based, not oil-based. Oil-based lubricant, like *Vaseline*, skin cream and baby oil, makes condoms weaker. The condoms might not *look* any different, but they might have little holes you can't see. HIV can pass through these holes.

What kind of lubricant should you use?

There are many kinds of water-based lubricants. *KY-jelly* and *Astroglide* are two kinds. If you buy lubricant from the store, the box will tell you if it is water-based. If you're not sure the lubricant is water-based, don't use it.

What about anal sex?

Anal sex is having a man's penis go inside someone's butt. The inside of the butt doesn't make its own lubricant. So it is *even more important* to use a lubricant from the store for anal sex.

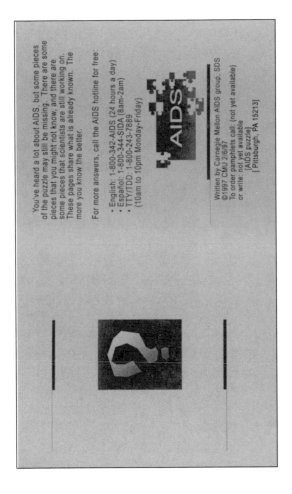

You've heard a lot about AIDS, but some pieces of the puzzle may still be missing. There are some pieces that you might not know, and there are some pieces that scientists are still working on. These pages share what is already known. The more you know the better.

For more answers, call the AIDS hotline for free:

- English: 1-800-342-AIDS (24 hours a day)
- Español: 1-800-344-SIDA (8am-2am)
- TTY/TDD: 1-800-243-7889
  (10am to 10pm Monday-Friday)

Written by Carnegie Mellon AIDS group, SDS
©1997 CMU 2/6/97
To order pamphlets call: (not yet available)
or write: not yet available
[AIDS puzzle]
[Pittsburgh, PA 15213]

is knowing your
partner enough?

is knowing your partner enough?

Sometimes people think that as long as you *know* your partner, having sex with them is safe. Or they think you can tell if your partner has HIV (the virus that leads to AIDS). Other people think that they can be *extra sure* by knowing *all* the people that their partner has had sex with.

But there's more to know than that. You need to know:

- if your partner ever had sex before
- all the people your partner had sex with
- all the people these people had sex with
- if your partner used a condom every time
- if your partner ever shared needles
- all the people your partner shared needles with
- all the people these people shared needles with
- if your partner cleaned the needles every time
- if your partner ever had a blood transfusion
- all the people who gave this blood
- all the people these people had sex with or shared needles with

And there's more to know than that!

There's just no way you can know all this about someone. Even if your partner wants to tell you all that, they may not remember everything.

How can you know for sure?

Even if you "know" your partner, you don't know if they have HIV or not. Even if you ask them and even if they tell the truth, you still can't be sure. Your partner may not know for sure that they *don't* have HIV. And if *they* don't know they have HIV, there's no way for *you* to find out by asking them.

If you really want to know for sure if your partner has HIV, they can get an HIV test. You can read about HIV tests in the booklet called "How can you tell if you have HIV?"

327

You've heard a lot about AIDS, but some pieces of the puzzle may still be missing. There are some pieces that you might not know, and there are some pieces that scientists are still working on. These pages share what is already known. The more you know the better.

For more answers, call the AIDS hotline for free:
- English: 1-800-342-AIDS (24 hours a day)
- Español: 1-800-344-SIDA (8am-2am)
- TTY/TDD 1-800-243-7889 (10am to 10pm Monday-Friday)

Written by Carnegie Mellon AIDS group, SDS
©1997 CMU 2/6/97
To order pamphlets call: (not yet available)
or write: not yet available
[AIDS puzzle]
[Pittsburgh, PA 15213]

Appendix D

This appendix reproduces examples of transcripts of mental model interviews from our first mental model study, which was of radon. The guidelines offered in Chapter 4 reflect our experiences in this and later studies and were not all followed completely in this first study. In these transcripts, you can see where the interviewer has completed the first-phase follow-ups and gone on to more specific questions. You may wish to copy the interviewer worksheet reproduced in Figure 4.1 and try using it to keep track of the topics covered in these examples. Note that one of the interviewees asks the interviewer a question designed to obtain information, but the interviewer defers the answer.

Sample Interview 1
Male homeowner in Pittsburgh, 40–60 years of age, completed high school and some college or trade school

Q: When I bring up the word *radon*, what kinds of thoughts does that bring to mind?

A: It brings to mind a thought of an unsuspecting, young couple buying an existing home that has never been checked for radon, and they get in the house and get contaminated. I don't know what that contamination is, though. I really don't. I don't know what the effects are, or how you would notice it. I understand you don't smell it, you don't feel it. It makes you nauseated, sick, and can kill you.

Q: Some of the effects of radon are that it can make you nauseated?

A: Well, that's what I read in the paper. I've never been exposed to it, nor have I known anybody that's been exposed to it. I'm in the insurance business. When people buy houses, we ask if they've had the

radon checked, or whatever. Westinghouse makes them do it. Some
mortgage companies do, but I don't know if they all do. But I have
no idea what the long-term effects are, or, you know . . . what is it?

Q: I can give you a lot of information at the end. Can you tell me about
how radon gets into the house?

A: Can I tell you how it gets into the home? No, not really, other than
it's through some sort of seepage or something. I don't know.

Q: Okay, so if you think it were seepage, how do you think that would
happen?

A: Well, where the home sits, if there were contaminants, or toxic whatever . . . down in . . . and supposedly after the Second World War we
have really destroyed the environment, the grass, the land, the water,
the ground, everything, all the way down. I would presume that the
seepage would come from some sort of a waste or previous waste. I
don't know.

Q: How would that seep into the house?

A: Well, hell's bells, the house is porous. It could come in anywhere – up
through the drains, the . . . anywhere you're trying to excrete, that's
where you're going to get a return in.

Q: Would the radon level be the same in all parts of the house?

A: No.

Q: How would it differ?

A: It would probably be higher, up higher . . . in my mind. I don't know
if that's true, but that's just the way I would think.

Q: Can you tell me something about how it moves around in the house?

A: I don't know . . . other than it permeates any porous product, and it
gets in there and that's where it stays. I don't know how they get rid
of it, either, you know, or how they would dispose of it.

Q: Is radon found in all homes?

A: No.

Q: So what would determine whether or not it would be found in the
house?

A: What would determine? Do you mean who would determine it or
what existing conditions?

Q: What existing conditions?

A: Other than what I said, I wouldn't have any idea. But it has to do with . . . contaminants, as I said, and this doesn't have to do with asbestos or anything like that. This is in-the-ground contaminants. I don't know if that's landfill, such as Chambers over here . . . garbage, where there are gases and all of that. I don't know if that's it. It is a gas. I don't know if it's that type of gas. So I don't know what layering they have to do to protect or prevent this, if, in fact, they even knew it even existed when they did it. That's what we live with now.

Q: Where have you heard or read about radon?

A: In the *Pittsburgh Press,* in various insurance journals . . . and from several mortgage companies now. This, plus my own exposure . . .

Q: Where have you heard about things that can be done to manage radon risk?

A: I haven't, other than the *Press,* and I really don't remember what they were. I know they have a system of checks and balances for . . . I guess they have a radon safety level, which . . . I don't believe in safety levels, but they'll say, "It's here, but it's not bad," or, "It's here, but you can live with it." I don't think you can live with any of that. How do you get rid of it? I don't know.

Q: Have you heard about any government or private programs to deal with the radon risk?

A: Yeah, I did. You want the name of it, I guess.

Q: Generally.

A: I did . . . pertaining to . . . not the FHA Yeah, but two or three months ago I was reading an article about this, and there was something of a federal nature, that . . . of course, there's always something of a federal nature. I can't tell you what it is, though. They always have something because they have to answer the problems.

Q: Is there any way for someone to learn what the level of radon in his home is?

A: Yeah, they have tests . . . Westinghouse, in particular . . .

Q: Westinghouse Corporation?

A: Yeah, because they have a real estate division. In this real estate division, they have a radon test. Every house that they take, let's say you worked for Westinghouse, and you get transferred . . . the deal is, they work with a two [inaudible], and if you don't move it, then they buy it. But they test for radon. They test them all, and they test the one that you're going to buy. Who they get to do that . . . it could be CMU, I don't know.

Q: If someone finds she has a lot of radon in her house, is there anything she can do about it?

A: Sell it. For most things, other than AIDS, we have, maybe not a cure, but a safeguard. I'm sure there's something they can do. I've never been confronted with it. I'd sure find out if I had a test and it turned out positive, I mean to a degree . . . and I don't think there's any safe level right now, in my mind. If there's a tenth of 1 percent of whatever the parts per millions, or whatever they give you, any would be bad.

Q: So the measures that one would take to take care of the radon, would they be effective?

A: No.

Q: Do you think radon is a significant risk, or is it one of those risks that's not at all important?

A: I think it's very significant because it's new to the buying public. Anything new that accumulated for, let's say forty years, is a definite, definite problem. It's not something you can sweep under the rug and let fall between the cracks.

Q: Can you give me any idea how the risk of radon compares with other risks, such as the risk of smoking?

A: I guess, I don't know. I'm trying to think now . . . what are the symptoms . . . headaches, nausea . . . they had all those in the paper, and I don't remember.

Q: Okay, but symptoms and risk are different. Like, do you think . . . well, you smoke . . .

A: There is no Surgeon General's warning on a house.

Q: This is true.

A: This is definite. Cigarettes will definitely kill. And there is a correlation between the two because that will too, I understand. I don't know if there have ever been any deaths from it. If there have been, they keep it sort of quiet. This, naturally, causes cancer . . .

Q: This, meaning cigarettes?

A: Cigarettes, yeah. Cigarettes definitely cause cancer, heart attacks, high blood pressure, lack of oxygen in your system, and all these nice things . . . to say nothing of the addiction of nicotine and tar . . .

Q: So, if you compare the risk of smoking to the risk of a radon exposure, how would they compare?

A: One you know and one you don't. You can't compare them because the other one hasn't been brought to bat yet. We haven't seen the long-term effects of one hundred years of radon. We've seen a hundred years of this since Sir Walter Raleigh started growing . . . okay, we know this. There's a difference.

Q: What can you tell me about radon in your own home?

A: I don't know if I have it or I don't have it. I've never had a test for it, and I think I will.

Q: You think you will?

A: Yes.

Q: Where will you call to get your kit?

A: Probably the Environmental Resources people, I guess. I don't know. A federal agency of some kind . . . that's where I'd call. I don't know if I'd get the right lady, but I'd get guided right to it.

Q: Do you have any reason to believe your own risk of radon is low or high?

A: I've nothing to compare it to . . . other than I've lived here all my life and I've never had a radon . . . whatever. But as I said, I've never known anybody whose house has been contaminated, or whatever it does.

Q: So none of your friends or neighbors you know of has problems?

A: No. And I don't know if mining or old mines have anything to do with this. I don't think they do. That's methane that seeps in. You know, people have drained toilets into mine shafts a lot around here because this is all mined.

Q: This area has mines?

A: All through Turtle Creek. Yeah. They drained their drains together rather than putting in long pipes. They just shot them into the mine. Now this produces a methane buildup and whatever else is down there, and this shoots back up . . .

Q: So what did they used to mine around here?

A: Coal. They have Rentin (?) mines still up here. There are a couple.

Q: How many miles from here?

A: Three.

Q: Okay, I think we're done with this part of it.

Sample Interview 2:
Male homeowner in Pittsburgh, over 60 years of age, completed undergraduate college

Q: So when you think of radon, what comes to mind?

A: It's a heavy gas that seems to float around in some people's basements. It's radioactive, and it can cause some trouble in heavy concentrations.

Q: Can you describe the gas for me?

A: It's a radioactive gas. That's all I know.

Q: Can you tell me where it comes from?

A: It comes from the earth.

Q: How does it get into homes?

A: Seeps through the ground and comes into the basement walls. You can put detectors in there to see how bad it is, and if it's bad, you can move out. I understand you can buy detectors to sit in your basement. I saw them advertised somewhere. It's what you have to do if you buy a home, to make sure you're clean and don't have any radon gas in it. It's one of the things a homeowner should examine, as well as the leaky basements and all the other things that go along with it.

Q: Can you describe for me, a little bit, how it seeps in?

A: I really don't know. It comes through the gas, I guess. You see, radon gas . . . maybe lead can stop it, and certain concentrations of concrete probably can. A radioactive material is pretty hard to hold. They usually use lead.

Q: Can you tell me about the kinds of things that determine how much radon there is in a home?

A: No. All I know is you can buy these detectors, and they measure any concentration of radon, if there is any.

Q: Can you tell me how radon moves around in the house once it gets in?

A: No, it's like the radioactive wave when x-rays are taken. The technician moves out of the way because it moves everywhere. There's nothing really that can stop it.

Q: Is the level of radon usually the same in all parts of the house?

A: No, it's a heavy gas, so it would stay in the basement.

Q: Is radon found in all homes?

A: Oh no, not that I know. Maybe it is, but not in any concentration that's of any consequence.

Q: What would determine how much radon is in a house?

A: I don't know how it's measured. I understand you can buy something to put in your basement to detect radon. How it measures it, I don't know. It's the same way with people who work in any radioactive area. They carry a pencil, and each night the pencil is checked to see how much radioactivity the workers were exposed to.

Q: So that measures the level in the house. What determines how much radon there is in the house to begin with? If all houses don't have it, why would one house have it more than another?

A: Depends on the geographical area.

Q: Can you tell me more about that?

A: No, I don't know. I'm assuming my house doesn't have it, I don't know. I haven't heard of any consequences in our area, but I know in some areas people are very concerned about it. Why in some areas it is, and in some areas it isn't, I don't know.

Q: Tell me more about the harm that can result from radon exposure.

A: Well, I guess it's the same as any radioactive material exposure. It can cause cancer.

Q: Anything else?

A: Not that I can think of.

Q: Can you tell me anything else about the cancer?

A: I understand that overexposure to any radioactive material can cause cancer. But what kind of cancer, I don't know. I do know if I go to the dentist and he wants to x-ray my teeth, I insist on the lead blanket. I'm very much concerned about the number of x-rays I get. Every time I got a physical, they want to give me an x-ray. Sometimes I agree with it, sometimes I don't. So I guess the level of concentration can build up in a person, and the technician gets behind a door to get out of the way.

Q: Does radon affect some people more than others?

A: I don't know.

Q: Where have you heard about radon?

A: In the newspapers . . . and in just reading. You know, there are people who have had trouble with radon in their basement. But they do advertise you can buy detectors if you're concerned . . . if you live in an area with radon. I guess the only place I got this was from reading newspapers or magazines.

Q: Have you heard about things that can be done to manage the risk?

A: No, I wouldn't know how to manage it. If you had a radon exposure in your house . . . What little I know about any radioactive material . . . They do use lead to contain it. You can't let lead lie in your house or basement. I don't know. I guess if I had a house that was exposed to radon, I'd have to find out what to do with it probably.

Q: Have you heard about any government or private programs to deal with the risk?

A: No.

Q: Is there any way people can learn what the level of radon is in their houses?

A: Yeah, like I said, you can buy detectors, commercially available. I've heard some people say you ought to do this. I imagine the people who are pushing this, to do this to see if you have any radon, I imagine this is one way you do it. How this gizmo works, I don't know. It probably works like the pencils people in nuclear power plants carry to see how much material they're exposed to.

Q: So how would you go about getting one of those kits?

A: I don't know. If I were interested, I'd call the Public Health Department and ask for one, saying I saw them advertised.

Q: If people find they have a lot of radon in their house, what can be done about it?

A: I don't know. I really don't know. When a nuclear power plant blows up you generally let it settle down, pour concrete on it, and forget it. I don't know how you can do that with your house. I don't know of any way you could cleanse your house of radon. If I had that problem, I'd have to look into it.

Q: Do you have any sense of how certain or uncertain scientists are about the risks of radon?

A: No, I would guess they're pretty certain about it because being exposed to radioactivity can cause problems, and it can accumulate in your system. I think they are certain about it.

A: So is radon a significant risk in society, or is it one of those risks that's not all that important?

Q: It's a risk in certain areas, so I would say it's an important thing to beware of.

A: Can you give me any idea how the risk of radon compares to other risks, such as the risk of smoking?

Q: Well, I would say the risk of smoking is greater because I don't know how many cases or incidents they do have with radon, whether, geographically. I guess it's just located in certain areas. I would say it depends on how much you smoke. You can't compare it unless you define the extent of both the radon and the cigarette the exposure of a person.

Q: What can you tell me about radon in your own home?

A: I assume I don't have it, so I don't know. I haven't checked it.

Q: So what is your reason to believe you don't have any?

A: I don't have any reason to believe that. There have been some houses sold in our neighborhood, and I would assume the purchasers might want this checked before they buy. You check everything else. It's quite possible they would ask for that check. If there were radon in our area, we'd know about it. I guess we don't have any radon, but I don't know.

Q: Is there anything else about radon that I haven't asked you that you would like to say?

A: Not particularly. I would say the Health Department should identify the areas where radon has been found. Just as you check areas to see if there are coal mines, so you might as well check the area for radon.

Sample Interview 3
Female homeowner in Pittsburgh, 40–60 years of age, completed some college or trade school

Q: Can you tell me what thoughts you have about radon?

A: I don't know very much about it except what I've read in the newspaper.

Q: What have you read?

A: That in some houses it is found in the basement after a house has been checked with certain instruments . . . that it's noticeable in the basement. According to what it shows on the instrument, they'll know whether it's really dangerous or not.

Q: Can you describe radon?

A: No. It's a gas of some sort.

Q: Can you tell me how it would get into the basement?

A: From underground mines, I think.

Q: Can you describe how the mines allow the gas to come into the basement?

A: Well, there's mining under a good part of Pennsylvania, and when you sign a lease, you're notified that this might be the case, that there was mining under your house. You can't sue someone if you have any subsidence.

Q: So how is that related to radon?

A: Well, the radon gas apparently filters through and gets into the house through the foundation.

Q: Anybody specific about the foundation?

A: I don't know.

Q: Can you tell me about the kinds of things that determine how much radon there is in a home?

A: I suppose the only way they can do that is through certain instruments.

Q: Is the level of radon usually the same in all parts of the house?

A: No, it's more concentrated in the basement, I think.

Q: Why would that be?

A: Because it comes out of the ground.

Q: Is radon found in all homes?

A: We don't think so. No, no, it's not.

Q: So what would determine the variation from home to home?

A: I suppose the underground mine areas. If there's a home that does not have any mines underneath it . . .

Q: Can you tell me what harm can result from a radon exposure?

A: Only what I've read in the newspapers. I suppose headaches, nausea, something like that. I don't know if it's cancer related or not.

Q: Are some people affected more than others?

A: Sure, I think some people get a little more excited about things, and a little more panicky because they don't know a lot about it. It's like going to the hospital for surgery, and you don't know what they're going to do. Then the doctor explains things, and you get more relaxed.

Q: Do you have any idea how certain or uncertain the scientists are about the risks of radon?

A: I think they're still uncertain. They're still investigating it.

Q: So tell me more about why the investigation, or about why they're still uncertain.

A: I don't think I can say any more about it. I think they're still doing some scientific research and I suppose they're finding out more and more about it. The deeper they get into the research or find more ways to research it . . .

Q: Tell me again where you've heard about radon?

A: Newspapers.

Q: Anyplace else?

A: I might have heard something on television.

Q: Where have you heard about things that can be done for the radon risk?

A: In the newspapers and television.

Q: Have you heard about any government or private programs to deal with these risks?

A: Yes, I think they were also listed in the newspaper with addresses you could contact. I suppose you could call also . . . the Harrisburg line. You could look in your telephone book and find someone who might direct you to somebody else, which might take days. There's a lot of red tape in getting information.

Q: What kind of information would you ask for?

A: Probably that we feel uncomfortable, and if there were any chance of radon in our house we would just have somebody come out and check it. It would be hard to determine what company, or if there's a company in Pittsburgh that does it, I don't know.

Q: How would they check?

A: Tests to show whether there's radon present.

Q: Do you know anything else about those tests?

A: No.

Q: If someone finds they have a lot of radon in their house, is there anything they can do about it?

A: I think I read that they insulate the house better. I'm not quite sure about that.

Q: How effective do you think these measures would be to reduce the risk of radon?

A: I don't know.

Q: Is radon really a significant risk in society, or is it one of those risks that's not all that important?

A: Oh, I think it's important, but we just don't know a whole lot about it. We should investigate it.

Q: Do you have any idea how the radon risk compares with other risks, such as the risk of smoking?

A: I don't know how to answer that.

Q: OK, so what do you think the health risks of smoking are?

A: I think it's very bad.

Q: So how would you compare the risk of radon?

A: I think you should be concerned to do something about it if you thought there was radon in your house, or you wanted to have it checked. If you had your house checked by a reputable firm, you'd ask what to do about it.

Q: Can you tell me about radon in your own house?

A: I don't think we have any. We've never had our house checked.

Q: Have you ever thought about having it checked?

A: We thought about it when there was an article in the paper. I asked my husband if we should do anything about it. He didn't think so. He didn't have a reason not to have it checked. If I asked him to have it checked, he'd never give me a reason not to have it checked. He didn't seem too concerned about it.

Q: Have you had any friends or neighbors that have had radon problems?

A: Not that I know of.

Q: Is there anything about radon I have not asked you that you would like to say?

A: No.

INDEX